STUDIES OF THE HISTORICAL JESUS

STUDIES IN BIBLICAL THEOLOGY

A series of monographs designed to provide clergy and laymen with the best work in biblical scholarship both in this country and abroad.

Advisory Editors:

C. F. D. MOULE, *Lady Margaret Professor of Divinity in the University of Cambridge*

J. BARR, *Professor of Old Testament Literature and Theology Princeton Theological Seminary*

PETER ACKROYD, *Samuel Davidson Professor of Old Testament Studies University of London*

FLOYD V. FILSON, *Professor of New Testament Literature and History McCormick Theological Seminary, Chicago*

G. ERNEST WRIGHT, *Professor of Old Testament History and Theology at Harvard University*

STUDIES IN BIBLICAL THEOLOGY

STUDIES
OF THE HISTORICAL JESUS

ERNST FUCHS

SCM PRESS LTD
BLOOMSBURY STREET LONDON

Translated by Andrew Scobie from the German

ZUR FRAGE NACH DEM HISTORISCHEN JESUS
(GESAMMELTE AUFSÄTZE II)
(J. C. B. Mohr (Paul Siebeck) Tübingen, 1960)

FIRST PUBLISHED IN ENGLISH 1964
PRINTED IN GREAT BRITAIN BY
W. & J. MACKAY & CO LTD, CHATHAM

CONTENTS

PREFACE TO THE ENGLISH EDITION

FRANKLY, I get annoyed whenever a scholar stresses the point that we ought not to equate our conceptions with the conceptions of past ages. For whom is this sort of thing written? Surely any right-thinking person is aware that his grandfather thought differently from him.

Of course, the point can also be made that the logic of our grandfathers was subject to the same laws of thought as our logic. That is true. However, as a rule, our grandfathers applied the logic to different events from us. And it seems to me that this is also true of the generations who wrote the New Testament.

Therefore we must distinguish between the events. There are past events that we understand without any difficulty. Poets make use of this—for example, Shakespeare, in his historical plays. The New Testament is in a more difficult position. For it talks of a man, Jesus, as if he were still alive. What is the significance for us of this basic statement of the New Testament?

I am convinced that the question of the immediate meaning of Jesus for us cannot be answered apart from the question of the 'historical' Jesus. We are not interested in exchanging this Jesus for some idea about Jesus. The New Testament—particularly in the Gospels—claims to talk of Jesus himself. We must therefore attempt to examine, and indeed to fulfil this assertion on the part of the New Testament. The following studies show how I do this, in particular the one about 'Jesus' Understanding of Time'.

In research there are two obstacles to our understanding of Jesus. The one is the opinion that the context of earthly events has been interrupted by the resurrection of Jesus, and by this alone. However, this is not the opinion of the New Testament. For there both the Holy Spirit and faith break in upon the earthly reality or the context of earthly events, with the result that many things change, including things in our daily life. The other obstacle lies in the opinion, also widely held, that the disciples were reduced to despair by the crucifixion of Jesus. This opinion confuses even the Bultmannian school. It reduces Jesus and faith to a phenomenon for psychological examination, and through the assertion of an ostensible 'Easter faith' it also devalues the early Christian confession of Jesus' resurrection. What emerges, once all modern prejudgments of this kind are cleared away? It is this exegetical question that I have pursued.

How can the very texts, which have become sources for the analysis of the historical-critical method, again become texts of a proclamation? What do we have to do at our desks, if we want later to set the text in front of us in the pulpit? What is meant by a 'text' of proclamation? Why does preaching need a text? Those who ask these questions are confronted by the 'hermeneutical problem'. This problem is not exhausted in the technical question of how we translate, or how we explain words. Historical reconstruction is not enough to render the New Testament comprehensible. We do not abandon the historical question. However, we do guard against the naïve opinion that it might be possible to understand the New Testament without reflecting on its purpose. This purpose is preaching; at least it includes preaching. What is the result of this for the exposition of the New Testament? What events gave rise to the New Testament? Are they not the events that are meant to be repeated wherever the New Testament is still read? What have these events to do with the historical Jesus?

I wish to thank the SCM Press, and in particular the Rev. Andrew Scobie, who has undertaken the strenuous task of translation in a truly hermeneutical fashion.

The first nine of these studies appear in German in Volume II of my Gesammelte Aufsätze, *Zur Frage nach dem historischen Jesus*, Tübingen, 1960, pp. 143–67 and 219–430. The final study appears in substantially the same form in *Theologia Viatorum* 8 (Jahrbuch der kirchlichen Hochschule Berlin), 1961–2, pp. 38–51.

ERNST FUCHS

Marburg,
15 November 1963

ABBREVIATIONS

BZNW   Beihefte zur *Zeitschrift für die neutestamentliche Wissenschaft,* Giessen

ET   English translation

EvTh   *Evangelische Theologie,* Munich

FRLANT   Forschungen zur Religion und Literatur des Alten und Neuen Testaments, Göttingen

par.   parallel(s), paralleled by

RGG   *Die Religion in Geschichte und Gegenwart,* 3rd ed., Tübingen, 1956ff

SBT   Studies in Biblical Theology, London

TWNT   *Theologisches Wörterbuch zum Neuen Testament,* ed. G. Kittel, Stuttgart, 1933ff

TZ   *Theologische Zeitschrift,* Basel

WA   Weimar Edition of the Works of Luther

ZNW   *Zeitschrift für die neutestamentliche Wissenschaft,* Giessen

ZTK   *Zeitschrift für Theologie und Kirche,* Tübingen

I

THE QUEST OF THE HISTORICAL JESUS[1]
1956

THE quest of the historical Jesus has existed ever since New Testament scholarship became aware of its task—in the eighteenth century the complete revolution of the Church stemming from the Reformation began to affect theology also. Even as a result of its concern for the correct form of the text, and especially through the quest of the historical Jesus, the new philological study of the Bible had been compelled to criticize dogmatic theology for pronouncements which overstepped its limits. The new method was obliged to protest against the supremacy of metaphysics in theology which, in spite of Luther, had hitherto remained unshaken. Many people thought it possible to set off on new paths hand in hand with dogmatics. But even so a tension remained between the philological tradition of biblical scholarship and the metaphysical tradition of dogmatic theology. As a result of this tension, for example, the discipline of Church history, closely related to the philological exegesis of the Bible, developed into an independent science. It became apparent in our time that even the historical consciousness is metaphysically conditioned. Perhaps new opportunities of discussion between the various disciplines and philosophical stimuli have brought us a little further. In any case, for methodological considerations regarding the nature of the sources, and for reasons of friendship, I am beginning at the point where New Testament scholarship is still in close contact with dogmatic theology, namely with the early Christian faith in Jesus. Then in a second part I shall raise the question of Jesus himself, having prepared the ground for this by discussing faith in Jesus.

[1] Guest lecture at the University of Zurich, on 25 May, 1956; published in *ZTK* 53, 1956, pp. 210–29. As contributions to the discussion, cf. E. Käsemann, 'Das Problem des historischen Jesus', *ZTK* 51, 1954, pp. 125–53 (ET in his *Essays on New Testament Themes*, SBT 41, 1964, pp. 15–47); and N. A. Dahl, 'Der historische Jesus als geschichtswissenschaftliches und theologisches Problem', *Kerygma und Dogma* 1, 1955, pp. 104–32; also the works of R. Bultmann, J. Jeremias and W. G. Kümmel.

I. FAITH IN JESUS

(*a*) A Christian of the period beginning with the Apostle Paul believes in Jesus as his Lord. He confesses that Jesus is Lord over all lords or cosmic powers (cf. Eph. 3.8–12; Rev. 17.14; 19.16; I Cor. 8.6 *et al.*). *Confession* of Jesus belongs to *faith* in Jesus—confession as it was made immediately before baptism in the presence of witnesses in those communities which had come under Pauline influence.

Thus Paul writes to the Romans (10.9f), clearly alluding to a baptismal confession with which they also were familiar, and in a liturgical style:

(v. 9) *(ὅτι) ἐὰν ὁμολογήσῃς ἐν τῷ στόματι σου κύριον Ἰησοῦν,*
καὶ πιστεύσῃς ἐν τῇ καρδίᾳ σου
ὅτι ὁ θεὸς αὐτὸν ἤγειρεν ἐκ νεκρῶν,
σωθήσῃ·

(v. 10) *καρδίᾳ γὰρ πιστεύεται εἰς δικαιοσύνην,*
στόματι δὲ ὁμολογεῖται εἰς σωτηρίαν.

(Because) if you confess with your lips that Jesus is Lord
and believe in your heart
that God raised him from the dead,
you will be saved.

For man believes with his heart and so is justified,
and he confesses (publicly) with his lips and so is saved.

The first verse combines the confession with a verse quoted from Deut. 30.14 in the previous verse. The fact that Paul, influenced by Deut. 30.14, gives first priority to confession with the mouth at this central point of the letter to the Romans, does not militate against the previously asserted sequence of faith and confession. In the very next verse (10), which I have quoted, Paul indicates the sequence which he prefers; the δέ is not adversative, but cumulative. Faith is *iustitia passiva,* pure obedience, a life-long obedience, a full acceptance of God's action (Rom. 4.13). Confession is none other than the public beginning of such obedience (or a beginning which has to be carried through in public), in which the baptized, like a soldier, pledges himself with a military oath to the name of his captain. We note the incidental thought that a confession with the mouth without the faith of the heart is in any case valueless for the confessor himself. God wants to enter into the heart. *That* the heart should believe, and *what* the heart believes, are the decisive things.

Paul stresses with liturgical emphasis the article of faith: 'that God has raised him (Jesus) from the dead'. This implies, first, that faith is substantially faith in the dramatic news that God has raised Jesus from the dead and, secondly, that this faith is not the mere repetition of a fact, which can also apparently be 'reported' without faith, but that, in fact, only the heart can grasp the message that God has *already* raised this Jesus from the dead. Faith is not the opposite of doubt, but *the consequence of a new beginning*. We must at once emphasize that faith affirms something new. The third point is that faith affirms that this Jesus who has been raised from the dead has become Lord. Both points are to be stressed: that he has become *Lord*, and that he has *become* Lord. Whoever believes in Jesus has found the one whom henceforth all are to call upon as Lord (Rom. 10.11–13).

Thus the confession expresses the new thing which faith both has and gives, if faith is truly a faith of the heart. Jesus must first be made known to me as Lord. But the decision takes place in faith. In the Shorter Catechism Luther stresses, indeed correctly: 'Be my Lord.' But Paul affirms more precisely: 'He is by faith *already* my Lord.' Jesus is Lord either already or not at all (cf. I Thess. 5.5). If the preaching has 'reached' me, and Jesus is already my Lord, then I can also *name* him as Lord at all times, and this means that, as at baptism, I can *confess* him and declare to my fellow men that at the last day this Lord must and shall be Lord of all men and Lord of all things. Furthermore, in the famous chapter on the resurrection of the dead (I Cor. 15) Paul assumes along with the confession the personal relationship of the witnesses to the Lord. A heated discussion about the logical aspect of early Christian apocalyptic introduces a captious note into the argument, from which Paul extricates himself with difficulty. But in our passage (Rom. 10.9f) the Pauline concept of faith dominates the context from the outset. Here every man must himself be the witness to his own faith (cf. also Rom. 14). It will be agreed that Paul comes nearer to us in this way.

If the news of the new Lord is reduced to the statement that Jesus is risen from the dead, we are, of course, immediately involved in doubt.[1] But really there is no question of discussion between faith and unbelief. Paul, and the early Church as it embarks on the Gentile mission, both agree that the resurrection of Jesus must be presented in connexion with faith and confession. The question of the source of the declaration of the resurrection must not be separated from its kerygmatic context. Hence there is no point in meaning to say anything significant about the resurrection of Jesus apart from faith in Jesus (cf. II Cor. 4.13). We have just seen that Paul speaks of faith in Jesus as a matter of the heart. Hence the most that criticism can do is to enquire how Paul came to the point of *believing* in the resurrection of Jesus.

(*b*) Here we are certainly confronted with a real historical problem. It is concerned in the first place with Paul's personal faith, and not immediately with Jesus himself. The historian's first question is concerned with his source, and only thereafter with the subject for which his source provides the evidence. We do this also. In our case Jesus is the *subject*. All affirmations, such as that Jesus is Lord, or that he is risen from the dead, certainly relate to their subject, Jesus. The first consideration of a careful analysis will be to avoid a hasty classification of Jesus under any of the affirmations or titles of honour which have been assigned to him. Our primary *source* is the literary legacy of the Apostle Paul. It may occasion surprise that my immediate appeal is not to the Gospels, since all of them in their last chapter (John 21 is a later addition) appear to give a direct account of the resurrection of Jesus. But this would be wrong, from the point of view of method. There is general agreement that Paul is the earlier source, since, taking all the Gospels together, they are at least twenty years later than Paul, and were probably written still later. This means there is the passage of about half a century between them and the earthly life of Jesus. It will do no harm to keep this fact clearly in mind. It may be that the Gospels are often using very early traditions; but those who transmitted these traditions remain anonymous.[2] On the

---

[1] Doubt may then quantitatively augment the first statement by further statements, so that we get whole collections of 'confessional declarations'. But the negative beginning of such a series of declarations is betrayed by the fact that new declarations are repeatedly produced for the simple reason that none can suffice of itself. The true confession of faith rests in its object, whereas doubt proliferates in a restless way.

[2] Cf. my book *Hermeneutik*, 1954, cited from the 2nd ed. of 1958, pp. 177ff.

other hand, we have in Paul a witness who is responsible for his own assertions.

How did Paul reach his faith in the resurrection of Jesus from the dead? It is well known that Paul was at a disadvantage as against the disciples of Jesus, inasmuch as they, generally speaking, were engaged in apostolic missionary activity. If we use rather more guarded terms, we may say that, in relation to the limited circle of the apostles, Paul's activities were those of a late-comer, if not the opposite of an apostle (I Cor. 15.8; II Cor. 11.5, 13 or 12.11 belongs to another context). Paul had certainly never known Jesus (cf. I Cor. 2.2 with II Cor. 5.16). As a zealous Pharisee he was hostile to the missionary proclamation of the new faith (Phil. 3.4ff), and even persecuted its adherents (I Cor. 15.9; Gal. 1.13); but on the occasion of one such persecution in the neighbourhood of Damascus he himself came to faith. For Paul his conversion meant a complete reversal, since he now accepted what he had previously passionately rejected. What he accepted was faith in the raising up or exaltation of the crucified Jesus, the very faith which he had previously rejected (cf. Gal. 1.23). In Acts there are three accounts of the conversion of Paul (cc. 9; 22; 26); incidentally, they are not wholly consistent with each other, and are to some extent legendary. But Paul himself writes about it on one occasion—a single sentence, which is therefore of special significance for us. In I Cor. 9.1, defending himself against certain attacks on his claim to be an apostle, he writes, in the form of a rhetorical question : οὐχὶ Ἰησοῦν τὸν κύριον ἡμῶν ἑόρακα; Have I not seen Jesus our Lord? An interesting remark! For according to the context, it is clear:

1. That it was generally accepted at that time that Paul had, in fact, experienced a vision or appearance of Jesus;

2. That it was not absolutely necessary for an apostle to have previously known Jesus personally (cf. also II Cor. 5.16);

3. That such experiences were probably the mark of each of the apostles, for the circle of those who had such experiences was considerably greater than the circle of those apostles who were at that time not included with the twelve (I Cor. 9.1, 5; cf. with 15.5–8). The appearances of the Lord were evidently spread over a long period of time, to entirely different persons and circles, and were in no way limited to a single place.

4. We have in I Cor. 9.1 a confirmation of the statement in Rom. 10.9 that at that time *only* the resurrected Christ was regarded as Lord. In the same way we also find in Acts 2.36 in an early saying, 'God has made him, that is the crucified Jesus, both Lord and Christ.' *God* has done this; we find the same statement in the pre-Pauline 'Christ hymn' in Phil. 2.9. As with the designation Lord, so also we learn from Acts 2.36 that the designation of Jesus as Christ was regarded at first, and to some extent still consciously in the New Testament, not as a name, but in good Jewish fashion as a title of honour, and indeed also as that of the resurrected Jesus. The same holds good of the title Son of God, which is similarly applied to Jesus rather later, a title derived from oriental royal ceremonial (Rom. 1.3f; cf. Mark 1.11 *et al.*). Briefly, the affirmation that God has raised Jesus from the dead implies that after the death of Jesus God has installed and revealed him as Lord and Christ, and consequently as the representative of God and heir of the rule of God (cf. also Heb. 1.2).

This designation of Jesus as king in the early community is earlier than the theology of Paul. Paul therefore came to faith since *he too* had experienced Jesus as Lord, and hence had learned to yield obedience to the self-same Lord whose followers he had previously persecuted. His conversion was evidently just the initial impulse for all else that followed from it (Gal. 1.12–24). The decisive point was that for all time Paul surrendered himself in utter obedience to this Lord as his δοῦλος (Rom. 1.1; Gal. 1.10; Phil. 1.1). This is illustrated by other sayings in his letters; e.g. the well-known passage in Rom. 14.7–9:

(v. 7) οὐδεὶς γὰρ ἡμῶν ἑαυτῷ ζῇ, καὶ οὐδεὶς ἑαυτῷ ἀποθνῄσκει·
(v. 8) ἐάν τε γὰρ ζῶμεν, τῷ κυρίῳ ζῶμεν,
     ἐάν τε ἀποθνῄσκωμεν, τῷ κυρίῳ ἀποθνῄσκομεν,
     ἐάν τε οὖν ζῶμεν ἐάν τε ἀποθνῄσκωμεν, τοῦ κυρίου ἐσμέν.
(v. 9) εἰς τοῦτο γὰρ Χριστὸς ἀπέθανεν καὶ ἔζησεν,
     ἵνα καὶ νεκρῶν καὶ ζώντων κυριεύσῃ.

None of us lives for himself alone, and none dies for himself alone;
for if we live, we live for the Lord,
and if we die, we die for the Lord.
Hence, whether we live or die, we belong to the Lord.
For Christ died for this reason and rose again (for this reason),
that he might be Lord over dead and living (together).

Paul never demanded of his hearers that they like him must have

a vision of Christ. It was enough that each should learn to accept
Jesus as Lord (cf. Rom. 8.4ff). Hence, without being obliged to
depend on Rom. 7, we are fully justified in speaking, as Bultmann
does, of a new self-understanding in Paul. The object of Paul's
missionary activity was to enable his hearers to participate in the
same self-understanding that had been disclosed to him when he
confessed Jesus as Lord.[1]

(*c*) But what actually happens when someone learns to accept
Jesus as Lord? Hitherto we have omitted mention of one word
which was specially stressed in that passage in Rom. 10.9f from
which we began. It says there: 'If you confess and (thus) believe
from the heart σωθήσῃ, then you shall be saved' (jussive). This
salvation means salvation from *God's judgment*. If we compare the
traditional conception with what was in Paul's mind, it is again
clear that here also Paul is thinking of something very personal.
According to the Jewish apocalyptic tradition current in Paul's
time, the primary meaning of judgment is the judgment of the
world and the wrath of God (cf. I Thess. 1.10; 5.3; I Cor. 15.50).
Then it will be decided if a man is to be assigned to eternal life or
to eternal death (cf. Rom. 2.7–10). But in view of the fact that
Christ now sits upon the throne of God (II Cor. 5.10), Paul draws
this conception right into our daily living and dying, as Rom.
14.7–9 has already shown. For him life really means the joy which
can unite an individual with God (cf. also Rom. 14.17), and death
means the anxiety that must separate a man from God (cf. Rom.
7.24; 8.15, *et al.*). He who believes in Jesus as Lord is free for
such joy, and free from such anxiety, as the letter (or letters) to the
Philippians show in particular. This agrees with our previous
observation that for Paul faith is a faith of the *heart*. For it is now
quite clear: according to the experience of Paul, he who accepts
Jesus as Lord has thereby himself become lord over anxiety, and
indeed over that terrible anxiety in face of God, from which
nothing can give security, least of all works (cf. also I Cor. 3.21–
23). But when Paul says that such faith *saves*, he assumes that he
who is *without* Christ has every cause to suffer from this hopeless

[1] This self-understanding can be discussed ontologically only as an understanding
of being. In Bultmann, therefore, the concept of the self-understanding leads into the
ontological, as soon as it is used formally. It is nevertheless true that the sinner really
has no self-understanding—Rom. 7.24 is interpretation.

anxiety in face of God. It is necessary to emphasize *both* the anxiety in face of God, and also the freedom from such anxiety.

It would be interesting to examine this paradoxical statement in detail in the light of Phil. 2.12. For at this point our very selves are summoned, even though in many of us the phenomenon of anxiety lies concealed beneath the quest for greater personal security and a more brilliant career. Every man of conscience knows quite well what a degree of fear and trembling can be involved in responsibility as a radical responsibility in face of God; and that there is more to conscience than just assent or dissent for what we do or have not done. Hence we can all very well understand what hopeless anxiety in face of God must be like; our restless age cannot fail to appreciate that desperate attempt at flight from God, which Ps. 139 so vividly rejects, the attempt at escape from the sole Judge, before whom every conscience is self-condemned. But he who believes does not take flight (cf. Isa. 28.16 in the Hebrew). According to Paul, faith in Jesus manifestly leads to the paradoxical truth that in the very God from whom man once fled or had to flee he has found a refuge which he now loves. Paul's conversion implies no change of direction, in the sense of turning from a God of wrath to seek a merciful God. The only kind of change that conversion can imply would be the attempt to flee from God in the wrong direction. But it is the merciful God who himself desires to be found in the God of wrath, who wills that life should be found in the place of death, joy in the desert of anxiety. It was with this in mind that Paul appealed to the crucified Jesus as the risen Lord. Paul preached in the name of this Lord that for every man the *time* for such faith had come with the utmost urgency, the time for faith in the merciful Judge (Gal. 4.4ff; II Cor. 6.2). Whoever has understood this message knows that there must be no delay in obeying it. The Lord could, in fact, pass by.

But what has all this to do with the *historical Jesus*? Paul never even once met Jesus before he was crucified. May it not be quite within the bounds of possibility that Paul substituted for Jesus a totally different person, or even the creation of his own faith? There is a popular tendency today to claim that what must be preserved is the identity of the crucified Jesus with the risen Lord. This demand is not unconditionally implied by the freedom from anxiety in face of God of which we have already spoken, or a well-founded understanding of Paul's faith. It remains to be seen whether an enquiry into the problem of the *historical* Jesus will enable us to develop further from the position so far reached.

2. THE HISTORICAL JESUS

(*a*) Before we embark on this question, it is again necessary to say something about the sources. For the question of the historical Jesus our first source can only be the Synoptic Gospels. New Testament scholarship today is generally agreed that these Gospels owe their form to kerygmatic considerations, and that their matter subserves this form. The evangelists were not mere compilers of their material, but had what may be described as a theological plan. For example the author of the Gospel of Mark did not simply collect all the available material, but undoubtedly selected what his plan demanded (cf. Mark 4.33).[1] It is possible to separate the material from its framework. This framework, especially in Mark's Gospel, has a resemblance to the Pauline theology. There are also features, both in the Gospel of Matthew and in that of Luke, which correspond to the Marcan framework. But, apart from the fact that John, too, includes a passion narrative, his Gospel, viewed in terms of its framework, is quite independent as regards composition. Hence, in spite of certain historically interesting details, we place John's Gospel in a class by itself, and therefore reject the view that all the Gospels were from the first expanded passion-narratives. Let us then, for the moment, substitute the Pauline theology for the synoptic framework, and by the Pauline theology we mean essentially what has already been said about faith in Jesus. The synoptic material will have to show if this is possible.

(*b*) If we continue our enquiry along the lines of the kind of faith which Paul understood as faith in a merciful God, we can in the first place disregard all the *traditional* statements in the Synoptic Gospels about Jesus and his fate, and simply establish what Jesus himself said (not only about his own, but) about our relation to God. As our first example we choose a parable which is, in any case,

---

[1] For Luke cf. H. Conzelmann, *Die Mitte der Zeit*, Studien zur Theologie des Lukas, 1954 (ET, *The Theology of St Luke*, 1960). For Matthew cf. my study 'Jesu Selbstzeugnis nach Matthäus 5', *ZTK* 51, 1954, 14–34; also the collected volume by G. Bornkamm. G. Barth and H. J. Held, *Überlieferung und Auslegung im Mätthaus-Evangelium*, 1960 (ET, *Tradition and Interpretation in Matthew*, 1963).

significant for Jesus' proclamation; for reasons both of method and of content it is legitimate to refer to it here, even if it was attributed to Jesus later. It is the parable of the prodigal sons, Luke 15.11–32.[1]

The story is well known. The younger son demands his inheritance, receives it, and squanders it in the foreign country. The elder son stays at home and works hard. When the father joyfully welcomes back the younger son, after he has repented and returned home with an open confession of his guilt in order at least to receive his due at home, the elder son is furious at the father's extraordinary behaviour. The father, however, points out to the enraged son that he also has cause for rejoicing, because the family is together again. A servant is actually the first to tell him very simply the motive for his father's behaviour. So much for the content of the parable. The usual interpretation tends to argue somewhat too hastily from the father's conduct to God's. Closer examination shows that Jesus is defending his own conduct. He does this because he rejected no sinner, and he bases his conduct on the will of God. It is true, he implies, that God must be severe, but he will nevertheless be merciful if a sinner flees for refuge to that God from whose judgment he had previously to flee in fear. Jesus therefore implies that God, despite his severity, mercifully receives the returning sinner, as he himself does. Hence it is not the prime purpose of the parable to explain the conduct of Jesus, although Jesus does vindicate himself in it; on the contrary, Jesus' conduct explains the will of God, by means of a parable drawn from that very conduct. For it is not usual for fathers to act in the manner of the father in the parable, and such conduct was hardly to be expected of the God of wrath. Moreover, other passages in the proclamation of Jesus, as, for instance, in the Sermon on the Mount, contain warnings of judgment, and even direct threats, such as the calls of woe.

With regard to the parable of the prodigal sons, which, of course, also contains a warning, we find here essentially the same attitude which we have come to recognize in the Apostle Paul. But if Paul, as we now see, after all coincides with Jesus, then, speaking undogmatically, we are certainly confronted by a very

[1] The German words *Gleichnis* and *Parabel* can both be translated 'parable', but where it seemed valuable to preserve the distinction *Gleichnis* has been rendered as 'similitude' and *Parabel* as 'parable'. See Bultmann, *Die Geschichte der synoptischen Tradition*, 3rd ed., 1957, pp. 188f (ET, *The History of the Synoptic Tradition*, 1963, p. 174).

daring line of conduct on the part of Jesus: he dares to affirm the will of God as though he himself stood in God's place. Jesus validates the will of God in exactly the same way as a man must do if he were in God's place. Certainly no man can *judge* another in God's place, since no man is omniscient. But when pardon is sought, man *can* undoubtedly *forgive* like God. True forgiveness never judges, but helps, as, for example, is shown in the parable of the unmerciful servant (Matt. 18.23–35). We can be like God, not in wrath but certainly in love. This is the only way it can be meaningful to speak of God in faith. Nevertheless, Jesus' conduct remains audacious—so audacious that he was put to death before the gates of the by no means godless city of Jerusalem, because men disputed his right, as a man of no official standing, to place himself in God's stead; they could not tolerate his claim to assert through his own conduct that God's will was a gracious will. That we are justified in saying this can be seen from pericopes like Mark 11.27–33, or from sayings like Luke 12.8f; 7.23. The circumstances of the arrest and execution of Jesus are shrouded in such obscurity that it is difficult to be certain what forces were at work; but it is at least clear that the decisive factor was this claim implied in Jesus' conduct (cf. also Matt. 5.48).

(*c*) From this it follows that *Jesus' conduct* was itself the real framework of his proclamation. We need not appeal to the miracle narratives, although these narratives in the Gospels do, as a rule, give expression to the same claim. Similarly, it is unnecessary to adduce the ascriptions of lordship in the Gospels, whose occurrence there is due to dogmatic considerations; nor is it necessary to speak of such titles as Son of God, or Son of Man regarded as the future or present wielder of divine power. All this, taken by itself, reveals to us not more but less than Jesus' own conduct. If our surmise is correct, it is only to be expected that the words of Jesus rather than the titles provide an historical record of Jesus' conduct. We are by no means directed to paradoxically formulated sayings. It will suffice if we find agreement between Jesus' words and his actions. This must be clearly understood, since the study of early Christian forms of language involves the search for traces of the concepts and doctrines of the time in the proclamation of Jesus, and thus may easily lead to our being entangled in the broader problems of the comparative study of religions. But all these concepts and doctrines, such as the recently rather hack-neyed idea of the 'messianic' Torah, of which there are barely a couple of rabbinic examples, and which, moreover, represent not stricter but more lenient prescriptions (Gal. 6.2 is quite a different matter)—all these belong to the inessential elements of the tradition rather than to the actual content of the words of Jesus. Strictly speaking it is impossible to speak of a 'sermon' of Jesus. Apart from parables or similitudes we have only isolated sayings. They are most consonant with Jesus' conduct. This conduct is neither that of a prophet nor of a teacher of wisdom, but that of a man who dares to act in God's stead, and who, it must always be remem-bered, draws to himself sinners who, but for him, would have to flee from God. It is a mistake to draw conclusions about the sociological type of speaker from the style of his sayings, unless, with a view to material of widely varying style, the intention were to emphasize a 'neither-nor'. It must, however, be admitted that the style of the sayings, which in Jesus' case also was determined by tradition, has facilitated their collection and preservation in the oral tradition. On the other hand, the situations reflected in the community debates and discussions preserved in the Gospels might well cast doubt on the genuineness of a particular saying; but they might equally cast light on Jesus' conduct. For actions are more likely to stimulate imitation than words.

(*d*) It is, of course, tempting to draw attention to certain sayings which express a consciousness of eschatological forces at work; e.g. Matt. 12.28 par. Luke 11.20, 'If it is by the finger of God that I cast out demons, then the rule of God has come upon you', or the obscure saying about taking by storm in Matt. 11.12 par. Luke 16.16, 'Everyone enters the rule of God by force'. But, in regard to this first saying, we would be forced to describe Jesus' relation to the coming rule of God so paradoxically that his conduct would become unintelligible. With regard to the second saying, the one about the use of violence, we would by contrast have to lay so much stress on Jesus' conduct that the question would arise of why he taught anything at all. It is safer to begin from the point that what Jesus, in fact, demands of his hearers is a *decision*. This is the object of the searching criticism implied in his interpretation of the law, with its insistence on the indivisible nature of the divine will. The same appears in the well-known, perhaps already traditional, precept which places love for one's neighbour on the same level as love for God. It is expressed in the so-called 'conflict-sayings', such as Mark 7.15, 'the things which come out of a man are what defile him', or Mark 3.4, 'is it not lawful to do good on the sabbath?' It is seen in the searching antithesis in Matt. 5.27f, where the heart is shown to be the seat of adultery; and it is found above all in some of the Woes directed against the pious practices developed especially by the Pharisees (Matt. 23.13ff par.). These are amplified by the Woes already mentioned, or warnings such as Luke 12.54–56, asking why those who can foretell the weather cannot read the signs of the times; or Matt. 8.11f, declaring that those who are citizens of the rule of God by birthright will be cast out of it, for many are called but few chosen (Matt. 22.14). All these sayings fit in well with the parables which likewise call for decision, such as the similitude of the treasure in the field and that of the pearl of great price (Matt. 13.44, 45f). Thus the central theme of the sayings of Jesus is the decision which they demand. But this demand is simply the echo of Jesus' own decision. We have to understand his conduct as likewise determined by a decision, and we can infer what he did from what he demanded. At any rate this is the next step.

If the starting-point for the question of Jesus' own decision is taken as moral piety, which was no less common in Jesus' time than it is in ours, we are faced by a difficulty, since we are not warranted in supposing that Jesus experienced anything resembling a conversion from evil to good. But Jesus himself did of necessity face a problem similar to the one his disciples faced after his death. Jesus had lived through the experience of the violent death of the Baptist. But if at the time of his own baptism Jesus without doubt recognized the gravity of eschatological judgment implied in the Baptist's message, then after the Baptist's death he would have to decide what this death meant for him. The tradition underlying Matt. 11 (John 3 can be disregarded) makes it clear that, in fact, Jesus not only furthered the work of the Baptist, but that he even made it more radical. But so far as the preaching of judgment was concerned this was hardly possible, because it was so radical already (cf. Matt. 11.11a par. Luke 7.28a). All that Jesus could do was to grasp the *time* of the rule of God in a new way; i.e. he could attempt to make the time of the rule of God his own.

That Jesus did not offer a political programme is apparent from the sternness of his proclamation with its almost impossible demands; although the political element which was always certainly inherent in the idea of the rule of God induced men to interpret him in this way. But Jesus did go up to Jerusalem. The sight of his followers could, in fact, make this appearance look like an insurrection. Indeed, the attitude of the authorities suggests that they *did* regard the whole business as an uprising. Scenes like the cleansing of the temple could hardly be called anything else. Jesus was thus dependent on the degree to which he was understood. The partial defection of some of those who had understood him was bound to happen. For the politically minded do not take into account the transformation of an unknown heavenly figure, unless this figure were thereby to become calculable. But this possibility was excluded. It is inconceivable that Jesus could come to terms with the authorities of a religiously organized state. He certainly did not share the definitely political aims of the Zealots, but on the other hand he did not avoid a clash with the Temple authorities.

(*e*) Jesus revealed his own decision by his action in gathering together the unorganized group of the eschatological community in the midst of a perverse generation (cf. Matt. 11.16f). This community cannot yet appear under the guise of faith in Jesus. The malicious description of him given by his opponents in Matt. 11.19 par. Luke 7.34 establishes the fact, in spite of Mark 14.25, that Jesus celebrated eschatological feasts with those whom he had called to the rule of God. Sayings such as Mark 2.19a (the bridegroom celebrates with his companions) are an echo of this. We may ask what similitudes or parables are fitting as table-sayings. Jesus is consistent. He does not look back (Luke 9.62). He knows that his conduct is dangerous: the dead must be left to bury their own dead (Luke 9.60 par. Matt. 8.22). Whoever would save his life will lose it (Mark 8.35a par.). The episode of the rich young man (Mark 10.17–22; cf. Mark 2.14) shows that those who would follow him must either follow completely or not at all. In my opinion the community disputes about sabbath-breaking, fasting, and such like, can be traced back to the situation of Jesus. This alone explains the continued persecution of the early community and the admission of Hellenists; and also how it happened that Paul the Pharisee was at first a passionate persecutor of their cause, and that in the name of the Torah he made common cause against them with their opponents in Jerusalem.

All this, however, is only the consequence of Jesus' decision, not the real heart of the matter. The example in Luke 15.11–32 shows that this is to be interpreted in a purely religious sense, and that it concerns his relationship with God. Once again a reference to Paul will make the situation clearer. Paul, too, stressed the wrath and judgment of God, but he also contrasts them with his mercy, as we have seen. Conscious as he is of being an innovator, he nevertheless holds fast to God's faithfulness to Israel, and never abandons the promise to the fathers, above all to Abraham. The new faith and the baptism of the Gentiles were manifested to Paul in the well-known collection for the poor in Jerusalem, and this was clear evidence of the revelation that God had fulfilled the promise in Jesus Christ and was now fulfilling it. The only objection that could be made was that Paul had made faith too easy for the Gentiles. But this Judaistic objection is countered by the fact, recognized by others as well as Paul, that faith in Christ involves suffering. The Mosaic law was thus transformed into a law of suffering. It was now made clear that the way of salvation for everyone was not by the works of the law but by suffering for the faith. God comes to meet man on the very way on which, as a rule, man has to expect God's judgment, and Paul, too, could say that whoever loses his life will gain it. Love is the fruit and, from another point of view, the paradigm of this situation. We leave aside the structural problem here, since we have already found the framework of interpretation in the conduct of Jesus. It is certainly possible to raise the objection against Paul that his way of salvation through suffering is a secret and hence more fateful relapse into justification by works. The objection might hold good were it not that the issue was directly that of the relationship to God and not a securing of this relationship.

(*f*) We can now speak of Jesus' own suffering. But we do not use just psychological methods, nor do we depend on the passion-narratives.[1] From the outset Jesus' relationship to God pre-supposes suffering. We should not be misled by the note of

---

[1] To speak of suffering psychologically would mean to speak of the *spiritual course* of suffering. The analysis which is carried out here has nothing *at all* to do with this form of consideration.

completeness of the parables. In them the result is only parabolically presupposed or anticipated, as in the parable of the prodigal sons. The same holds good of the parable of the labourers in the vineyard (Matt. 20.1–16) and also of the parable of the sower (Mark 4.3–9 par.). The end is only seen by the one who comes last; the first-comers do not see it. In the parables this way of regarding the situation is on occasion interchanged aesthetically, but not materially. In spite of the eschatological meals, the secret turning-point of truth is really still death (cf. Mark 8.35). But the revelation is not limited to those who follow afterwards, who perhaps are in a position to assess in what light their predecessors died. God's faithfulness ensures that the revelation shall include the predecessors, too. God loses no one. Hence resurrection takes the place of death. Apart from resurrection the suffering of faith would be pointless (cf. also I Cor. 15). On the other hand, resurrection would be no real goal, were it not preceded by suffering; for resurrection is both grace and faithfulness (cf. also Matt. 6.1–18). Therefore, when Jesus directs the sinner beyond death to the God of grace he knows he must suffer. Precisely because Jesus himself assumes the standpoint of God's grace, he assumes also for himself the standpoint of suffering. His threats and calls of woe, and also the severity of his demand, all stem from his stringent will to suffer. For in all this Jesus opposed his adversaries, even though he was fully aware of the violent death of the Baptist.

In support of this thesis I am not now reverting to the theory that the Gospels are passion-narratives with extended introductions, although I could now accept this theory with the modification that nothing needs to be extended. However, the Gospels are, in fact, not just narratives of suffering; they are, from the very beginning, proclamation of the resurrection. They explain Jesus' relationship to God by turning it round, as the introductory narratives in particular show. The subject of resurrection requires further elaboration, in order to round off what has already been said. Therefore I add a concluding section to what has already been explained.

3. THE PROCLAMATION OF THE RESURRECTION

(*a*) Jesus' prophecies of suffering in the Synoptic Gospels, which stem stylistically from the kerygma of the community, cannot be imagined without the announcement of the resurrection. Nor is it possible to conceive that the Gospels would have been written without Easter chapters. Research is thereby involved in a hermeneutical problem which is by no means easy to master in practice. The problem would be easier to deal with if it were possible to prove exactly that the Gospel pericopes were from the outset meant to subserve preaching. But why is the situation different in the case of John's Gospel? The problem that I have in mind consists of the fact that the proclamation character of the gospel has been obliterated by the appearance of the literary Gospels. It is impossible to place a complete ban on the attempt to isolate as 'salvation facts' the dramatic passages of the revelation in these Gospels, especially as Luke, in spite of his more refined project, has already done this. Thus everything finally becomes so massive that we are no longer able to gain a direct view of Jesus' own conduct and decision, unmolested by dogmatic interests. But since the advent of the historical-critical analysis of the New Testament, the problem has never come to rest. It should not be said that what can be read in the Gospels is sufficient for the simple church member. This is not correct. The simple member has special need of the means of access to the gospel, which the spoken word of preaching provides. Whoever fails to see this shows that he has no knowledge of Jesus' own concern.

(*b*) Without doubt Paul regarded Jesus' resurrection as a firm fact. But Paul did not isolate this fact. He always viewed it in connexion with Jesus' crucifixion and the future of the world, even in I Cor. 15. Paul was not alone in this view; he was in agreement with all the apostles, and also with James the brother of the Lord. Thus Jesus had not died in vain. His death signified more than just a personal event for Jesus himself, which might not concern us at all. In the same way, it would be both too much and too little to say that the disciples' inevitable shock was overcome by Jesus' resurrection. Nor is it sufficient to refer to the early formula that Jesus died for our sins. Jesus was instead addressed as our representative in the extremity of death itself, and as a result there was an awareness of being bound to him in suffering for the faith.

However, this was only one aspect of the statement. The same

Jesus was recognized as the risen Lord and therefore as God's representative. For those who believed in him as God's representative, his execution necessarily remained an offence which had constantly to be overcome anew (Gal. 5.11). This offence was by no means finally removed by the Easter experiences of the first generation. For there was no renunciation of the need for every believer to face the experiences of suffering. The suffering of the Christian believer was by no means alleviated. Faith remained obedience in face of a message, and the message continued to be a claim to this obedience, which was founded solely on God. In spite of confessional refinements, we can say that faith itself remained a *decision and risk*. The believer would certainly find help in the community of the faithful. But even this aid remained (cf. I Thess. 4.13–5.11) at the decisive point a reminder of baptism and of Jesus' death (I Cor. 11.23ff). The representation ideas— Jesus being both God's representative and also ours—were not yet fully worked out. Jesus could certainly only be our representative if faith in him as God's representative already existed. Faith for its part had to accept full responsibility for the decision about his being God's representative—a decision that was manifest only 'before God' (cf. also Rom. 6.8). This is why the message of Jesus' resurrection still remained basically a statement of faith, which was to be believed either 'from the heart' or not at all. This means that the Easter experiences had only personal significance for those concerned. They were an aid from God and hence a working of the Holy Spirit. Just as the action of the Spirit thereupon proved to be a much more comprehensive aid, so the early Christian faith itself gained all the more the marks of decision, and became a parallel to Jesus' own conduct (cf. Phil. 2.6–8; Rom. 15.3). The familiar triad of faith, hope and love is based on this feature of the revelatory event which aims at decision.

(*c*) We must then say that just as Jesus was the representative of faith, so faith became the representative of Jesus. To have faith in Jesus now means essentially to repeat Jesus' decision. This is why faith cannot be separated from suffering (Mark 8.34–38). The repetition of Jesus' decision was certainly something new, inasmuch as the adoption of an attitude to Jesus was automatically involved. Jesus' opponents had already taken care of this. However, it remained the old decision, because its task was to make its own claim to God's will and God's name. Jesus' person now indeed became the content of faith. This happened entirely in God's name; for God had acted towards Jesus and in Jesus, and as the confessional formulations, their Pauline exposition, and later the Gospels all show, he would act along with Jesus all the more in the future. All this always has the implication that God has acknowledged Jesus and will acknowledge the believers who have faith in this. Thus there is always something open in the original conception of faith. It follows that Heb. 11.1 can, in fact, be applied as the classical definition of faith: it is the conviction of things not yet seen.

(*d*) Faith therefore seeks to be pure faith. The result is certainly a new concept of faith which could hardly have existed previously, in spite of the traditional-sounding formulation even in Heb. 11.1. However, this does not mean that we have to be content with faith's characteristic as a risk. Faith certainly has a content, but one which must always be transformed back into its original form. This is why faith ever and again needs preaching. For the most dangerous enemies of faith are now those experiences which were a help to the believers. As a rule they do not take these experiences into consideration for the proper transmission of faith, for they are not the experiences of those who are to attain to faith after them. For this same reason a final word must be added about Jesus' suffering: Jesus himself must not be an obstacle to the faith of those who followed him. Just as he faced up to his opponents, so he had to prepare his own for the struggle which lay ahead of them, too (whether he was successful is another question). His proclamation had therefore to anticipate their temptation, and it had to be able to do without Jesus' own certainty. This feature constitutes the special secret of what he said. John's Gospel treats the same theme in a different way (John 16.7).

(*e*) As far as the resurrection is concerned, this means that it is possible for a person to venture on faith in Jesus' resurrection only when he ventures along with Jesus to claim God's grace as God's *true* will, and to persist in this right up to death. The venture both is and remains a risk. There are only two possibilities, either to make the venture or not to—*tertium non datur*. There are, of course, external impulses. As the Easter events once did, so today the clarity and boldness of a preacher can contribute towards a person resolving on the risk of faith. But the real aid to faith is in faith itself. For pure faith is response. It responds to the question, which originally Jesus could decide only for himself, and which today we must each decide for ourselves, even though in community with Jesus we may still receive marvellous clarity and certainty. The question is this: *Is it God's will that we should summon up freedom in face of him to appeal directly to him,* despite our well-founded fear of his judgment, which we have all long since recognized in secret? The decision of the historical Jesus affirms just this. This is why he called sinners to follow him (Mark 2.14), and gave them preference to the just. For the person who hears and follows, Jesus is indeed *already* the Lord.

The early Christian proclamation is distinguished from Jesus' proclamation by the fact that it knows about this 'already' in Jesus, and has sought to integrate the experiences of faith into its knowledge of Jesus.[1] Is this not then a return to knowledge about Jesus in place of pure faith? *The proclamation loses its character when it anticipates confession.* There is certainly an extensive network of cognitive statements running through the whole New Testament. These not only obscure Jesus' own decision, but also, for example, repeatedly suppress Paul's concept of faith. Nevertheless it remains the case that Jesus' lordship, in just the same way as the purity of faith, must repeatedly be newly ventured upon as one and the same thing. If faith is response, proclamation is a question—that question which asks what God wants of us. God's will for us is that our being (*Dasein*) should hinge on God. Our being (*Dasein*) should retain the Godward direction, so that we learn that we are 'of God'. If faith, because of its decision, is termed the representative of Jesus, preaching is now revealed as the new representative of God. *God comes to us in his question to us, as in Jesus so through the preaching about Jesus.* Far from putting an end to this question, the proclamation of Jesus' resurrection repeats it. The repetition of this question does not mean that we are diverted from the answer of faith; in the proclamation the entirety of the relationship to God revealed in Jesus demands our decision all the more. Then faith knows that in the proclamation of the resurrection the historical

---

[1] G. W. Ittel's study 'Der Einfluss der Philosophie M. Heideggers auf die Theologie R. Bultmanns', *Kerygma und Dogma* 2, 1956, 90–108, diminishes the theme of this 'already', both in Bultmann and in Heidegger.

Jesus himself *has* come to us. The so-called Christ of faith is none other than the historical Jesus. But what is much more important is the statement that God himself *wants to be encountered* by us in the historical Jesus. The quest of the historical Jesus is now essentially transformed into the quest of the reality of the encounter with God in *preaching*.

It is evident that the quest of the historical Jesus leads to theology, rather than diverting from it. The dogmatic continuation of exegetical analysis would have to be a doctrine of the word of God which keeps its sights firmly trained on the historical Jesus.[1]

[1] The close relation of exegetical and dogmatic theology must be maintained in particular in regard to John's Gospel. At this point Bultmann's collaboration with Gogarten is incontrovertibly correct and significant. Cf. also my contribution on 'Das christologisch begründete Existenzverständnis', *Hermeneutik*, pp. 239–48; and my paper given on the occasion of Gogarten's becoming Emeritus Professor at Göttingen, *Begegnung mit dem Wort*, Bad Cannstatt, 1955.

II

THE REFLECTION WHICH IS IMPOSED ON THEOLOGY BY THE HISTORICAL-CRITICAL METHOD[1]
1958

THE reflection which is imposed on theology by the historical-critical method arises above all from the work done in the disciplines of Old and New Testament study and Church History, relating to the historical Jesus and the historical churches; but also especially to the methods of theological dogmatics and the discipline of practical theology. In this paper I confine myself in the first place to that particular trend of the reflection which is imposed on every theological student as soon as he has to present the draft of a sermon on a New Testament text. I choose as an example the parable of the labourers in the vineyard, Matt. 20.1–16.

Once the student has received or chosen his text, he will first of all wish to read it carefully. He knows that the usual Lutheran text is a translation of Matthew's Greek text, and he himself will now venture upon a translation of the text. For this purpose he uses the lexicon and also commentaries and the literature which discusses the text in detail; in this case, therefore, the standard works on the parables of Jesus by A. Jülicher and J. Jeremias, and perhaps also the special contribution in G. Bornkamm's paper on the 'Idea of reward in the New Testament'.[2]

In the very first sentence the translation confronts him with decisions: Does ὁμοία mean 'same' or 'similar'? Or should one say, in the case of the βασιλεία, 'the situation is like . . .'? What, then, does βασιλεία τῶν οὐρανῶν mean? Should the translation be 'the

[1] First published in *EvTh* 18, 1958, pp. 256–68. This paper was originally given to a gathering of ministers in Berlin. The choice of theme was occasioned by Bultmann's remarks about the historical method in a study on the problem 'Ist voraussetzungslose Exegese möglich?', *TZ* 13, 1957, pp. 409–17. Regarding the problem of the historical exception, cf. my study *Das urchristliche Sakramentsverständnis*, 1958, pp. 36ff.

[2] 'Der Lohngedanke im Neuen Testament', *EvTh* 6, 1946–7, pp. 143–66, reprinted in *Studien zu Antike und Urchristentum*, Gesammelte Aufsätze II, 1959, pp. 69–92.

kingdom of heaven'? Or are the more recent scholars correct in translating it as 'the rule of God'? But what does 'the rule of God' mean? Is it some great miraculous force which is coming, or promises to come, or is near, or has indeed already come? Yet the text seems to be a parable, in which a distinction has to be made between two parts—the 'image' and the 'matter'.[1] From that it might be deduced that the very intention of the image part is to answer questions such as the meaning of God's $\beta \alpha \sigma \iota \lambda \epsilon i \alpha$. The translation is therefore dependent on the understanding of the parable, even though the understanding of the parable in all its detail in turn presupposes a translation.

The 'image' introduces us to the story of the householder who gathers together hired labourers in the market (as we are told later) for his apparently sizeable vineyard. This procedure is repeated almost to the point of absurdity, for the man snaps up and engages some who have remained without employment up to the very last hour. The day is over, and the lord of the vineyard gives payment. They are paid by the day. Originally the agreement was for one denarius, which was not much, and everyone receives that, first and last alike. Up to this point the lord's behaviour has been striking, to say the least, but now the narrative rises to a climax of dramatic tension. It achieves this by means of what might be called a device of dramatic technique, inasmuch as the last are paid first, so that we, too, share the inevitable reaction of the first. The first see that the last receive the whole day's wage, and naturally they hope for a higher rate for themselves. But in fact they receive the same. Immediately they reveal their bitter disappointment, because it seems to them that the lord's action is unjust. They say, 'These last worked only one hour, and you have made them equal to us who have borne the burden of the day and the scorching heat.' Thereupon the lord replies to one of them, and this again cleverly adds to the dramatic effect: 'Friend, I am doing you no wrong. Did you not agree with me for one denarius? Take what belongs to you and go.' However, this stern pronouncement is

---

[1] Translator's note: *Bildhälfte* and *Sachhälfte*: This distinction between the two aspects or 'halves' of a parable is not easy to render into English. '*Bild*' means the 'image' which is immediately represented, and in the absence of an adjectival form the phrase 'image part' has been used. '*Sache*' means the subject-matter, the real 'thing' which is complementary to the image. It is with reference to this 'matter' that the phrase 'material part' is used.

not his last word on the matter. The lord offers a further explanation, although he has really no need to do so. 'I choose to give to this last as I give to you. Am I not allowed to do what I choose with what belongs to me?' With these words the objection is finally dismissed. Every judge would have to take the side of the lord. It is not permissible to bring in modern viewpoints. But the lord has one more thing to say: 'Or is thine eye evil because I am kind?' If this were translated 'good', the point would be lost, because a kind person does not do anything that might remain beyond the reach of an evil person, whereas a good person might well do. This translation is linguistically possible.

The dialogue is at an end. An application follows, which could be omitted, and which represents an independent logion (as Matt. 19.30 shows immediately before). Verse 16b, which in Nestle is eliminated for reasons of textual criticism, is identical with Matt. 22.14, and so also an independent logion, and it interprets v. 16a with a warning. But the narrative is not necessarily of a warning nature. It may well reject an unjustified claim, but it thereby underlines not just the freedom of a great lord, but also his real kindness; and those who want to know what is right are the very ones who ought to understand this kindness. To this extent the narrative solicits understanding, even though it makes no concessions once the die has been cast. The application in v. 16a will then arouse suspicion, for it selects a standpoint which is no longer within the trend of the narrative. As v. 16b shows, it raises new questions.

But what of the parable as a whole? What is the point which makes possible the comparison between the two parts, the 'image' and the 'matter', supposing that we are in the first place prepared to admit the validity of the introduction, i.e. the reference to the βασιλεία? Are we to say that the 'image' stresses the right of kindness? But then we would have overlooked the fact that the 'image' very definitely tells of an individual or exceptional case. It is, in fact, expressly intended that it should not bear a general parabolic character.

The style of the whole parable is significant: the circumstances surrounding the hire of the labourers; the minute attention to detail, almost from hour to hour; then the correspondingly quicker acceleration in the development of the text; its relentless course, leading to the release of tension in the dialogue; the use in the dialogue of the general only as a foil for a word which singles out the individual and grasps him deep down—this all indicates that, just as the narrative summons the individual to reflection, so also the person who is speaking wants to be considered and respected as an individual. What has to be kept in view is a particular and unique conduct.

Therefore we should not jump prematurely to the conclusion that the parable is referring to God and his kindness. If the 'image' and the 'matter' do, in fact, agree, the parable indicates rather a particular conduct of God. This is certainly to be termed 'kindness', not with the intention of expressing a divine property, but rather indicating that we have to think of an *act* of God's kindness. This act is characterized by the fact that none the less it both is and indeed has been contradicted by those who do not understand, but who really ought to know better. This is shown by the warning in v. 15b, which stirs the conscience and almost oversteps the bounds of the 'image'. It is also noteworthy that Matthew regards the parable as special material and introduces it at an important point in his Gospel. The βασιλεία τῶν οὐρανῶν, then, means a particular conduct of God which, by virtue of being an act of kindness, aroused opposition, although for right-thinking people it ought really to bring great joy. At any rate, the evangelist seems to have understood the matter in this way.

We now quite naturally ask which particular conduct or bearing of God is meant to be stressed by the parable. Since the evangelist uses it as special material, and indeed lays emphasis on it, as is shown by the context in which it stands, and since this evangelist trains his attention in particular on God's judgment as one which is already operative in regard to Israel (cf. Matt. 5.17ff; 22.7 *et al.*), it is worth considering whether at least the application in v. 16a might refer to the distinguishing of Gentile Christians before the Israel which ultimately rejects the Gospel. However, Jesus himself was rejected by Israel, at least by its official section, which was so conscious of its own right. There is no convincing reason for denying that this is one of Jesus' parables. Even if its introduction were the work of the evangelist, it is quite possible to say of Jesus himself that he could indeed refer to a particular act of God's kindness in terms of the βασιλεία. For on more than one occasion he celebrated a meal with the publicans and sinners which, though not a messianic meal, was certainly one which celebrated God's βασιλεία. This conduct brought upon him severe accusations from the strict Jews, and eventually even death on the cross. (Matt. 11.18f stresses this meal as a characteristic of Jesus' conduct, in contrast to that of the more monastic Baptist, who likewise died a violent death.) We can hardly be mistaken in concluding that Jesus' meal—or his entire conduct towards publicans and sinners who did 'penance'—comprised in Jesus' eyes anyway a specific act of God's kindness, or that his conduct was at least comparable with such an act (Matt. 4.17). This also means that sinful man is dependent on God's kindness. In particular it means that Jesus in any case held out as a prospect this act of God's kindness and ordered his conduct towards sinful men accordingly. Certainly Jesus repeatedly underlines God's demand clearly and severely, as the first antitheses in Matt. 5 show. He appeared not simply as the preacher of some possible kindness of God, of which all stood equally in need. Instead Jesus clung to this kindness, as to an event known to him; and he did not shrink from demonstrating the correspondence between this event and his own conduct towards those under judgment. Jesus acted in a very real way as God's representative, and said himself, 'Blessed is he who takes no offence at me' (Matt. 11.6). A declaration of this kind relates not to Jesus' personal qualities, nor to a dogmatic assessment of his person, but to his conduct and to his proclamation. Coming from Jesus, the parable then declares: *'This is how things stand with regard to God's kindness—I know it and am showing it to you—it is like a great lord who once . . .'* And its unwritten introductory saying is ἀμήν, λέγω ὑμῖν, inasmuch as the parable effects and demands a decision. But to be able to preach the parable properly the student must now ask whether Jesus' claim to be God's representative still possesses validity today. He should not allow this question to be answered by any dogmatic system, not even by that of the Gospels. Instead he must first of all remain on the same plane which had been opened up to him by his comprehending translation. He must also look for the answer to this question in the parable. Up till now we have, in fact, looked only at one aspect of the concept of the βασιλεία. What has now to be done is to explore its temporal meaning in greater detail.

The parable itself tells us that Jesus intends to be understood. Indeed, he solicits understanding, by giving us to understand his conduct as God's conduct. *It is up to the person who understands the parable to give the verdict on the truth of Jesus' claim*. It is the person who understands who has to decide. Jesus encountered opposition, and thus, by means of a parable of this kind, he handed himself over to the judgment of those who understood him; for they were aware of the demand laid upon them to relate God's conduct to themselves in the very same way as it met them in Jesus' conduct. Just as the right-thinking man has every reason to understand God's kindness as an exceptional act, so Jesus meant to say that we should all found our hope and trust on this exception, as surely as we are directed to this exception. According to Jesus' proclamation, which went along with his conduct, it depends entirely on our own hearing or faith, whether we today gain the opportunity of trusting along with Jesus in God's kindness for us.

However, have we not included ourselves prematurely in these considerations, which originally applied to Jesus' hearers and those about him? The objection only underlines the fact that Jesus was the first to require of his hearers this faith in the exception, while equally surely they all stood under the rule of a law which they must have been aware involved their condemnation. But those who hear will indeed realize that by means of his conduct Jesus has staked his own life for this faith. The parable by no means simply contains the pallid requirement that sinful man should believe in God's kindness. Instead it contains, in a concrete way, first Jesus' *pledge*, which says that there will be no disappointment for those who, in face of a cry of 'guilty', nevertheless found their hope on an act of God's kindness; and, secondly, Jesus' *determination* to give up everything else for this faith. Ultimately those grumblers are the reverse picture of those who really understand—the dialogue brought that to light. Jesus himself was one who understood. Must we not, then, say, 'He lost his life so that we might win God'? The proof of this parable was finally revealed only on the Cross; and this was for all who were to hear in the future. For this word holds good right on beyond Jesus' death. It demands faith alone, and nothing else. Thus, in view also of this insistence on his word, the meaning which the $\beta\alpha\sigma\iota\lambda\epsilon\iota\alpha$ gains in the context of Jesus' proclamation is revealed. It is the expectation that Jesus' proclamation will find faith, and that the fulfilment of this expectation will recognize in the very fact of the proclamation an act of God's grace. Then the hearers will no longer be dependent on Jesus' actual conduct, because the declared kindness of God in the acts of the proclamation continues, at least *as* an act of the proclamation. God himself 'will' then become our Lord. The rule of God really consists of the fact that Jesus' word finds faith in the future. But it does not mean that everyone will believe. Instead the astonishing thing will be just how adversely people make up their minds; as a result, the two comments in v. 16 will always be true. (This verse is fully accepted by Luther.)

On this basis it is certainly possible to preach, assuming that the expositor examines his heart at the same time. The ultimate exposition of the parable will be this sermon—that God's kindness, which was proclaimed by Jesus, continues beyond Jesus' death and demands our faith and summons us to decision also.

What are the consequences of this example for our theme? I think there is a single thesis. The exposition has endeavoured quite briefly to pursue its course analytically, one step at a time, as the historical-critical method demands, and has tried simply to help the text speak in the context which is authoritative for it. The result has been an orientation for the preaching of Jesus' word, which demands faith. Therefore my thesis is as follows:

The historical-critical method of interpretation of New Testament texts has done its duty when the necessity for preaching arises from the text.

What follows is simply comment.

1. Years ago I resisted passionately what a preacher, then rated among the best, said from the pulpit, about his text, that at this point we came specially near to Jesus, because the text was a word once spoken by Jesus himself. However, I myself have just said that the result of exposition was 'an orientation for the preaching of Jesus' word, which demands faith'. The difference should nevertheless be clear. For we do not come nearer to Jesus through having a word of the historical Jesus preached; what should be preached is that Jesus' word demands faith. In faith I am not only near to Jesus; in faith I await the occurrence of God's kindness *together with Jesus*, and this is just as certain as my need, in faith,

to pronounce the word 'guilty' about myself. We are not concerned with a nearness to the historical Jesus; in company with
him we are concerned with the nearness of God, with the 'near'
God. In my opinion the understanding of the proclamation of the
rule of God in the Gospels which is to be worked out by the
historical-critical method agrees in other respects with this view,
as Bultmann, for example, has shown in his book on *Jesus*.

2. In his article already referred to, Bultmann says:[1] 'All
decisions and all actions have their causes and consequences, and
the historical method assumes that it is basically possible to
demonstrate these and also their connexion and thereby to understand the whole historical course as a closed unity.' For 'the
historical method includes the presupposition that *history is a unity*,
in the sense of a closed relationship of effects, in which individual
events are linked through the succession of cause and effect'. But
this linking is one thing, and our understanding of historical
phenomena another. This distinction leads to the insight which
Bultmann stresses, 'that *historical knowledge is never final and definitive*'.[2] There are certainly events which can be fixed by dating. But
what they 'signify as historical (*geschichtliche*) events cannot be
definitely fixed. We must therefore say that an historical event will
be recognizable for what it is—in fact, *as* historical—only in the
future. Then we can also say that *the future of an historical event
belongs to the event*.' Man plays his part in this. The *understanding* of
history presupposes our responsibility for history, and therefore
our personal decision by which we avail ourselves of this responsibility. This has its consequences for faith in Jesus' word, because
this faith is aware of its responsibility for the message of God's
nearness. The consequence is that faith also accepts its responsibility for the message of God's nearness in the form of responsibility for history. Faith will then have to be specially on
guard against the temptation to dissolve the historical correlation
of effects. For what faith cannot allow is the idea that this correlation of effects is 'interrupted by the thrust of supernatural other-
worldly powers', nor even that this is possible.[3] Instead faith
—while remaining entirely *within* history, i.e. in its responsibility

---

[1] 'Ist voraussetzungslose Exegese möglich?' *TZ* 13, 1957, pp. 411f.
[2] *Ibid.*, p. 415.
[3] Cf. Bultmann, *op. cit.*, p. 412.

for history—must be concerned with the whole of history. If we assume that history, as a closed causal unity, stands under a law (which, of course, is not to be confused with a natural law, because history's future nature demands not simply our observation of historical processes, but principally our co-responsible understanding of history)—assuming this, the thought then occurs that faith considers history in terms of Paul's word about Christ being the end of the law (Rom. 10.4). God's nearness then indeed means the proximity of the end of history. This does not imply that Jesus expected the imminent end of the world—the decision about this conception depends on what consequences Jesus intended to have drawn from his proclamation of God's nearness. The conclusion is rather that faith in Jesus' word is true faith in so far as it respects the compulsory character of historical connexions as God's will, with the result that faith can only appeal from God to God (cf. II Cor. 2.17). If it does this—and without this appeal faith would not be faith—faith then has to do with God himself in history. Does this imply that it is just the 'meaning' of history that changes? The meaning of history certainly is different for faith, because faith is now aware of being led from God's judgment to God's grace, and is, for example, able to bear suffering, as Paul stresses (e.g. II Cor. 1.5). But history is not everything. Alongside and together with it we find nature. As far as we ourselves are concerned our real life begins with faith. This life is rightly understood as life 'before God', for instance by Luther, but also by Paul. The 'end' of history, which is not the same as the end of man, is therefore identical with the 'beginning' of life, inasmuch as faith gives its verdict (Rom. 8.24). In this connexion the New Testament speaks of the resurrection of the dead. But does its talk of the resurrection of Jesus Christ not make clear that faith, in its understanding of history, intends to hold firmly to the origin of life as an event within history. The one question which remains is whether theology is right in maintaining it is true to Jesus, even though it usually considers the coherence of history to have been disrupted by the resurrection of Jesus. Is theology not then constructed from the beginning on the basis of unbelief? For the paradox—that the end of history is not seen but believed—corresponds to the unity of faith and word, and therefore to an understanding of history.

3. However, at this stage of the reflection a new objection seems to arise. It should be accepted that a theology which maintains that the historical correlation of effects has been shattered by the resurrection of Christ is erected on a foundation of unbelief. For in this view God's law is not fulfilled, but rather suspended, and therefore the paradoxical character of the sentence 'Christ is the end of the law' is misunderstood. This kind of massive theology is nevertheless interested in defining history as a causally conditioned correlation of effects. It would not consider itself as mythology, but, so to speak, as contra-historical scholarship which lives by the 'historical' method, because it can salvage its theme in the sphere of historical knowledge only as a paradox; for faith history then only becomes history completely when it is necessary to speak of the unity of already comprehended history (Gal. 3.23). An understanding of history is also involved in the formula which says that historical knowledge assumes a causally connected correlation of effects—i.e. which has in mind basically the closed nature of history. The objection to this formula is as follows: Surely this understanding of history, which is apparently entirely secular and which certainly appears everywhere in the historical method—surely this is from the very beginning theologically conditioned. Then it would not be surprising that the misuse of the causal understanding of history necessarily strikes back at theology itself and falsifies it. The causal understanding of history is comprehensible on the basis of the idea of God's judgment, particularly if faith considers God's judgment is revealed and confirmed by the message of grace, and therefore submits itself to the actuality of this judgment. It follows that there is only one 'closed' unity of history, and that comes under the heading of death. However, history which is understood in this way is to be distinguished from the person of the believer. This understanding came about because faith, being faith in Jesus' word, was aware of the summons coming from Jesus' person, henceforth to insist along with Jesus in relying on the event of God's kindness. It remains the case that this event of God's kindness announces itself within the history which is to be understood. But according to the verdict of faith history is only properly understood when it is drawn into the light of God's kindness. The event of faith is itself also causally linked with history. For faith considers itself to be the response to Jesus'

proclamation. But in faith the event turns to what happens between God himself and man himself. Surely we must then say that the causal understanding of history remains essential, but at the same time it is essentially history which of itself is not understood.

4. The causal understanding of history is essential, wherever and as long as it is possible, because its analysis makes clear the nature of our action as decision. To this extent there is no objection to the historical method. However, this method is for two reasons basically unable to cope with the future character of history: firstly because every phenomenon already has its future belonging to it, in so far as it is impossible to know what further effects the phenomenon will later reveal from its understanding; and secondly because there are without doubt phenomena which drop out of history, so that their effects are no longer discernible. Causally explained history is quite simply the totality of what remains, in some cases more, in others less, and, seen as a whole, very little, when one thinks of the fullness of previously present possibilities of life. For this reason the causal explanation of history —and this understanding is no more than an explanation—is tailored to the standard of transitoriness, with the result that it can at least demonstrate to us God's judgment. The historian who follows the historical method—and also the exegete—must therefore make up his mind whether his material (in our case the New Testament texts) makes claims on his understanding, for he would eliminate them if he wanted to explain them causally. If the hermeneutical problem consists of this, i.e. the way the text is to be questioned, we have now to say that the historical method can be only an aid to exegesis. The possibility of its application is limited by the actual phenomenon to which the text bears witness, supposing the phenomenon still belongs to life. The correlation of effects which is presupposed by the historical method is therefore itself basically limited and is thus only occasionally closed. But if this viewpoint is extended to the idea of a generally closed history, this ignores the fact that, although life itself on occasion runs on into history, it is only one direction of history which points to the past, whereas its 'matter' always comes newly from the future—from life itself. With a view to the future, history is therefore quite open. However, if a person is aware that he is under the constraint of history, if in faith he sees that all life is indeed threatened by this force, talk

about an end to history will then certainly be meaningful for him; for he is himself aware of being freed from this force, and is able, for example, to hold firmly to Jesus' word. Expressed in inner-historical terms, this means that man stands over against himself, though faith says that man now stands before God. This shows that the historical method is a foreign influence on the exposition of the New Testament, as soon as the relation of the text to preaching is eliminated. (For we can only stand before God if we are called before him. It is the text, and not the historical method, which knows what meets us there.)

5. But we must go one step farther. Is not history, for example of the Germans or the French, primarily what has transmitted itself to us from the past? The historical method may establish what things were once like. But the stock of history which is explained in this way is of itself something different from the results which are to be expected from the historical method. A race for its part speaks of tradition and heritage. History which has not been violated by the historical method admittedly also includes the sphere of the past. This method will not even be able to make available to us the material with which as a result of our heritage we have to come to terms. The history of which it tells us will normally be essentially an incomplete obituary notice. Therefore if we are looking for a better concept of history we ought not to have as our starting-point the idea of history which comes to light in the historical method. The historical method can only show us history in the form of power. However, it is for this very reason that it fits into the sphere of work of theology, assuming that theology keeps to its theme of faith in God in the way that this faith was demanded by Jesus. Such persistence in faith is, in fact, only possible if Jesus' word remains operative subsequent to his death. The historical transmission of Jesus' word is involved here, and also the recognition that this word has been handed on because of the claim it makes. The power of history, which became identifiable at Jesus' death, was not able to separate Jesus' word from faith; instead it bound this word the more firmly to faith. Jesus' word alone, in the sense of his action, has remained the ground for faith in his word. If Jesus claims to be God's representative in the future also, then faith in Jesus' word about the event of God's kindness will always derive its understanding from the selfsame time,

43

i.e. from the time as it was claimed by Jesus—and this is the time of faith (cf. Gal. 3.25). But the application of causality presupposes the unity of time, for cause and effect can only be fixed in terms of the difference between a 'before' and an 'after' which modify the same time. (This is also the basis for distinguishing between epochs of history, because in every epoch a time which coheres in itself is modified.) If one wanted to speak with justification of history as an idea, as the historical method must do if it intends to understand and explain history as a closed unity and as the one correlation of events, then history must always deal with the same time. Does history which is to be explained in this way presuppose the time of causality itself? The power of history is then the power of causality. However, although this power certainly makes faith comprehensible as an event, nevertheless only faith can see it as the power of history. The historical method is formally based solely on the unity of time, even if this is the unity of the time of causality.

6. With a view to Christian faith we must then say that the understanding of history is determined by whatever power is operative in it: i.e. whatever power so determines our life that for us past and future divide in relation to it. If the power operative in history is defined as the power of causality—there are, however, other quite different powers operative in history, e.g. the power of the German or the French language—it then appears as if history is determined by a standard which is really operative in nature in the form of natural law. This is why stress was laid on the fact that our enquiry concerns history that is understood. In comprehended history the power of causality is something different from causality in nature.

In nature we are indeed concerned with a correlation of effects which is closed by the power of causality, but this is ultimately not the case in history. If faith considers history to be a correlation of effects which has fallen under the power of causality, it does this because faith itself is comprehensible only on the basis of Jesus' history. Does this mean that freedom is bestowed in faith? Freedom from the power of causality which threatens our life, and yet at the same time always determines it and is even helpful? Certainly—as long as we look at this power of causality not in nature but in history, as long as we keep to our texts in the sense that our life itself is decided in faith. (The causality operative in nature can also be interpreted by faith as an aid.) Within the work on the texts which we have to expound, this freedom will appear at the point where the text urges the need for preaching about the power of causality. If Jesus' word—i.e. his claim that we should attend to the occurrence of God's kindness—is to be termed the origin of faith, then the fact of this concrete correlation of effects must be understood as the origin of life in faith (cf. Matt. 5.17). History would then indeed be the sphere within which the origin of our human life is at stake. In comprehended history this origin is known as freedom. If this thought is assessed in relation to man as he is—and the phenomenon of faith recommends this—then it can be said that history is the sphere of man's decision, or rather that it would be, if men believed in God. Even that consequence of faith which Gogarten rightly interprets in terms of the secularization of the world cannot be logically followed out. Similarly the historical method is not in a position to get right home to the nature of history. It is applicable to the exposition of the New Testament only to the extent that the analysis illuminates the texts in a concrete way, i.e. in the context of the time which makes them cohere. Then we understand why they have been handed down to us. The texts force us to develop our understanding of faith in relation to their understanding of faith, by virtue of the fact that they leave the power of causality undisturbed.

7. The enquiry about causality in the form of power can now be outlined in the following way. In this discussion we are not concerned with any causality other than that in nature, for there is only one kind of causality. This means there is no place for miracle *within* causality. So in all these considerations causality is to be seen in the first place as it appears to the man who understands. He for his part lives within causality, but has noted that it is precisely because of this that the choice of free decision between various possibilities of conduct is laid on him. Causality appears to him as power both in nature and also in his daily experience; in scholarly work and, it is to be hoped, in his conscience. Care, anxiety, despair, and indirectly hope also, are all possible forms of human conduct, only when we presuppose causality as power. This is the basis on which our chances of understanding other people are also determined, if we want to know what was compelling

for them. Like Luther, the expositor of the New Testament must consult in particular the experience of conscience, if he wants to find out not just the generally possible motives of the people who find expression in the texts, but also the context into which in their own way the texts fit. It is not as if the true content of the texts were discovered by referring to the experiences of conscience. If faith is concerned with what believers and their contemporaries understood historically, with what they intended when they gave an account of those personal experiences which the texts either report or presuppose, such as their experience of Jesus or his disciples or faith itself, then the experience of conscience is the key to their and our understanding of causality as power, which had become active in all these things. The real New Testament understanding of history emerges from this alone. Conceptions about possible courses of history or courses the reality of which was anticipated, which traditionally are considered to have operated in the New Testament, do not say clearly enough what the people of the New Testament were concerned with within history.

In the New Testament this kind of understanding is most clearly marked in the fragments of Jesus' proclamation that are still recognizable to us, and also in the Johannine writings. The Pauline distinction between law and gospel, which is expressly orientated towards the conscience, also points in this same direction of understanding. The object of faith is not to sharpen the conscience, but in fact this is what it does. If the New Testament is concerned with faith, the experience of conscience (for this reason, too) will be the hermeneutical principle of its exposition. This principle leads the way from historical analysis to preaching, and yet for this very reason makes historical analysis essential. What matters is the task of transferring a 'succession' (*Nacheinander*), which is historically developed by the power of causality, back to the 'relation' (*Beieinander*) which is demanded by the situation that determines the nature of our texts—to the relation of the preaching of faith. Time yields a more basic knowledge of itself in relation than it does in succession, because succession discloses the unity of time and space less readily than relation. We must therefore ask whether the relation will not do more justice to the nature of history than the succession which is operative in causality. This is why the so-called existential interpretation denotes a corrective to the historical method. For existential interpretation examines the possibilities of existence not simply on the plane of the succession but on the plane of the relation, and balances these two possible aspects of an event; and this is because it understands man primarily on the basis of language rather than of nature.[1] These theses will certainly have to stand the test of a radical analysis of being (*Sein*). If, as I think, it is necessary to say: 'Being is, and . . .', if therefore being simply expresses something like 'appending', and in this way affords the possibility of language, then the relation might simply express the nature of existence. For all existence is historically conditioned. But surely something like historicality (*Geschichtlichkeit*) always arises on the basis of hearing.

[1] At this point the conversation with Bultmann might be continued on the basis of his Gifford Lectures of 1955, published as *History and Eschatology*, Edinburgh, 1957. There Bultmann, with regard to historicism, considers causality and personality in relation to each other, so as to see the meaning of history realized in the *eschatologically conceived* present. But it seems to me that we have first to consider the 'language-character' of our existence, so that the relation (*Beieinander*) peculiar to the present does not disappear in the individual. I conceive the word of love to be the true *principium individuationis*, and I think that Bultmann would have to agree with this.

III

JESUS AND FAITH[1]
1958

THE interest of New Testament scholars has recently turned again to the general subject of the historical Jesus.[2] To what extent is theology concerned with the historical Jesus? In order to bring into the picture the contribution of New Testament scholarship to this question which has been so far accomplished, I should first like to expound my theme in a somewhat simpler form.

The purposely general formulation of the theme 'Jesus and Faith' may easily be put in a narrower way by adding to the word 'faith' the two words 'in him', so that it runs 'Jesus and faith in him'. In this narrower form the theme presents us with a familiar problem of New Testament theology: How did early Christian faith in Jesus account for itself, and can it be justified even though the historical Jesus made no demand for faith in his own person? The question can also be put in this way: How did the faith of Jesus become faith in Jesus?

It was and is possible to try to avoid the problem of this question by simply questioning the validity of the historical-critical analyses, for example of the Synoptic Gospels, which lie at the root of it. At this stage I do not wish to concern myself with such an objection. But even if the analyses are accepted at least in their essentials, mediating theses can be drawn up. One could, for instance, say that Jesus possessed a messianic self-consciousness, that he proclaimed himself, or that his call to decision implied a

---

[1] A lecture, delivered at the invitation of the Theology Faculty in Münster, on 13 June 1958. First published in *ZTK* 55, 1958, pp. 170–85.

[2] I refer to the contributions in *ZTK*; and also to Ph. Vielhauer 'Gottesreich und Menschensohn in der Verkündigung Jesu', *Festschrift für G. Dehn*, 1957, pp. 51–79; to James M. Robinson, *Kerygma und historischer Jesus*, Zurich-Stuttgart, 1960, being the expanded German edition of *A New Quest of the Historical Jesus* (SBT 25), 1959; to the supplement to the 2nd ed. of my *Hermeneutik*, 1958; and also to my study, *Das urchristliche Sakramentsverständnis*, 1958.

christology. But the early Christian kerygma or, as has also been said, the 'kerygma-dogma' (Schlier) of the crucified and risen Lord, is nevertheless threatened by the historical approach of exegesis. As soon as the interest of research is concerned with the historical Jesus, one must basically reckon with the fact that the early Christian kerygma of the crucified and risen Lord not only says something that Jesus did not say, but also adds something new that Jesus could not have said. The indisputable terminological difference between Jesus' proclamation and early Christian theology—not just the theology of the Apostle Paul—increases the suspicion. And the difference between the proclamation of Jesus in the Synoptics and Jesus' proclamation of himself in the Fourth Gospel seems to confirm it.

It can, of course, be said that this is quite in order. With the death and resurrection of Jesus something new did, in fact, take place, and it follows that the proclamation of the historical Jesus never intended to express the relation between Jesus and faith in him. But the Synoptic Gospels did nevertheless feel the need to combine Jesus' historical proclamation with faith in him. The so-called kerygmatic sections in Acts are an approximate parallel to this procedure. Obviously faith in Jesus would not and could not in the long run simply relinquish what had once been said by Jesus. On the other hand, the earnest and increasing efforts for a gospel which also contained the proclamation of Jesus shows that a difference certainly existed between Jesus' proclamation and faith in him.

We must not obliterate this difference. But we would do so if we tried to argue somewhat as follows: the Easter kerygma speaks of the risen Jesus and therefore demands faith in him. However, the risen Jesus is none other than the historical Jesus. Everything that belongs to Jesus, including his proclamation, belongs to faith in Jesus, if the Jesus in whom we believe is really the same Jesus who gathered disciples around him, performed miracles and preached. This popular argument of identity fails to recognize the weight of the question—how the difference of language between Jesus' proclamation and the theology, for example of Paul, but also of the Fourth Gospel, is to be explained historically and theologically. Philological devices and sociological and geographical considerations about the progress and needs of the early

Christian mission cannot lessen the weight of the theological question, which is at the same time an historical question.

The above-mentioned argument of identity without doubt by-passes the *essence* of faith. For faith always means something invisible; it is by no means a matter of seeing. Faith in Jesus was not really possible in relation to the historically visible Jesus; unless the historical Jesus had, in a Johannine fashion, made a distinction between what could be seen of him and what he was for faith. If, despite the historical-critical analysis, one wanted nevertheless to say that the synoptic Jesus did indeed speak of what he would at least *become* for faith, there would still remain a considerable difference of language between the Synoptic Gospels and the Fourth Gospel.

We will admit that, in fact, the historical Jesus can be none other than the risen Jesus, if faith is to be faith in Jesus. However, if faith in Jesus is to *begin* with Jesus' resurrection—as, for example, Paul certainly says and means when he comes to speak of baptismal confession—then faith in Jesus implies that Jesus is made present in a new way for faith in him. And the post-Pauline return to Jesus' proclamation, for example in Mark's Gospel, would just be a demonstration of the fact that only faith in Jesus is in a position to assess the historical Jesus properly. The life of the historical Jesus would certainly then remain open to almost unavoidable misunderstandings (Käsemann), as only faith in Jesus would acquire an appropriate understanding of him. By means of this kind of consideration we certainly avoid the all too clumsy alternative that either Jesus deceived himself about the future or the early community or Church misunderstood Jesus when and because they began to believe in him. Instead there is laid upon us the new obligation of interpreting faith itself as a struggle against misunderstandings, and asking to what extent these misunderstandings were seen and overcome by the New Testament and even by Jesus himself.[1]

In this paper we will tackle at least one stage of this task. Therefore I intend to speak firstly about the struggle of faith in Jesus, and in a second part about Jesus himself. The starting-point must be the struggle of faith in Jesus, because the real meaning of the historical Jesus comes properly to light only in this struggle—

[1] This would be a kind of test as a check to Vielhauer's study, see p. 48 n. 2.

assuming the correctness of the thesis that only faith in Jesus acquired the possibility of a full understanding of Jesus.

1. THE STRUGGLE OF FAITH

The familiar passage II Tim. 4.7 speaks of a struggle of faith: 'I have fought the good fight, I have finished the course, I have kept faith.[1] Henceforth there is laid up for me the crown of righteousness, which the Lord, the righteous judge, will award to me on that day, and not only to me but also to all who love his appearing.' The passage sounds like an encomium, like an obituary notice for the apostle who has died a martyr's death. It need only be transcribed into the third person to recognize the style of the declaration: 'He has . . .' We find this same confidence expressed in Rev. 2.10: 'Be faithful unto death, and I will give you the crown of life.' And correspondingly the warning in Rev. 3.11: 'Hold fast what you have, so that no one may seize your crown!' At that time practically all the leading Christians became martyrs.

However, it is necessary to guard against a possible misconception of martyrdom. Martyrdom was not so much the struggle as the victory of faith. The Johannine writings show this; cf., as well as the victor's sayings in Rev. 2 and 3, I John 5.4; John 16.33. The faithful have at their disposal spiritual armour which they donned at baptism, with the result that they are fundamentally insensitive to all the fiery barbs of the devil (Eph. 6.14–17; I Thess. 5.8; Rom. 13.12). For Paul there is no alternative to moving forward on this course (Phil. 3.13f), and if he has to wrestle, then it is with himself, in order to be in good training like an athlete (I Cor. 9.27). The early Church does not doubt that faith will reach its goal. This is the only way to understand why the Letter to the Hebrews allows no rest: one is either completely a Christian, or not at all—*tertium non datur*. The believer has chosen correctly between life and death (II Cor. 2.15f; 4.1–4). He has gained a Lord for whom he lives and dies (Rom. 14.7–9). The daily conduct of the Christian, intent on progress in what is worthy, may come under the heading of a '$\pi\epsilon\rho\iota\sigma\sigma\epsilon\acute{\nu}\epsilon\iota\nu$ $\mu\hat{a}\lambda\lambda o\nu$' (I Thess. 4.10) (reminiscent of the Stoic '$\pi\rho o\kappa\acute{o}\pi\tau\epsilon\iota\nu$'), but in all this the Christian conduct of life

---

[1] In my opinion the translation of $\pi\acute{\iota}\sigma\tau\iota s$ as 'faithfulness' is too weak in this case, although, as Rev. 2.10 shows, it is easily suggested.

clearly has one intention—to have God's will and indeed God's right on its side (I Cor. 7.19; II Cor. 1.12; Rom. 12.1ff, etc.). A person does not believe because he cannot live as a Christian (as many think today); in the New Testament a person lives as a Christian because he believes. It is self-evident to Paul that the outworking of faith is love (Gal. 5.6). Faith is not a stop-gap for ethical insufficiencies, but the source of an ethically exemplary life, which, of course, includes forgiveness. Paul demands discipleship. The early Christian exhortation has no need to fight shy of comparison with its heathen equivalent the Stoic ethic, which commands its respect. And it is aware of this, as Paul's terminology shows (cf., e.g., I Cor. 6.12; 7.29–31).[1] Faith certainly practises the good, as the Stoic does also. But faith does not spend long struggling over the good—it does it. The world can and should recognize Jesus' disciples by their deeds; so says the Johannine Jesus (John 13.35). Here I may point out that the *iustitia civilis* in Luther's doctrine of the Two Kingdoms has the same meaning in reference to the freedom of a Christian.[2]

What, then, is the struggle of faith? If, as in Abraham, faith refers to the invisible, then the struggle of faith is concerned with the difference between the invisible and the visible (Heb. 11; Rom. 4.18–22). We miss this aspect if we start out from moral or ethical needs. Therefore, before what must naturally follow, I have inserted a survey of what in the New Testament is the unequivocal Christian conduct of life. Faith does not speculate, nor does Paul idealize. The idealizing Lucan Book of Acts stands right on the fringe of the New Testament. Certain elements of a dualistic tradition in the New Testament should not blind us from seeing that the process of demythologizing—or, as can also be said, of de-demonizing of the world—had then been carried to its furthest in the realm of the conduct of life. This is also very clearly shown by the matter-of-fact household lists (Col. 3.18–4.1; I Peter 2.13ff, etc.; Eph. 6.12 is only apparently an exception).

But faith certainly fights against sin, death and the law, as *powers*. What does this mean? Exactly what the word 'powers'

---

[1] The fact that the formulation in I Cor. 6.12 has in view the discussion with Gnostics still does not invalidate its Stoic ring.

[2] I am thinking of passages like the one in the Argument of the *Commentary on Galatians* (WA 40.1, pp. 50f.), and also of the question of what is removed from the decision of conscience (cf. *RGG* II, col. 1357).

describes. From now on sin and death are no longer to 'rule', and
in the future the law is to serve life. These powers are the powers
of the world, as Paul shows in Rom. 5.12ff. The struggle of faith
is a struggle for the world. However, the struggle with these
powers does not take place anywhere, but in the Christian himself.
The inner life of the individual is the arena of the struggle for the
world. This inner life should certainly not be confused with
something like inwardness. Paul develops an anthropology in
order to avoid this; i.e. it does not stem from ethical needs. The
familiar Pauline imperative encourages faith rather than throwing
it in question. I now propose briefly to investigate the Pauline
anthropology.

Faith gives freedom. For this Bultmann has coined the phrase
'freedom from ourselves for ourselves'. This formula is very useful for our purpose if we understand freedom for ourselves as
freedom for faith, and freedom from ourselves as freedom from
the three powers of the world mentioned above. The three powers
of sin, death and the law do not have equal standing. According to
Paul, certainly, the last enemy death (I Cor. 15.26; Rom. 8.21) is a
rival to sin (cf. Rom. 5.12ff). On the other hand, sin and death can
be included together under the concept of the law of sin and
death (Rom. 8.2). By making the law a superior concept governing sin and death, Paul intends to stress the fact that sin and
death necessarily belong together, since they pervert God's
law. God really wills life (Rom. 7.10). Death operates with the
help of sin, because sin turns God's law against man (Rom. 5.20);
and sin operates with the help of death, because death turns God's
law against man (Rom.7.24). The real power therefore lies with
the law, not with sin or death (I Cor. 15.56). The Christian can
freely meet death, as the example of Paul shows, and he can understand dying as a gain (Phil. 1.21). The Christian can likewise claim
freedom from what is sinful, because in faith he understands himself
as a 'new creature' (II Cor. 5.17; Rom. 6.11; 8.10). The world can do
him no more harm (Gal. 6.14). But what is the position with
regard to the law? For faith the law has altered its function;
indeed, it has regained it, for it is now fulfilled in love (Rom.
13.8–10). Prior to faith the law led irresistibly to sin and death,
because it was misused; but now it serves faith in its function
as the divine power of order in life (I Cor. 7.19; Rom. 13.1–7).

It shows the believer that he has the freedom to remain indebted to someone else, provided he follows the rule of love (Gal. 6.2).

However, the new freedom of action which is given to faith is not an ethical maxim, but the conduct of life in the spirit of faith (Rom. 8.4; Gal. 5.25). Faith itself is the active quantity in this new relationship of faith and conduct of life, or of faith and spirit. As is well known, faith in Paul occasionally assumes the marks of conscience (I Cor. 8–10; Rom. 14). What does this mean? Freedom from sin and freedom for death as dying still does not destroy the world. But it provides each individual with a great, though always varying, opportunity of bringing his faith, seen as freedom for himself, into action in the conscience. Everyone is obliged to decide in his own conscience what it is for which he has concrete freedom. Everyone must himself make the test to see in what act he remains sure of his faith (Rom. 14.5, 22). As we have said, it is not a question of a struggle between good and evil, but of a struggle between weakness and strength. Indeed, Paul understands his weakness as strength (II Cor. 12.8–10). This paradox does not apply to everyone without further ado. But everyone should see to it that he conducts himself in such a way that, despite sin and death, the power of faith in him successfully opposes the power of the world—as if the power of the world, which is otherwise so fateful, no longer existed even outwardly (I Cor. 7.29–31). In this way everyone has to be like a star in the night and bear visible witness to the fact that the world has found its true Lord (Phil. 2.15); and therefore that, as Paul believes, the spirit already triumphs over the flesh rather than the flesh over the spirit (Rom. 1.25ff; 8.12–14). This is impossible without prayer. But every believer is able to cope with the world at least by calling out along with the community 'Abba, dear Father'. The faithful therefore by no means isolate themselves.

The struggle of faith, as understood by Paul and also maintained elsewhere in the New Testament, is, as Rom. 1.17 says, a struggle *for faith* (εἰς πίστιν), because it stems from faith (ἐκ πίστεως). It is a struggle for the lordship of Jesus Christ in the world. It is a struggle for time, and it takes place in time, in the sphere of freedom from sin and death which is spiritually effective and therefore spreads out into the world. The faithful, and indeed the whole world, now live in the time of this struggle.[1]

A warning like Eph. 6.12—that our struggle is not with flesh and blood—is also to be understood on this basis. But the misunderstanding which is here contested and which threatens faith arises from the struggle of faith itself. Faith is endangered not by its failures but by its successes. How is this to be understood? Very simply. A radical struggle of faith must be successful, because it need shrink from nothing, not even martyrdom. This is why faith will always almost unavoidably be transformed into experience, into sight. The experiences of faith first of all confirm the strength of faith. But because they are visible they also arouse a new discontent with what is, because everything that is visible is subject to criticism—we constantly strive for more than the eye can see. Thus the successes of faith immediately endanger faith itself. Faith is now spurred on not solely by the message, but also by the effects of faith. Thus it is degraded to the level of a means of being (*Dasein*), instead of remaining its objective—christology is exchanged for an anthropology, whereas anthropology should really serve faith in Jesus. This is why Paul, like all good theologians after him, strives for a *better* anthropology. He opposes the Gnostics' desire for sight and also the defective sight of the Judaists, so that faith may remain faith.[2] In spite of the obituary notice in II Tim. 4.7, Paul lost this struggle, in so far as the speculation of the Gnostics gained an influence on the incipient dogma, and the success morality of the Judaists gained an influence on the incipient order of the Church. However, with regard to the New Testament, the Apostle did win his struggle, because his letters on faith created the presupposition that enabled the Gospels to be written; and thus the picture or negative of the historical Jesus which saved faith did not simply disappear. The second part of the paper, which is now to be developed, is to provide the basis for this statement. We turn to the proclamation of Jesus, and look first of all at the Fourth Gospel.

[1] Cf. my *Hermeneutik*, p. 140: for this II Cor. 3.18. The popular and not entirely unfounded comparative interpretation of the ἐκ-εἰς in Rom. 1.17 should consider more resolutely how this comparative is to be justified; i.e. to what extent faith brooks a comparative. What comparative can there be of Rom. 3.28?

[2] This is the problem: how faith remains faith. The problem becomes meaningless if, through reference to Isaiah himself, faith is defined as 'that which endures'. Neither God nor faith are themselves something enduring. James 3.18 is a profitable starting-point.

2. JESUS

If we want to speak of the historical Jesus we must accustom ourselves at first to disregard the christological dogmas of the Gospels (which incidentally are not in agreement with one another), and to consider whether we can, in fact, find in the Gospels the decisive reference point for Jesus' proclamation. To what does Jesus' proclamation refer? There are two answers to this question, the synoptic and the Johannine, and both may be discussed. I begin with John.

John speaks of what it means to love Jesus. Bultmann formulates the Johannine answer in the following way: Man does *not* know 'what he *really* wants, nor that the revelation provides him with the possibility of attaining his reality, and thus confronts him with the question of whether he wants to be himself. There is one thing that he *really* wants, that he must want by virtue of being a creature who receives life through the Logos, and that appears in his desire for love; it is this: not to exist of himself and for himself. This finds its fulfilment when in faith in God's revelation he receives himself as a gift. Thereby he experiences the love of God and of the revealer.'[1] In faith in God's revelation man therefore receives himself as a gift, when he wants to exist in the love of God and of the revealer; then he lives no longer of himself and for himself. At the same time this life transposes man into the range of validity of the word (cf. John 11.25). The message which he believes is the word of love. The word of love is the word about the *event* of love. The two condition each other: love is proclaimed as an event, and this proclamation, which is itself an event, furthers the event of love (John 13.34f; cp. 14.25f). Therefore Bultmann's statement that man does not want to exist of himself and for himself presupposes love as an event. Considered formally and independently of the message, the concept of existence used by Bultmann means that every man needs a ground for his being (*Dasein*). It means also that man is always in a relation to himself in such a way that he is and remains man only in the knowledge of himself as one who needs a ground for his being. But it is clear that the one thing which fits in exactly to this formal concept

---

[1] *Das Evangelium des Johannes* (Meyers kritisch-exegetischer Kommentar über das Neue Testament 2, 11th ed.), 1950, p. 481, on 14.21.

of existence in Bultmann is the phenomenon of a love which has been understood. The human desire for love is thus divested of its biological and psychological features and conceived as a structural factor of human being (*Sein*) in general. Bultmann's interpretation of love is for its part not a random one, but is derived from the proclamation, or bound up with the proclamation. His structural analysis of human existence is certainly stimulated by Heidegger.[1] But it stands and falls not with a philosophy, but rather with the right to understand the revealer (i.e. Jesus) as the word of love which has become an event (John 1.14). As far as its content is concerned, the Logos in John 1.1 is to be understood as the word of love. This love appears as word, because love cannot survive of itself, but can only be handed on as word. In the Fourth Gospel Jesus and faith in Jesus, in fact, say the same thing; and this is because faith rests content with the ἐγώ εἰμι of the revealer. Jesus says: I am (love); faith says: thou art (love). But faith can only say this because it is capable of a special relation to *Jesus*' word. For faith Jesus' word has become the ἐντολή, the new command of love. As a result faith is able to desire, believe and hold out in love. Love is here the summons of a new being (*Dasein*). In John the proclamation of Jesus refers to an attitude which no future will affect, and which at the same time fulfils the being (*Sein*) of man (John 19.30). As the conduct of love this conduct is in harmony with the victory of joy (John 16.24). Whereas in Paul the various inflections of Christian existence take place in the interplay of weakness and strength, in John it is fulfilled in pain and joy (and this is not just in the parting address).[2] According to John, Jesus' proclamation is related in a concrete way to pain and joy.

What have the Synoptic Gospels to say, when we read them (critically, of course) as sources of Jesus' proclamation?

At first sight we find nothing comparable in the Synoptics. The joy over the recovery of what was lost (Luke 15, etc.) is something different from the Johannine χαρά, which lacks any object; and Jesus' cry of jubilation in Luke 10.21 (cf. Matt. 11.25) is confined to him alone. The joy of the disciples in Matt. 5.12

---

[1] I have carried on this structural analysis in my *Hermeneutik*, pp. 62ff; similarly in the supplement, pp. 7ff.

[2] The contrast between life and death is not adequate.

(and in Luke 6.23) remains a promise.[1] In the Synoptic Gospels we find an entirely different climate and atmosphere from that of John's Gospel. The synoptic Jesus expounds the law. He does this extremely strictly and he reproaches the teachers in Moses' chair because they are concerned with trifles and forget the important matters: 'Woe to you, scribes and pharisees, hypocrites! for you tithe mint and dill and cummin, and have neglected the weightier matters of the law, justice and mercy and good faith!' (Matt. 23.23). This is simply the preaching of repentance. The thing that is significant for Jesus is that he assesses even the traditional teachers in terms of the need of the neighbour or fellow man. They had to be aware of their solidarity with this need, without having to spend long making up their minds. For the will of God, correctly understood, shines deep into the impure depths of man (Mark 7.15 par.). Man must admit his guilt as soon as he examines himself and sees how, in fact, he deals with the name of his neighbour, with his honour and with the truth (Matt. 5.21–37). One leads the other ever deeper into misfortune (Matt. 15.14; Luke 6.39). The profane epigrammatic wisdom, which often lies behind such penitential sayings, seems to me to be itself significant for Jesus' preaching of repentance.[2] Jesus' piety can hardly be distinguished from the piety of his environment, in so far as this piety was to be taken seriously (cf. Matt. 6.1–18). His conflict-sayings such as Mark 7.15 ('The impure comes from within you') or 3.4 ('Does the Sabbath serve life or not?') appeal in tone and content to truths which must sound familiar and obvious to simple people. The originality of Jesus is certainly not contained in one or other utterance of this kind, but in the relationship of his words to the entirety of his proclamation (as Braun correctly notes). The saying-source which Luke and Matthew follow hits the right note by linking Jesus' preaching of salvation with his preaching of repentance (Luke 6.20–36, etc.). Matthew has further stressed this note in his Sermon on the Mount: the promise and indeed the model of *God's* working applies only to those who want to examine themselves, and as a result they are relieved of care about 'being' (*Dasein*) (Matt. 6.19–34).

[1] Luke's correction (ἐν ἐκείνῃ τῇ ἡμέρᾳ) obliterates the peculiar character of the imperatives, which raise the present into the being of the future, but still remain address (v.11).
[2] For a different view cf. Bultmann, *Die Geschichte der synoptischen Tradition*, 3rd ed., 1957, p. 107 (ET, *The History of the Synoptic Tradition*, 1963, p. 102).

But does the eschatological aspect of his proclamation not show an entirely different Jesus? Is the present here not simply claimed as the 'time of decision' (Kümmel) for God's future? Leave the dead; do not look back; do not trouble about father and mother; sell what you have; gain by losing—what kind of emphases are these? The parables and similitudes expand this: kindness teaches love; repentance creates knowledge; the reckoning comes only at the end; do not be taken by surprise, etc. A person ought therefore to come to a decision, like this pearl merchant or that farmer who found the buried treasure, or like the godless householder who in his own shameless way knew well what would help him. What is the common denominator of this group, which at first glance is certainly not free from contradiction? Faith perhaps? The word faith certainly appears in the Synoptic Gospels. But in the sense of saving faith it belongs in my opinion to Christian linguistic usage. Within the Jewish tradition it is used only in contrast to doubt. Exceptions are provided only by the words 'unbelieving' and perhaps also occasionally 'of little faith', for they at least do not appear strange on the lips of Jesus, the preacher of repentance. The image of the mustard-seed faith that moves mountains may have been an eschatological conflict-saying or threat of Jesus (Matt. 17.20 par.). But the linguistic usage is not decisive, if the thing exists. Jesus appears not in his own name, but in God's name: whoever takes offence at him should beware lest he has taken offence at God's promise (Matt. 11.5f. par.). Everything is possible for God (Mark 10.27 par.), even what is impossible for men; if he wishes, God enters in at the very point where man makes as little progress as the camel through the eye of the needle (Mark 10.25 par.). What changes is the course of the human expectation of the future, for human expectation is attuned to calculating: God comes, perhaps with sudden impact (Luke 17.20f). Despite the scruples of Vielhauer and Conzelmann, it seems to me probable that even the parousia sayings about the coming Son of Man belong to Jesus' proclamation (Luke 12.8f *et al.*), even though in Jesus' eyes the relationship to the rule of God is certainly decided for everyone in regard to his person. This very relationship of Jesus to the rule of God belongs to those things which to normal sight seem impossible and contradictory.[1]

[1] The dispute about whether Jesus' relation to the rule of God should be

This is why the secular everyday aspect should not be missing from his proclamation. This same Jesus, in regard to whom the decision is made about whether God comes and how he comes, represents God's will in everyday life—in face of an unbelieving generation, and in company with a most unimposing collection of penitent men who were branded by their opponents as publicans and sinners (Matt. 11.19).

Jesus' proclamation certainly demands immediate decision. But precisely at this point it should be clear that under these circumstances it is impossible to speak of faith in Jesus which could in any instance dispense with Jesus' word. Jesus' own faith is all the more important, even though the Synoptic Gospels studiously avoid this formulation. They never say: 'My faith has saved you.' Jesus' faith does not refer at all to him alone having faith in God. In this matter he would not distinguish himself from any devout Jew. Nor does Jesus' faith refer especially to his conception of God's coming. Everyone in Israel at that time who gave earnest affirmation to the word 'the rule of God' expected that God would come and help Israel (Acts 1.6). They prayed for God's coming, as the Kaddish, for instance, shows. What was peculiar to Jesus in his attitude to the recipients (i.e. those whom God's coming was to benefit) was not just that he addressed them radically as penitents, but that, in contradistinction to the Qumran sects, for example, he also designated them and dealt with them as those who were unable to help themselves. It must remain an open question whether he called them the poor, or whether they were only later thus called (as the early community?). It seems to me that the traditional Jewish style of composition was responsible for their being contrasted with the rich in Luke and in Mark 10.24f. Matthew is correct in describing them as those who dispense with right on earth, and thus classing them along with those who for their part are intent on God's right, for example, on peace (Matt. 5.3-10; cf. James 3.18). They are bent not on themselves but on God's business, because they both suffer and have to suffer through God's business being distorted and mishandled in the world. It must again be stressed: in all this Jesus thinks about God

---

considered as 'near expectation', which would really exclude Jesus' death, could come to an end if Jesus' 'faith' were not thereby founded on conceptions rather than on the rule of God itself (see below).

no differently from the devout in Israel. But Jesus dares not just to announce or threaten God's coming, but to single out and separate those men to whom God will come; and he does this by including himself with them, as soon as they listen to him seriously. Nor does he by any means shut himself up with them in monastic seclusion. What Jesus did was more than any other prophet or teacher had done in Israel. At least in the eyes of the Jewish tradition described by the evangelists, it is blasphemy and treachery to Israel; and as they present it, it must lead to catastrophe, as soon as Jesus and his company attract public notice in the temple at Jerusalem. This is why the synoptic authors are at pains to demonstrate the theological correctness of Jesus' proclamation. In particular the controversy dialogues during the Jerusalem days, from which Jesus emerges as victor, are meant to show this.

Jesus therefore dares to single out those to whom his proclamation is addressed. He does this, differently from John the Baptist, by beginning quite openly to solemnize and celebrate with them the rule of God, by eating and drinking with them (a matter that arouses the censure of his opponents), and by setting off with them to go from Galilee up to the feast at Jerusalem. It is not as though these first had already to be the last. But they will nevertheless be the first. It is noticeable that, apart from the healing of Peter's mother-in-law, not a single story of healing applies to one of the trusted disciples—we are here disregarding the Fourth Gospel and the wider circle of Jesus' surroundings (the remark in Luke 8.2 is legendary). On the other hand, according to the presentation of the Synoptics, the 'little faith' of the disciples or of Peter did indeed seek for miracles. In my opinion it follows that Jesus, in spite of his special ability to effect the miraculous, did not allow his own faith to be in the least dependent on miracles. Jesus was sure of God (cf. Mark 9.23).[1] But he could not know if his disciples would share his faith, or how they would; or rather, how they would see it through. Luke is conscious of this question, at least in relation to the Church, for after his exhortations to unlimited forgiveness he adds the words: πρόσθες ἡμῖν πίστιν, grant us faith for this (Luke 17.5). The saying, already mentioned, about the

---

[1] If the word is to be used, then it should be used as in Mark 9.23 and Matt. 17.20, but not as in Mark 9.24; for the *eschaton* admits of no further objection.

61

mustard-seed faith which follows on this rejects the request as a misunderstanding. In fact, how can Jesus confer anything as personal as faith? There is one thing he can do for them, in addition to his community with them: he can pray for them and let them take part in his prayer. The Lord's Prayer shows clearly enough that Jesus let his disciples take part in his *prayer*, however much it may have been expanded in the early community. The fact that Jesus prayed *for* his own does not require the special proof provided by the parting situation in the passion story; it emerges from a whole series of parables and similitudes—I call to mind not just the friend requesting food (Luke 11.5–8), but also the two debtors (Luke 7.41–43), the prodigal son (Luke 15.11–32) and the sower (Mark 4.3–8 par.). God's faithfulness seeks the response of man's obedience. This is well known to the person who stressed the saying about putting the hand to the plough (Luke 9.62). With a view to his disciples, Jesus' prayer, his intercession, is the most eminent part of his own obedience in faith (Luke 22.27); and the Gethsemane scene is right in representing Jesus going straight from his prayer to the Cross and to drink the cup. Jesus certainly distinguishes himself from his disciples, because he suffers the struggle of faith for them. He remains separated from them in this most personal matter. He knows their temptation. But it thus becomes clear that he has risked faith in God's coming *for them*. Thus the words of the Lord's Supper which are a later ecclesiastical formulation, and also the prophecies of suffering which are similarly a later formulation, both express Jesus' self-understanding.

We have now reached the point to which, according to the witness of the Synoptics, Jesus' proclamation refers. One thing must still be taken into consideration: the death of Jesus and the Easter message did not usher in the whole future, to which Jesus and his own were aware of being directed. The early community was well aware of this, for they now looked forward to the crucified Jesus coming as the Son of Man from heaven. However, it would be wrong to deduce disillusionment about Jesus' proclamation from this increased expectation of the end. On the contrary. Increased expectation does not arise from disillusionment, but rather prevents it. (At this stage we are disregarding the special problem of the apocalyptic Easter experiences of individuals.) It was on the basis of Easter that the community was first really aware of being under Jesus' protection, and deemed its election to be confirmed by God himself: God had confirmed that the faith of Jesus was a faith which would benefit them. In the future everyone who committed himself to the community could himself believe in his election by God; he could number himself among the κλητοὶ ἅγιοι and hence himself receive God's Holy Spirit as the power for faith.

The starting-point of Jesus' proclamation in the Synoptics is Jesus' full authority to gather a people for God under the banner of the rule of God (cf. Matt. 9.8). This authority does not answer the question: What can you do?—which was significant for the faith of Paul—nor the Johannine question: What do you want? Instead it answers the question: What do you pray for? or, For whom do you pray? Jesus' faith leads him to prayer for the heavy laden, for the poor and for the disciples (cf. by contrast the unmerciful servant, Matt. 18.23–35). In the future faith in Jesus will continue this prayer, even though Paul is undecided whether or not he should at once pray for the day of the Lord (Rom. 8.26). For faith it is sufficient that God has listened to Jesus (Heb. 5.7; John 17.10).

I now sum up: That early declaration about Jesus interceding for us before God (Rom. 8.34; Heb. 7.25; I John 2.1) is precisely what gets to the root of the historical life of Jesus. Is it nevertheless fantasy or mythology? It can be, if it is misused in the form of a conception *about* Jesus. But faith in Jesus, in so far as it is faith, really refers only to the one conception—that God has listened to Jesus' prayer for his own. Is this conception also mythology? This is at any rate not true of faith when faith holds fast to Jesus' prayer, because it believes that God will also listen to our prayer and intercession. The result is that by means of this prayer faith keeps the future open. For then we no longer really bring ourselves to the fore; instead we present ourselves along with the historical Jesus before God. Like Jesus we then relate the invisible to our universally visible need, without embellishing or gilding anything. Jesus' conduct becomes for us also the new command of love. For now we know along with the evangelists that Jesus' love was the word of intercession. To believe in Jesus means to believe *like* Jesus that God grants prayer. Jesus calls God Father, our Father, and the Father is certainly the one who grants prayer. But our faith is distinguished from Jesus' faith, because since Easter we have been told in Jesus' name that God *has* granted prayer. We can hand on this word if we further it with our own intercession, so that one after another rejoices in the love of Jesus. Jesus believed that God would grant prayer (Matt. 11.6; cp. 11.25–27). Faith in Jesus confesses that God has granted and will therefore continue to do so in the future (John 16.23f). Because of this temporal sequence, faith in Jesus stays close to Jesus' prayer and sees to it that faith remains faith in the granting, as long as it is time to pray out of need to God as Father (Matt. 7.11). Faith has its unlimited sphere in this prayer (John 17).

Since I have spoken of faith, I must add a word about the concept of dogma. Does not a living faith which leads to prayer resist every dogmatization of the historical Jesus? Can dogmas be more than hermeneutical principles of scriptural exposition? Must they not quite simply be directions for prayer, if indeed the New Testament is also a prayer book? Then it should be possible for everyone to see clearly that theology is concerned with the historical Jesus, and why this is so. Theology is concerned with the historical Jesus because it has to teach according to scripture that the prayer of faith takes place in the name of Jesus—and that it is granted. Now it is true to say: Whoever believes in the granting can wait (I Thess. 5.11). Jesus waited; he waited for faith (cf. also Luke 18.8). If we have faith, we wait for the glimpse into Jesus' joy.

IV

LANGUAGE IN THE NEW TESTAMENT[1]
1959

LANGUAGE is communication. Whoever wants to talk about language in the New Testament must, of course, say, or at least attempt to show what it is of which the New Testament is speaking. This can be done in very different ways. I opt for a procedure which is meant at the same time to indicate the unity of the New Testament, which has become problematical for historical reasons and for reasons of content.

This paper is arranged in three sections. The first section is introductory and will concentrate my examination on a thesis that requires discussion. Then there is a second section dealing with the language-character of the rule of God, and finally a third section about the language tendency of the New Testament with regard to the theology of faith.

I. THE THESIS

The New Testament does not reflect upon language because it is itself concerned to speak. It could nevertheless be the case that the New Testament prepares for the phenomenon of language a destiny which can also be observed elsewhere. Let us make a comparison with what precedes it. Jesus did not write anything; nor did his disciples. The Apostle Paul possibly occupies an intermediate position. But even he wrote reluctantly. It is true that after Paul a whole literature springs into existence. We find the Gospels on the fringes of this. What comes later acts, at least within the New Testament, as an appendage.

In view of the Gospels we cannot say that in the New Testament the words of Jesus simply disappeared. Nevertheless we are confronted with a new phenomenon in the New Testament:

[1] From 'Das Problem der Sprache' in *Theologie und Kirche*, Berlin, 1959, pp. 21–35.

theology has now assumed an interest in faith, whereas Jesus had spoken of the rule of God.

In a certain sense the New Testament owes its existence to theology. For this reason we cannot merely say that it is just the product of the early Christian mission; that it had to proclaim or interpret Jesus in a way that Gentiles could understand him. There is more weight to the argument that the events at Jesus' death raised the person of Jesus to a level above his historical word. However, the Gospels took up Jesus' word again. Faith in Jesus could not dispense with Jesus' word. Why?

The New Testament writers have given a theological account of faith. They could only do this by reflecting on Jesus. If, then, Jesus' word recedes for a time, the thought readily occurs that this might be due to Jesus' word itself. Not only in the sense that Jesus was, in fact, no longer there, with the result that he would be, so to speak, struck dumb. What is more important is the consideration that Jesus' word had consequences, which also had to be taken into account, if Jesus was to be understood. In fact, the very death of Jesus precludes a one-sided isolation of Jesus' proclamation. His death and other consequences of Jesus' word had to be compared with what caused them. Anyone who was accounting for faith had to engage in this *thought-process*. The New Testament has done this. Not only Jesus' proclamation but also the theology which appears after Jesus was a phenomenon of life, of a life which seems to have been thoroughly coherent in itself. However, in order that we may arrive at a useful thesis, our reflection requires still further expansion. The New Testament cannot simply be added on to theology.

It is not permissible to think of the process as if an oral tradition, as it were, came to an end in the New Testament and died out there. For this reason we must first of all note that in the New Testament life, seen in terms of language, is expressed in a new way; and we must also note how this happens. The now literary Gospel may serve as an illustration of this. The New Testament developed in the literary Gospels a completely new stylistic genre, which should not be labelled 'minor literature'. The evangelists set about the task of working out the Jesus tradition in a literary form. But this task was not easily accomplished. To cite but one instance: how were they to deal properly with the multifarious logia, of which, after all, at least one collection was already at hand? A comparison of the Synoptic Gospels at once shows that this difficulty was indeed experienced. Matthew can serve as evidence for this. He preserves the stylistically correct form of the logia better than Luke, whereas Mark includes only a few logia in his Gospel, because he cannot deal with them properly. The logia were in themselves too heterogeneous to be reduced to a common denominator. They required to be divided and interpreted according to content. Matthew, the stylist, interprets his material by dividing it into several themes, thus consciously composing. Indeed, all three evangelists interpret their subject-matter variously by means of their respective composition. If the compositional technique of the evangelists is to be properly appreciated, then we must take good care not to regard it prematurely as an historicizing tendency. Nevertheless, this tendency is not entirely absent. However, it takes its place among definite theological patterns. Matthew looks back on Israel with Jesus' eyes, even though he wants thereby to warn the Church. Luke, on the other hand, looks back with the Church on Jesus, in order to strengthen the Church's hope. Mark endeavours to provide a foundation for faith in the words and deeds of Jesus and of the Spirit, and thereby to create a firm hold for the enquiry about Jesus. But these tendencies do not make the characteristic features of the subject-matter unrecognizable. It is a sign both of the toughness of the subject-matter and also of its characteristic quality that all three evangelists try expressly to put their own composition into parenthesis—Mark in Jesus' prophecies of his passion, in the apocalyptic chapter and in Peter's confession, Matthew going beyond this and elaborating points made by Mark, in reflective quotations and summaries supported by them; Luke too follows a programme which is theologically conceived and laid down in both 4.21 and 24.26. Even though there is operative in all this the traditional idea of prophecy which is to be fulfilled and which has been fulfilled, there is nevertheless no mistaking that the entire composition of the Gospels is raised like a drama to the level of language. Everything that happens and that will happen is at the same time revelation in word—even the death and the resurrection of Jesus. Apart from the passion and the beginning of the Gospel, the external attendant circumstances recede or remain veiled, while the store of language forges to the fore. Even the miracle stories show the same tendency towards the word. This trend towards language is emphasized christologically in John's Gospel by the 'Logos' concept, if, in fact, it is not over-emphasized. The Gospels are meant to be appreciated in general as language phenomena. They are also language achievements of a unique order (Auerbach).

What holds true for the Gospels can also be said of the early Church: just as the Gospels defy any literary classification, so it is impossible to fit the early Church into any sociological category. The early Church is itself a language phenomenon. It is precisely for this reason that it has created for itself a memorial in the new stylistic form of the Gospel. Even the Apocalypse of John, and more than ever the apostolic epistles, are creations of a new language that transforms everything with which it comes into contact. Linguistic assimilation first makes itself conspicuous on the fringes of the New Testament, in the Pastoral Epistles, for example, and after the New Testament, when ecclesiastical institutions and ecclesiastical dogma began to develop. Even if the express collection of the New Testament into a canon was due to the need for an ecclesiastical legal formulation which wanted to be sure of its *regula fidei*, the content of the New Testament canon had long since been given and now towers far above the Apocrypha like something alien, something which could no longer be overpowered, and reaches into the entire period after the New Testament. A comparison with the modern 'life of Jesus' novels could bring the facts home to us very vividly. Even passion or nativity plays have failed to catch the power of language of Jesus and the early Church; I may here leave out of account the possibilities of musical presentation. Obviously the content of the New Testament coincides to a great extent with its form. We must therefore ask how the substance of the New Testament, Jesus' speaking about God, could be translated forthwith, even demanded that it be translated, but obviously reached its goal with its first translation as the New Testament. To what extent are we concerned here essentially with a new language?

The answer is obvious. The language of the early Church recorded in the New Testament was not, in fact, primarily a language belonging to the early Church itself, which would then later have had to be replaced by another language. I previously described the early Church, too, as a language phenomenon. By that I mean: the new language did not serve the early Church but the early Church was there for the sake of the new language, and had served its purpose when the New Testament was written. Thus far the proposition that the early Church erected a memorial in the Gospels was merely provisional and not literal. We must change our thinking in this matter. Jesus spoke of the rule of God. It is not true that the Church came *instead* of the rule of God. Nor is it true that the Church came *with* the rule of God. Rather: *the New Testament came through the rule of God.* This thesis must now be developed. The means of doing this will be the theological thinking achieved in the New Testament.

2. THE LANGUAGE-CHARACTER OF THE RULE OF GOD

(*a*) The Kaddish prays: 'And may he let his kingdom prevail in your lives and days and during the life of all the house of Israel, now and in coming times. Amen' (Fiebig). Would the rule of God not, in fact, bring the *end* of this world? The resurrection of the dead? The beginning of a new creation? Are we guilty of a spiritualization of the Jewish eschatological hope, when we say that the New Testament came with the rule of God? Or are we to say more cautiously that in the place simply of a *conception* of God's future, the future itself appeared? This future proves itself to be a present power, inasmuch as it determines our existence in the present. Hence the New Testament must be quoted as an example of the working of this power. The rule of God would then in part be understood in terms of an analogy with the power of death. Death, too, can exercise its power only as future, whereas its power is at an end once death has occurred. The Pauline understanding of baptism announces further to this that death has indeed already been disposed of in Christ, and it then gives *faith* in this into the future's keeping. As a result we can hope in faith to endure every sorrow and the hour of death in such a manner that Christ emerges victorious from our life, suffering and death. We know that Paul proceeded to make the entire apocalyptic conception of the rule of God subservient to his message about Christ. However, the Apostle cannot be accused of spiritualization of the expectation of the rule of God, because the central Pauline concept of pneuma is in no sense spiritually conceived—quite the contrary. Pneuma, which for Paul was entirely bound up with the rule of God, implies that for the Apostle Christian faith already operates within the rule of God. This motion on faith's part is indeed identical with the all-powerful working of the rule of God, so that where faith becomes effective—that is in love—righteousness, peace and joy in the Holy Spirit at once gain ground as the forces of the rule of God, and, as the Pauline charisms show, also work miracles. The experience of conscience, which is likewise bound up with faith, is not in opposition to this. Faith, as understood by Paul, certainly keeps within the experience of conscience, because only within the experience of conscience does it take place as faith in God's mercy. As a result man always confronts himself also in faith. But the powers of the past which are present as conquered forces in the experience of conscience are, of course, the powers of the flesh, of sin and death. These powers are for their part powers of the world, so that faith which witnesses to the fact that these powers have been overcome always also affects the world itself. Positivistic psychology makes the mistake of viewing the declarations of faith about the powers of the world as mere *interpretations* of the world. As a result it is compelled to view the *power*, which indisputably rises up against us in the experience of conscience, merely as the power of sensuality directed inwards into consciousness, and hence to limit the power of the world to sensuality. However, this is opposed by every deeper under-standing of anxiety as an '*existentiell*' determination through the world's transitory mode of being. In faith as it is understood by Paul, the experience of the frightened conscience is not evaded, but rather penetrated, with the result that fear and trembling become experiences of faith. Because faith is equal to the ex-perience of conscience on the plane of the experience of the world, it does not content itself with some kind of penitence or feeling of guilt; instead faith *brings home* the nothingness of the world in the conscience. Consequently faith never by-passes conscience, but respects the measure of strength which every man, as an in-dependent consciousness, can in faith oppose to the nothingness of the world. Concrete freedom for a particular form of conduct confronts the power of fear, and then one person becomes brother and succour to another. The struggle with the world does not become easier or more abstract but more earnest and concrete when it is fought out in the conscience. It is also clear that the Christian can easily be in the situation of the loser if Christ is to be the winner. In Paul's view Christians have to be able to become a byword for good losers, right to the very arena.

It is most remarkable that this struggle of faith does not in any way neutralize the world—unless one were speaking in a different context about an ethic of neutrality—but much rather that it concentrates the world. Indeed, faith must constantly renew its struggle with the world, since not faith but faith's Lord is to be victor. Consequently it sees itself in its struggle more and more directed to the same work of God, which already made faith possible in us. The perfect end would be a 'spiritual' body, a being (*Dasein*) that had been fully freed and had left behind the 'dead' body—dead because of sin—i.e. which had left its past behind. This is not an '*existentiell*' possibility in this world in which we have instead to make our way struggling towards the goal. Nevertheless in faith man is confronted not only with himself. Instead Paul is aware that he has surrendered himself to the Lord.

The language-character of Pauline existence appears at this point. For Pauline faith the entire working of God has been concentrated from the point of view of language on the *name* of Jesus Christ and thus on the person of Christ the *Lord*. For Paul the theologian there follows from this concentration of God's working on the Lord Christ Jesus the task of declaring Jesus' lordship with regard to everything, τὰ πάντα. However, he does not acquit himself of this task chiefly by the use of theorems, although Paul still uses the traditional doctrinal statements current among the Israelites and the early Christian community. Rather Paul strives beyond this to interpret anew human existence itself. The means of doing this is for him the law. It is not correct that the Pauline Christian is still the man *under* the law. He certainly fulfils God's commandments, but he does this in freedom, whether he be slave or master in the world. The law of God which is understood as love thereby becomes the very instrument of freedom. The law *serves* the Christian, so that everyone wills what God does, and sows where *God* sends the harvest, whereas previously man did not do what God wanted. For Paul therefore, Christ's lordship can indeed be perceived from the concrete fulfilment of the commandments.

What is still missing will operate in the community of believers only indirectly as suffering, but in the world directly as a judgment, so that in the end it will indeed be God's law that triumphs. Paul certainly says that whoever lives in the Spirit must also lead his life in the Spirit. But this imperative does not cast the believer back under the law but awards him his freedom anew. For the Spirit in which faith leads its life is the Spirit in which we keep in sight God's law, as the law which has been carried out by God himself in Christ. God will also carry out his law in the future along with Christ; however, it will then no longer be against us but for our benefit. The daily decay of the old man now creates the continuity of the new man, until God will be all in all; i.e. God's rule will be the only rule in all things. This extremely vivid conception of the rule of God as a power already effective in history determines the Pauline statements through and through, above all in concrete thanksgiving and in concrete petition. For Paul the Kingdom of God is inconceivable without *prayer*. But does this not already prove that it is in essence a phenomenon bent on finding expression in the word?

(*b*) With Jesus, too, the rule of God belongs to the realm of prayer. Even if the Lord's Prayer, as reproduced by Matthew and Luke, has been formulated as a community prayer, it can hardly be disputed that this prayer reflects and assumes Jesus' attitude. The fifth petition as it occurs in Matthew and Luke certainly carries a legal emphasis, which Matthew even underlined. Nevertheless here, as in Paul, the reference to the law is merely put to the test. The Lord's Prayer is an eschatological prayer. It awaits the rule of God, but it also summons it and thus to all intents and purposes takes it for granted as a present reality. Certainly the rule of God, regarded as the power which has drawn nigh, is enjoined both by the Baptist and also by Jesus in conjunction with the admonition to conversion; for Jesus also motivates conversion by pointing to the nearness of the rule of God. It must, of course, be noted that the call to conversion is really issued to those who are not to come under judgment. God's judgment and the demands of the law are to be distinguished in the case of Jesus also. Although he opposes the abuse of the law, he by no means opposes the law itself. He even formulates it anew in God's name. Jesus rejects the *ex opere operato*, but not the faith that God rewards. He knows the joy in

God which goes along with the law. What Jesus really wants is this joy. But such joy is a gift; it cannot be taught. When Jesus associates with penitent publicans and sinners, he certainly lays claim by means of this conduct to a full authority which, though it is not forbidden by the law in all cases, is nevertheless not vouchsafed by the law. Indisputably Jesus was even able to heal and acquired power over maniacs.

For us and in face of a critically viewed tradition, Jesus' authority manifests itself above all in his language, in his scarcely surpassed parables and in his pointed logia. Modern stylistic research on the parables has led to the rejection of allegorizing and has established the principle of discrimination between two parts, the 'image' and the 'matter'. Nevertheless Jesus' language is not to be assessed first and foremost in terms of an artistic outlook. Its images come preferably from the everyday happenings of rural life. They are, however, not provincially conceived but almost always paradoxically pointed. From this we are easily misled into thinking that Jesus' understanding of the rule of God was likewise paradoxical. Nothing could be further from the truth. We must consider the verbal daring of this image language, even though it does formally develop the imagery technique of the Semitic proverb. Not the image itself but its meaning, its implicit application, is daring. In his parables and similitudes Jesus does not merely start from the idea of the rule of God; and it is immaterial whether or not he expressly mentions the rule of God. Instead, by means of this procedure, by the altogether clear choice of image, he makes the audience share in his own authority, although he must surely know both that he is different from them and also in what way he is different. However, it is significant that Jesus does not make his hearers share in the experience of the rule of God reserved for him personally, but that he only allows those experiences of it which one and all can have, when they give ear to him. He inspires confidence in God's action by drawing pictures of resolution, of daring, of the power of nature, of certain reward, of surprise and of unexpected compensation. In all this Jesus wants his hearers to gain freedom, and then to meet their neighbour anew. But he knows that this way of living can be attempted only with God and not against him, just as the peasant must work with nature and not against it if he wants to wrest anything from nature. The rule of God thus begins with the adoption of a new attitude by man, in a conversion, which acquires command of God's language just as the peasant acquires command of nature by his toil. The rule of God is already there, *because* this language has become possible. It induces man from now on to do justice to God and man, by the one taking the other at his word, like the Syrophoenician woman. Indeed, only in this way can a word that is binding among men be attempted. This is why Jesus' language is so natural and unaffected, now critical, now full of exhortation, deliberate and yet without any restrictive stipulation, resolved on letting God be master. As a result complete lucidity prevails among men. Such a thing can only happen in full freedom. Thus Jesus' language is above all a testimony to his freedom. This freedom could by its very nature remain restricted to him alone just as little as the pneuma of the Apostle to Paul. The Fourth Gospel also expressed Jesus' freedom terminologically.

Although we must take into account the strong influence of the Baptist's movement on Jesus' disciples and followers, the distinction between Jesus and the Baptist is significant enough. Jesus' proclamation of judgment is not, as it were, the first step towards his freedom (nor should the Baptist's proclamation of judgment be interpreted in this way). Jesus' proclamation of judgment is instead the consequence of a freedom which far exceeds the power of a charismatic prophet. The clearness of his interpretation of the law may indeed derive from the knowledge that God's ways admit of no half-measures. If it is polemically pointed, it obviously opposes foolish objections. But even the pointed antitheses of the Sermon on the Mount are nevertheless really only images and are of a dialectic, didactic nature, in so far as any kind of conduct different from that contemplated by Jesus, for example towards one's enemy, is of no service at all for love. Jesus recommended neither an interim ethic nor indeed any code of ethics at all. He has no thoughts of following man into the intricacies of his machinations. The only thing he cares about is the new attitude itself, and how it will become an event among men (Bornkamm). He who knows the rule of God pities those who want to make do without it, and resists those who deny it or deform and abuse it.

What is it, then, about the nature of this rule of God if it appears in Jesus as freedom and is protected and proffered in freedom? As has been indicated, it bears in Jesus' case also the features of the phenomenon which in Paul is looked upon as pneuma; i.e. the features of the power over everything that normally remains unavailable to man. If the word faith was really used by Jesus, then talk of the faith that moves mountains is still the most appropriate for Jesus. But with Jesus' faith it is not a question of power in general, in opposition perhaps to powerlessness, but rather of the power of God which now enters the everyday life of man. Just as in the literary Gospel the new theme brought forward by God of the life and death of Jesus was linked up with the language of the people, so, too, for Jesus himself the power of God was linked up with everyday life. It is here that the emphasis lies in Jesus' appearance. Because the then prevailing Jewish theology sacrificed everyday life in favour of sacral illusions or entangled itself in legal machinations, Jesus turned against the reprehensible behaviour of the scribes on Moses' seat. In so far as apocalyptic was interested in guarantees for the future, Jesus certainly opposed its arithmetic fantasy. Nevertheless, Jesus was not simply a man of the people. But he kept to conditions which held good if God's rule was to be an affair of the people. We can draw parallels at this point: Jesus made God's cause entirely a matter of the free word, whereas Socrates had to withdraw in contemplation. Jesus' word acquires its authority not only from its images and similes, nor like Paul from discussion about the law, nor like Plato from the power of the idea, but primarily and more basically from the phenomenon of justice itself, which man owes his fellows and consequently God (Käsemann). Justice is not confined to property, as in the case of the right of inheritance, but rather it means man himself. This is why in Jesus' case it is always connected with the free word. It is not just the right to speak freely, as in the case of the Greeks and then also in the early community, but rather the right that comes and goes with the free word, like sunshine and wind or rain. Whoever pays attention to this realizes that Jesus' word is really a word that creates justice, though, of course, it was distorted the moment it was transformed into juridical regulations for the community. The justice created by Jesus' word is in truth the free *essence* of the rule of God, God's sentence in the present. Here man grows towards his destiny of being God's image in freedom. Thus God's power or justice is in Jesus' case full authority for freedom.

The freedom of Jesus holds true as the word which puts God right with man and man right with God.

Thus it comes about that Jesus risks everything on his word. He cannot be silenced. Consequently the danger lurking round him became greater and greater. But Jesus pays no attention to this. Nor does he worry about the theological arrangement of his terminology, especially as in true Jewish fasion he prefers the simile or the image to the concept. For Jesus God's rule is not exhausted either in an idea or in a concept; it is where it is, be it in heaven or on earth. Whoever recognizes it will pray for it all the more. He is then praying God for the word. With Jesus it is not a question of *homo coram Deo* but of a *Deus coram homine*.

3. LANGUAGE AND THE THEOLOGY OF FAITH

If we again view the New Testament as a homogeneous whole, it should have become clear that it describes a curve, which no longer coincides with its literary beginnings. This curve starts historically from Jesus' word and, as literature in the Gospel, returns to Jesus' word. By this route Jesus' word traverses the plain of the theology of the early Church or (expressed with regard to content) of the theology of faith. The first formulae of faith designate Jesus as the object of faith, whereas Jesus himself had only demanded faith in the power of the word, of the word which he himself spoke and proffered, because it was God's sentence in the present. From now on Jesus himself becomes the word that faith believes and speaks by confessing it (Bultmann). But that is not the end of the matter. Jesus' word becomes effective once again in the Gospels. Thus we witness the peculiar spectacle of Jesus and his word appearing to compete with each other in the New Testament.

(*a*) In the first place the confession of Jesus who died for us and rose from the dead (ἐγήγερται) stands in the foreground. In this confession the emphasis lies on the *pro nobis*. Through the *pro nobis* God's justice is proclaimed as grace which gives man the right to faith. The human right of faith is freedom to have faith. It is true that the theology of faith appropriate to this is developed only by Paul. However, the core of this theology, the same freedom to have faith, unites the entire early Church. Freedom to have faith was doubtless understood not only as freedom to confess faith, as done in baptism, but far beyond this as freedom to speak, or 'freedom for the word'. It was not reserved for any office, although from the beginning recognized testimonies of faith were preferred, as Paul also shows. Whereas the theology of faith was a charismatic product of the early period, the offices which looked after doctrine and discipline do not appear until late in the New Testament.

Nevertheless, the characterization of the theology of faith as a charismatic work still proves nothing about the necessity of such a theology. Neither the confession of Jesus by the early Church nor the faith which took its bearings from this confession could prevent the growth of a Judaistic movement and a speculative gnosis which were both able to join forces, indeed with a liturgical emphasis. The Pauline epistles were written opposing them, later the Epistle to the Colossians and the Epistle to the Ephesians, but probably the major Gospels, too, which once again brought Jesus' word into the foreground. The difference between the Synoptics on the one hand and John on the other hand explains the dilemma which had to be overcome by the theology of faith, and yet which could be overcome only on first principles. It was not enough simply to recall Jesus' historical word. After all, what did faith possess in faith? The question certainly was faced. It was also answered, and thus brought about the turning from Jesus to Jesus. For there was indeed a standard of faith. This standard was, in fact, Jesus himself.

On this point thinkers are divided in our day, too, although strictly speaking the separation is not quite clear. The controversy about demythologizing was not thought out to a conclusion, because the premise on both sides remained too similar. I mean the concept of the *fact of salvation* (*Heilstatsache*), which is found in Bultmann. Those who retain this concept should be able to show how facts of salvation are compatible with the phenomenon of a justice-creating word, which originally occurred only in the sphere of the spoken word. The concept of the fact of salvation favours the concentration of theological statements and also of the pro-clamation on the confession of the death and resurrection of Jesus. According to the New Testament formulation we are here con-cerned with the concept of the eyewitness (Conzelmann; M. Barth). This concept, too, restricts theological statements and the proclamation resulting from them to that minimum for which eyewitnesses can vouch. The danger is seen in the Johannine writings. But even in the tradition incorporated by Paul in I Cor. 15.1–11, it is evident that the message of the eyewitnesses had to be heightened by scriptural statements. It is remarkable that it is really the eyewitness who drives the historical Jesus into the background. We must begin anew. The earliest formulae of faith were combined with the historical Jesus first in the kerygmatic sections of the Acts of the Apostles. The account of the raising of Jesus from the dead probably had initially a much more comprehensive meaning than we imagine, we who are under the influence of the category of the fact of salvation or of the eyewitness, perhaps even of Peter. Even in the presentation in I Cor. 15.5–8 it is possible to pick out a kind of chain reaction of apocalyptic experiences and an eschatological appraisal (of the death and) of the resurrection of Jesus, which point to an essentially different context. Those who venture to speak of an eschatological disillusionment should check what it is on to which they are going to link this statement. The connecting link must not be from the first the historical Jesus. However, we have indeed to conclude that the apocalyptic hopes, or rather expectations, of this early period did, in fact, break down, even though they may have continued among fanatic minds, against whom the theology of faith then fights. As with the exact defining of the communion liturgy, so also the theology of faith, with regard to the death of Jesus and its significance for faith, has led under the constraint of antitheses to consequences, the outcome of which may not be accepted without discrimination. For the actual intention of this theology is a different one, as we immediately see if we look again at the whole.

The Pauline and Johannine theologies of faith both impel faith towards existence. Why do they do this? Because both hold fast to Jesus' freedom in the face of all fanatical joy in experience. When Paul had to explain freedom for faith to the congregation in Corinth, he preferred to depart and expose himself to mortal danger well known to them all, which was further increased by the journey, as he later confesses. He preferred this rather than having to force his personal authority on the congregation. In the case of John we can perhaps go the length of saying that he preferred to write the Gospel completely anew rather than have to abandon faith to an institution that had become traditional, and which could no longer cope with its fanatics. Between fanaticism and a tradition that loses the authority for the free word, the theology of faith attempts to travel its way along with Jesus himself.

(*b*) The objection of spiritualization thereby returns to us once more. Is the Jesus, with whom the theology of faith means to go, not of necessity a spiritualized Jesus? It certainly seems as if in Paul the Lord became the Spirit; he certainly became power, but was this principally the power of faith? In fact, this would be an objection if the theology of faith were not a theology of the cross all along the line. We can now also take the Epistle to the Hebrews into account in our considerations. Where it is a question of faith obeying like Abraham, because it walks in darkness—in other words, because and although the struggle with sin and unbelief becomes more and more acute—then, of course, Jesus himself becomes the symbol of faith and its power. On account of the danger of an evaporation of the visible, outwardly effective marks of faith, we must not overlook the much greater danger of the false objectification of the person of Jesus. Jesus' subjectivity is in relation to faith the objectivity of truth and spirit. The early Christian theology of faith did not content itself with representing in Jesus' cross a symbol of the God who enforces his justice. Paul in his understanding of justification does not content himself with the methods of juridical scriptural exegesis. And John more radically than the Epistle to the Hebrews has recourse to a language which cannot be shaken by any scriptural exegesis, hidebound by tradition. The connexions between the Old Testament and the theology of faith are not so insignificant that they may be reconciled with more or less allegorizing. Where history takes place language is no longer just an instrument for indicating all possible meanings; instead language itself becomes an event, world-forming and world-destroying.

Those who set out from the fulfilment of prophecy are certainly closer formally to the New Testament theology of faith. Only we must take care not to authenticate this view with the help of the defective concept of a *theology of history*. For this concept does not provide a defence against the secret scepticism which hovers round the theory of the fulfilment of prophecy. The theory comes from Judaism. It is modified in the theology of faith and that is done precisely by citing the prophecies whose fulfilment is to be claimed. Faith here decides in favour of the particular word that agrees with the results of faith. The main error in the debate of our times seems to me to be that *doubt* is the starting-point for the interpretation of faith. Instead of this we must set out from the fact that faith is *fruitful*. Not the frustrations but the achievements of faith give rise to the theology of faith. Faith yields experiences of faith. Those who know these experiences, however, readily see that the deeper *danger* of faith also lies not in its failure but precisely in its successes, and develops from these successes. Here lies the root both of fanaticism and of legalism. For the experiences of faith inevitably strike back at faith and almost always transform it into a kind of sight which does away with faith and is then soon no longer adequate. The theology of faith realized this. (Seen in this light the apocalyptic residual statements in Paul acquire a new interest. After all, they prevent faith changing at once into sight. The same holds good for the sacrament which was still understood eschatologically.)

Even the experiences with Jesus could stand in the way of faith in the future. Jesus was very well aware why he directed his hearers only towards those experiences which they were to have with his word. He was silent about the experiences peculiar to himself. Faith needs for its own sake a diacritical point at which it is recalled to itself as faith. In the theology of faith this point is Jesus' obedience unto death. Jesus' obedience unto death certainly does not balance the scales to such an extent that it makes amends for the disobedience of sinners. In this sense it is rather Jesus' death itself that balances the scales. However, the assessment of the death of Jesus which objectifies to such a degree must not tempt us into disregarding the conduct of the historical Jesus. Jesus himself becomes the standard of faith, because his *obedience* unto death illustrated this standard once for all, whether or not we view it simultaneously as the act of him who was pre-existent. Those who believe in Jesus do not surrender faith to their own experiences, no matter how extraordinary these may be, but look at Jesus' conduct, at Jesus' freedom, at Jesus' freedom for the word. Certainly the freedom of the historical Jesus has been strengthened in hymnic songs in praise of his conduct, his obedience, his love. But it is precisely those songs which, by virtue of being linguistic structures, themselves witness to the fact that freedom for the word is more important than every experience of freedom, because faith has a future whereas experience loses the future.

Even Jesus' words in the Gospels likewise become the symbol of his conduct, the symbol of his *freedom* for the word, the symbol of faith. As a result they, too, often compete with the Christ-hymns in quality and intrinsic value. What initially presented itself to us as Jesus' rivalry with his own word now proves to be an extremely relevant circle: faith is brought about as freedom for the word, freedom for the word is brought about as faith. Those who believe in Jesus will remain in faith. What is bestowed upon them in such faith *is* freedom for the word. They recognize this in Jesus, and thus are aware of being united with Jesus in faith. Freedom of faith does not interfere in God's working, but keeps to the freedom for the word given to it for the time being. As in Jesus' case, the word of faith remains the word of the justice that God gives to man and that man owes to man. If we are in this one matter fellow labourers with God, we will become all the more certain of God's working. Faith, like Jesus, wants what God does. And God wants us to believe in this fashion. In the freedom for the word faith trusts entirely in God's working, like Abraham; and it confines itself to saying what is true, like Jesus. But in this matter faith is now completely free. If faith becomes articulate, the mists divide and the rule of God appears.

The *thesis* was that the New Testament came with the rule of God and through the rule of God. The truth of this thesis depends on whether faith really becomes articulate in the New Testament. The New Testament teaches as far as Jesus is concerned that the freedom of faith is freedom for the word. Now it depends on whether faith becomes articulate with us, too. The New Testament consigns to us the responsibility for the freedom of faith; it does not relieve us of this. The New Testament does not want us to cede the word to it; instead it wants us ourselves to begin to speak, as Jesus began to speak. Thus the New Testament remains an autonomous language phenomenon in the statements which are characteristic of it. And because it points to that particular word which becomes an event in freedom for the word, it holds us to an understanding of language for which the word means the winning of freedom and freedom means the winning of the word. Faith begins to speak when we obey this language and make use of this freedom for the word. Thus it holds good that faith is derived from the word and that the word results from faith. But the word does not change into faith. *God* gives us faith in the form of freedom for the word. He sets man free in the word to be man. But then man has God in the word. In the freedom for the word man meets God. An exchange takes place: in the word God gives man a share in freedom; man surrenders to God his human, mortal part. For man is without doubt responsible for his freedom for the word, since the word seeks to become an event. But the power and the momentum of the justice-creating word remains with the word and does not pass over to man. Man himself is indeed aimed at. But it is God who aims at him and finds him, when the free word becomes an event. This is the only reason why the word is connected with the sacrament in the New Testament. For in the *sacrament* it is precisely that freedom which wants to take place, in which man shares in the word, but in which it becomes clear at the same time that God himself stands surety for the word of freedom. Thus the word reaches beyond the being (*Sein*) of the living. Indeed, there is no justice that could write off the dead. We now perhaps understand why the word in the New Testament forces us back to the word of Jesus. This word, because it is entirely and solely word, is not yet fully honoured, its freedom is not satisfied with the beginnings in everyday life; it awaits the hour in which *God* honours the right of the word, which we all owe one another and yet can never fully give. Our responsibility for the freedom for the *word* now turns out to be the pledge that God intends to vindicate before man his nature as God. Jesus awaits the hour in which man *must* acknowledge God, whether he will or no. Those who believe after the manner of Jesus know this. Our word cannot want to say anything other than Jesus' word: that we want to rejoice in God. The word remains the chief thing in the New Testament, because the New Testament knows, knows from experience, that the word receives its due here in faith, there in sight, because it is the word of freedom which recognizes as binding only the distinction between God and man. God is nowhere closer to us than in the word. Therefore we will be closest to him as soon as *everything* depends only on the word. It is of this that the New Testament is speaking.

Note. The debate induced me to supplement the paper orally as follows:

(1) In the New Testament also we must distinguish between language and languages, because, for example, even within the Greek New Testament that we have, linguistic alienations occur, which tear not a few words from their original context and make them the *vox theologica*.

(2) The phenomenon of language contains the question of how language relates to being (*Sein*).

(3) If we reduce the language of the New Testament to the word, it can be understood as that 'yes' which, in judgment and mercy, means the resurrection of the dead: God stands by his will.

(4) What will result from this for the understanding of the Church and of history must be asked anew. (The same holds good for the phenomenon of corporeality.)

V

WHAT IS INTERPRETED IN THE EXEGESIS OF THE NEW TESTAMENT?[1]

To Rudolf Bultmann, on his Seventy-fifth Birthday
1959

I. THE THEME

THE theme should first be explained. It is in the form of a question. The question is defined by what it does not say. But we begin with what it does say.

(i) What is exegesis? In its traditionally accepted form, exegesis investigates the meaning of a text. This meaning can find expression in the ascertainable *scopus*. The *scopus* then states the object at which the text was aiming. If our progress is more limited, we must be content to ascertain at least the 'intention' of the text. For this work there are various aids: the furthering of the history of word meanings with the aid of lexicons, grammar, literary and style criticism and parallel materials; research into the historical circumstances which produced the text; comparative examinations of the history of ideas and of the history of religion, etc. In all this the text itself is understood as a part of intellectual work, and this intellectual research is understood as a contribution to the discovery of truth. As a result every text must submit to being assessed in terms of its contribution to the discovery of truth. In this we assume that truth not only demands a clear and distinct knowledge of its subjects, but that in its declaration of truth it maintains the form appropriate to it. Because truth must permit of expression, a declaration ought to be true in itself. The meaning of a text would therefore be grasped at that point where the text is and can be understood in such a way that it reflects the truth contained in it.

Some texts will do this better than others. In this way an assessment of the *niveau* of the text becomes possible. The ideal type of

[1] First published in *ZTK* 56, Beiheft 1, 1959, pp. 31–48.

text would certainly be a mathematical text. For example, Spinoza chooses to develop his philosophy *more geometrico*. In the case of historical texts priority will be given to accurate documents of an authentic character. But narrative will also be highly regarded, if it is faithful narrative. On the other hand, religious texts are harder to assess according to this scheme of reference. Their meaning clearly presupposes an understanding of the phenomenon of religion. If such texts go so far as to claim to say something new, they must be responsible for providing their own understanding.

This last requirement, that the text itself must be responsible for its own understanding, is specially applicable to the New Testament collection of documents. Exegesis must now be largely promoted to interpretation, because of this responsibility for the text or its matter which stems from the text itself. This is because what the New Testament texts intend to establish is precisely the relationship of the exegete or reader to their subject-matter. As in the case of philosophical texts, the exegete must at the same time take into consideration the living tradition which was bound up with the texts. For these texts continued to influence the tradition, and the tradition for its part had an ever-increasing effect on the texts; i.e. it repeatedly influenced the choice and wording and meaning of the text. If we succeed in finding the original meaning of the text, the text will have all the more forcible effect on our attitude towards its relation to the subject-matter or the truth. But for this reason the text itself will also be exposed to our critical consideration of the subject-matter. Modern exegesis therefore demands interpretation in the sense of *'criticism of the subject-matter'*. For only then can exegesis do justice to the text *as* text. It is quite right to call this 'historical-critical' exegesis.

(ii) It might make for clarity if at least a methodological distinction were made between the task of exegesis and that of interpretation, although in practice the two cannot really be separated— this certainly applies in the case of New Testament exegesis, where the demands imposed by the criticism of the subject-matter prevent such separation. Exegesis is raised to the level of interpretation when the exegete, as expositor, undertakes to question the object of his exegesis as a declaration of truth. The interpretation explains what the position is with regard to the text's understanding of the subject. If we just sought out the meaning of the text, we could in many cases dispense with any critical questioning of this under-standing. But the situation is at once different when, for example, we have to preach on a text. The exegesis which conveys the meaning of the text will then be obliged to produce its knowledge of the subject, so that nothing essential is lost or hidden from the preacher. As the sermon has to adopt an attitude to the subject itself, the exegesis must place at the disposal of the sermon the various possibilities for a point of view which it has worked out in the course of its investigation into the meaning of the text. The exegesis will only be able to do this if it leaves itself open to the possibility of a point of view being adopted. It soon becomes evident that in many cases the meaning of a text would be abbre-viated if the text were, so to speak, left to its own devices. If this is clear, we can then use the words exegesis and interpretation interchangeably.

To continue: the text probably does not yield its meaning com-pletely, unless it is tested as a text for a sermon, or alternatively until it is expounded in terms of this test. There is, for example, the familiar idea that the intention of a parable is to disclose the matter to which it refers. But when we preach on the parable we soon see that this cannot be the case. Even Jesus' preaching was not con-cerned to bring enlightenment, for example, with regard to the rule of God. The fact that our hearers are in the main not attuned to the eschatological tempts us in our preaching to use a parable of Jesus to introduce our audience to the eschatological. This was not necessary for Jesus' audience. For them the parable would already be set *within* the eschatological situation, in such a way that something specific was to be said to them which arose out of the situation itself. We shall therefore also have to enquire about Jesus' own relation to the rule of God.

As it is exegesis which has to handle the tools for posing a question of this kind, it will have to decide to what extent the text may have arisen within a preaching situation—perhaps that of Jesus—which was significant for it. But as every sermon reveals also in its own way the situation of its audience, exegesis must explore to see in just *what way* an attitude to the subject-matter itself could or had to be taken at that time. This will not happen without the risk of the exegete himself becoming involved in the subject-matter which is to be understood. In a sense the exegete has to take sides, without neglecting the self-criticism which methodically is now very specially required of him. He then becomes an interpreter who is personally responsible for the subject-matter itself, and his exegesis becomes interpretation. This prevents the loss of the more or less clear preaching character of the text and guards against the assertion that the text has no preaching character at all. At all events the exegesis of the New Testament cannot act as if there were no Church which required preaching texts. (We shall return to this problem.)

(iii) Historical-critical exegesis certainly tends to guard against the demands of interpretation, for it has a tendency itself to strive towards one particular interpretation. It aims at a conception of history grounded on irrefutable facts, a conception which makes possible irrefutable statements about the historical connexion. This aim is not basically confounded by the lack of historical material. But there certainly are objections to the choice of material which this method enforces. Statements about historical facts are wanted. On the other hand, Bultmann, for example, makes the point that past events usually, and perhaps fundamentally, become comprehensible only in the future.[1] The historian is therefore forced to take into consideration the tension between past and future as the essential mark of history. This tension cannot be resolved by distinguishing between statements of fact and prophetic statements, as Cullmann tries to do.[2] We are concerned not just with those statements the actual wording of which refers to the future, but also with statements about a previous present, even when it is not at first sight evident that the future could be significant for such statements. The main issue is, of course, how the statement was understood by those originally concerned. As the bare words of the statement may well not convey what there is to say, we must examine the understanding of those concerned on the level of their self-understanding, in order to get an insight into the possibilities of their understanding. The history of words and conceptions can often contribute towards this. But man is mentally too active to allow the examination to come to an end there. Under certain circumstances words may say precisely

---

[1] Cf. R. Bultmann, *History and Eschatology*, pp. 120f.
[2] As in his book *Christus und die Zeit*, 1946, where on p. 84, for instance, he speaks of 'history viewed from the prophetic point of view' (ET, *Christ and Time*, rev. ed., 1962, p. 97).

nothing about what mattered, because the essential thing was either *that* something was said at all, or the person to *whom* it was said. In Matt. 4.17 Jesus repeats in his preaching the very sentence that the Baptist had proclaimed (Matt. 3.2). It was nevertheless possible for Jesus' words to mean something quite different, because he perhaps said them in a situation quite different from that of the Baptist. When the Gospel writer represents Jesus repeating the exact words of the Baptist, he is not so naïve that he himself is unacquainted with this kind of consideration. Even if the same meaning were nevertheless to emerge, this also will have its special significance. When words are repeated, the very fact of repetition indicates that something special happens, even when this event is only teaching. But in this case we are concerned with preaching or proclamation. The intention of the evangelist was obviously to determine our understanding of the rule of God as Jesus and the Baptist meant it. We shall learn the consequences only when we take into consideration the phenomenon of proclamation as such. This means we are not to imagine that either the Baptist or Jesus wished purely to offer to their hearers an explanation of the idea or concept of the rule of God.

But this is precisely what historical-critical exegesis is opposed to, for it has in mind its own view of history and it is therefore from the beginning based on ideas which fit with the least possible trouble into a factual system—even though it were just a history of the ideas themselves. Any enquiry about the self-understanding of those concerned is suspect, for self-understanding will normally only be conceived of as a psychologically comprehensible fact which inevitably lends assistance to the caprice and fantasy of interpretation. This is a crude prejudgment, though one that is, of course, significant for factual thought. The self-understanding of man is most certainly methodically comprehensible. What is required is a knowledge of those situations in which it comes to light. These situations are not tied to particular conceptions, as is the case with self-consciousness. They emerge rather at the point where man has to show how he behaves; we can then ask why he *has behaved* in a quite specific way. We avoid Jaspers' term 'boundary situations', and choose rather Heidegger's *existentialia*. Care and anxiety are examples. In care and in anxiety man must always reveal a quite specific conduct which expresses, with or without words, how he behaves in relation to care and anxiety—whether he is brave or courageous, whether he takes a risk or not, and so on. This is the point where we can understand him, because here he sets himself in motion, whether he knows it or not.

If our texts agree thematically with these phenomena, they then offer a quite explicit basis for this investigation. Another point that arises is whether we have due cause to class as *existentialia* other forms of being which occur in human existence. We discover that in these *existentialia* man is continually and urgently concerned with '*time*'—time that he has, and time that slips away from him. This means that his *practical* understanding of time contributes to his self-understanding.[1] We can then realize that the intercourse with time is linked with a practical understanding of the world, which is disclosed in ever-varying ways. We can also realize that in this matter 'language' acquires a special function; for whenever man himself is the issue at stake, the question arises of whether he has a word to say, and for what he has a word.

It is this interpretation, actuated by the *existentialia*, that we call '*existential interpretation*'.[2] Its special task has become the working out of this 'language-character' of human existence (and not just of its questionableness). In our investigation of the self-understanding we take note not only of the possibilities of human conduct, but in particular of the '*freedom for the word*', which a man can either have or lose. We ask how he understands himself, whether consciously or unconsciously, when he is assessed by this standard. The particular *existentiale* which the existential interpretation must now make use of, is not so much the 'understanding' but this 'freedom for the word' (which is the natural presupposition of every sermon). It is this which will have to contribute in particular to the search for Jesus' self-understanding, that is, to the understanding of his sayings.

Thereby I certainly take a step beyond the starting-point of Bultmann and Heidegger (that of 'questionableness'). The methodological justification for this extension may be shown by the fact that it is valid not only in theological exegesis, but that in general it necessarily appears wherever there is occasion for a real

[1] Cf. my *Hermeneutik*, §9.
[2] Vol. I of my collected studies, *Zum hermeneutischen Problem in der Theologie*, 1959, deals in detail with the existential interpretation and its connexion with the language-character of existence.

anthropological reflection, and thereby for an enquiry into the self-understanding of human being (*Dasein*). Incidentally it may be noted that in Luther the 'freedom for the word' in the sense of an *existentiale* is probably brought into play in the sphere of the exposition of the conscience. This is because he sees that the conscience can either hinder or free language, depending on what we experience in the conscience. This would necessarily appear in the relations between faith and conscience. These may not be restricted just to the plane of acting, but according to Luther concern primarily our being (*Sein*) as persons, or rather our being before God (*Sein vor Gott*). If God is concerned with something in the nature of a word, then our being as a person, or alternatively our being before God, ought to mean our relation to the word. The consequences of this for the phenomenon of language in general may meanwhile be left alone. What then is the object of interpretation in New Testament exegesis? Nothing less than its existence as a 'text', its function as 'language', especially in the situation of preaching or proclamation.

2. EXAMPLES

I restrict myself to two examples taken from the proclamation attributed to Jesus. Both examples belong to parable material.

(i) *The similitude of the mustard seed,* Matt. 13.31f; par. Mark 4.30–32 and Luke 13.18f. It is to be admitted that Matthew combines the versions of Mark and Q, therefore that Mark and Q begin with a double question;[1] further that the mustard seed served in Jewish terminology as an image for a very tiny item.[2] The conclusion of the similitude is a quotation from Dan. 4.21, i.e. it is stylized in an edifying way. All this precludes any doubt about its Jewish origin. It can then be reckoned that the similitude is a saying of Jesus, or at least that it was closely linked with a saying of Jesus.

However, there are reservations. At first the similitude seems to offer an explanation about the Basileia. Is it possible to credit Jesus with having first confided to his hearers about God's Basileia? Or

---

[1] Bultmann, *Geschichte der synoptischen Tradition*, p. 186; ET, p. 172.
[2] Strack-Billerbeck, *Kommentar zum Neuen Testament aus Talmud und Midrasch* I, 1922, p. 669.

had he to attack some other interpretation of the Basileia ? Hardly. If we follow Matthew, Jesus linked on, as has already been said, to the Baptist's preaching. Neither Jesus nor the Baptist had any need first of all to spread conceptions about the Basileia, for if one can follow the Kaddish, for instance, a pious Jew of that time sought this without any encouragement. But what did matter was to *proclaim* the coming of the Basileia *as* imminent, so that the demand for μετάνοια was readily understandable as the reality, and the baptism of John as a sign for the gravity of the situation. This applies in the first place also to Jesus' appearance, as is shown by the first beatitudes of the Sermon on the Mount (Luke 6.20f, par. Matt. 5.3–6); even if one or other of them may stem from the community. Jesus also did not first explain the Basileia; he proclaimed its coming. In relation to the Baptist there was a change of accent only in so far as the beatitudes laid a stronger emphasis on promise. In the case of the Baptist there was a gulf between the present and the Basileia, which a person had to acknowledge by means of baptism. Jesus' preaching, however, leads into the future, so that people who previously had no future now have one. While the Baptist stands almost in isolation, like a stranger, Jesus includes himself along with his hearers, as soon as they listen to him. This still applies, even if Lohmeyer, for example, has exaggerated by stressing Jesus' ceremonial meal.[1]

At first sight the similitude of the mustard seed seems scarcely relevant to this situation. People who were used to eschatological material like Mark 13 did not need to be told that God's miraculous action would of necessity have a magnificent final result. On the contrary. The pious conclusion of the similitude, and the precise reference to the smallest of all seeds, arouse the suspicion that it is made to measure in a rabbinic way. At the same time it appears to lack the urgency of the Baptist's style, and the concrete nature of Jesus' beatitudes, which do not just reflect on an event but themselves stand within it.[2]

But the question is whether the *scopus* or *tertium comparationis* of the similitude is correctly assessed by means of this kind of debate. Let us first of all ignore the style of its introduction and conclusion. *Must* the similitude be a recommendation of the miraculous ?

[1] In *Kultus und Evangelium*, 1942.
[2] Nor should we speak of 'parables of growth'.

Would it not be nearer the mark to allow the same God who effects such a marvellous conclusion to make a marvellous beginning? When at a later stage the community felt they could appeal to the resurrection of Jesus, they then transposed this miraculous act of God back to the beginning. Paul took great pains to demonstrate this with regard to Jesus' cross. Further: has miracle[1] a beginning at all? Is it a demonstrable process which permits interpretation according to a scheme of a small beginning and a marvellous end? If for the time being we exclude the idea of growth and look rather at the demonstration of two sides of one and the same thing, it still remains to investigate the direction in which the thought runs. If we follow the Sermon on the Mount, the Basileia comes, but does not grow, and the natural consequence of this is to turn the line of thought away from the 'image' towards the 'matter'. This means thinking not from beginning to end, but on the contrary thinking first from the end back to the beginning. The Basileia (assuming it is this we are concerned with) certainly remains on the other side. It is itself the end. What is then the beginning? Not simply the beginning of the Basileia. What is left is indeed to be temporally conceived. We are indeed concerned with beginning and end. But if the miracle is at the end (coming afterwards), then the beginning indicates not the miracle but rather our *relation to* the miracle. At the beginning the Basileia is lacking, inasmuch as it is not yet visible. However, in the 'image' the end depends on the beginning: No crop without seed. But what is self-evident in the 'image' is not self-evident in the 'matter'. The similitude chooses its image by contraries, as in fact Jesus often does. The relation between a tiny beginning and the miraculous conclusion is therefore certainly emphasized, but it is not self-evident *in the case* of the Basileia. On the other hand, it is self-evident and obvious that Jesus has in mind his own situation and that of his hearers, when he proclaims the Basileia to them.[2] What

---

[1] Translator's note: '*Wunder*': Fuchs, like Bultmann, would distinguish between two senses of 'miracle'. A 'miracle' which is considered to be objectively demonstrable is mythological; but 'miracle' may also be used in a non-mythological sense, referring to the action of God and perceptible only to faith. The context normally indicates which sense of the word is meant.

[2] Jeremias's category of 'parables of contrast' prevents him from even noticing this reversal of the direction of thought. In Jeremias, therefore, Jesus' disciples have still to remain a 'poor little band' (*Die Gleichnisse Jesu*, 3rd ed., 1954, p. 93; ET, *The Parables of Jesus*, 1954, p. 91). Why? The beginnings were by no means wretched.

else ought they to think of in face of such a message? Of themselves, of course. The Baptist also had this in mind when he demanded μετάνοια. But now they are told that the tiny beginning applies only in relation to them. Why? Because the message applies to this audience? To the people of the beatitudes? But why does it concern them? Why does God allow his Basileia to be preceded by such a small beginning, by such a meagre public? Does he somehow accommodate himself particularly to them? *Ought* the Basileia to begin with them in such a small unspectacular way, outside of themselves so to speak, *in order that* they, the insignificant, may be able to take part in its coming? This idea is very similarly expressed by Paul in I Cor. 15.36. So the similitude says that God in his coming accommodates himself to our circumstances; we are the seed from which the Basileia is to rise in a marvellous way—as come it certainly will. If we think of Jesus no longer in miraculous garb but in the solidarity of the preacher with his audience, then this meaning of the similitude corresponds exactly to the relation between Matt. 11.5 and 6. This appears when we understand v. 5 not as a collection of facts but as a promise; and the end of the verse would then disappear, or else foreshadow v. 6.

The following *scopus* would emerge: God's miracle is accommodated to our need, the great to the little, the saviour to the one to be saved, the judge to the sinner, etc. The *tertium comparationis* would not be the equation, 'small origin: vast results', but rather the inverse scheme, '*small stake: vast yield*'. The poetic means of expression and the choice of material are still, then, appropriate to Jewish linguistic style. The introductory double question indicates the need for caution in assessing the comparison, and the pious conclusion justifies the paradox of the comparison. But the similitude is no longer a pious address, nor is it a toying with irony; it has the effect of a sudden flash of lightning that illumines the night. It is now irresistible and self-sufficient. It has become a text, a preaching text. It gives to these people a context for which

---

Wretchedness comes to an end where faith arises, and this is precisely the point. Interpretation must not be bogged down in sociology, in the field of vision of unbelief. I wonder if Jeremias would agree with me here. Schlatter is not successful either, although he is right in wanting to see what Jesus saw (cf. *Der Evangelist Matthäus*, 1933, p. 442). However, Schlatter's anthropological connexion can be rendered fruitful with the help of existential interpretation.

they could *not* hope, *nor* even reckon with. This is why it has indeed something miraculous about it: what no one sees, he already hears: his call through God. He who has ears to hear, let him hear.

(ii) *The treasure in the field*, Matt. 13.44. While the previous form was 'small stake: great yield', the *tertium comparationis* may here be formulated as 'large stake: greater yield'. We can therefore immediately discuss this similitude after that of the mustard seed.

In his book *Jesus*,[1] Bultmann places this similitude under the heading of an 'either—or', and indicates that the hearer is asked if he will decide for the rule of God and sacrifice everything for it. But the men in the image part, both in this parable and in the lines about the pearl merchant (vv. 45f), know exactly what they are doing. There is no mention of a sacrifice. The gain corresponds instead to the stake and even exceeds it considerably. But where does the stake fit into the material part? Here again the Basileia belongs on the side of the gain. It is not the stake. The introductory caption 'Basileia' is then misleading, if it is naïvely thought that the similitude should explain the conception of the Basileia. Acquaintance with the Basileia is instead assumed. By what means is it concretely produced? By means of Jesus' preaching. He proclaims it. In the introduction to the similitude the caption 'Basileia' stands for Jesus' *preaching* of the coming Basileia, in the same way as the whole chapter is introduced by the parable of the sower—because Jesus' preaching is to be made meaningful *as* preaching.

But how much of a contribution does the audience make? They can only gain. Jesus the preacher is the only one who really invests anything. He it is, far ahead of them, who risks conflict with Jewish officialdom and also with the temporal powers who were party to the Baptist's execution; or with the Romans who were to execute him. Was Jesus, the expounder of the law, an ascetic?

We are therefore well advised in this case also to think along different lines from the 'image'. Jesus certainly risks what he stakes; the audience certainly gains, when they listen to him. But this means that Jesus *gives* them his stake. What he gives them is considerable, for him *and* for them. For him it is considerable because he risks his life, or at least this preaching, on them. For

[1] 2nd ed., 1951, p. 30; ET, *Jesus and the Word*, rev. ed., 1958, p. 30.

them it is considerable because they *receive* his word—the consolation that the Basileia comes for their sakes. They are to grasp it
by means of this word. This ought not to be hard for them. For
through his word, through his freedom to speak to them, they can
joyfully recognize that something great is under way: the Basileia
comes, it comes indeed, as surely as Jesus had the freedom to
speak with them in this way. Just as the man had first to acquire
the field if he wanted his share of the reward, so they had only
to accept the gift of Jesus' word in order to be sure of the Basileia.
What more do they want? What matters is not a general certainty
or truth, but *their* certainty, or God's call to them.

The 'that' of the revelatory event, which Bultmann speaks of
elsewhere, is here concentrated on the 'that' of Jesus' word. What
matters is not how much we sacrifice, but that we should place
our whole trust in the one word which proclaims to us God's
coming. It is only the announcement of the Basileia, the word
about it, which precedes the Basileia—when the Basileia means the
release of the tension between past and future, or the end of
history. Since it is only *faith*, and not our action, which corresponds to this word, faith in the Basileia will be the one form of
access to it. The Basileia comes to the person who believes in its
coming, who directs to its coming all the faith he can muster.
When? This is now no longer decisive, if I believe that it comes
to me. The Basileia itself needs no announcement for its coming.
The fact that it was nevertheless announced by Jesus simply means
that his audience were to be addressed as its recipients. Jesus gave
his pledge that the Basileia comes to those who believe in it and
who allow for their faith no other object—just as the men in the
picture wanted nothing other than their treasure and their pearls.

Whoever understands this will recognize Jesus' love in his
pledge for the word addressed in this way. He will also become
surer of his own faith when he understands and recognizes that
the love which is capable of such a word can be neither undercut
nor outdone by God's coming. For his hearers Jesus' word fills
the place where otherwise they could perhaps only with difficulty
perceive God. Will they want to keep this word to themselves?
Does it not break all the barriers at which otherwise man usually
gives in? Love never draws back. No matter where it has begun
it arrives at its goal. That is the secret of the rule of God, of the

love which stood by its word even after Jesus had been put to death.

3. METHODOLOGICAL DISCUSSION

Because my exegesis takes note of psychological matters, I have to expect the accusation that I let my imagination run free and fail to keep within the strict methodical bounds of an existential interpretation. In reply to the first objection, historical-critical exegesis cannot dispense with psychological considerations, for it always has to reckon with the probability of an event, and will make suppositions about the intentions which lie behind this event and the extent to which they are obstructed or fulfilled. This is self-evident. If, for example, we have to assess the question of whether Jesus was an eschatologically determined fanatic who was taken by surprise, overtaken by the actual course of events, then we shall have to elucidate Jesus' experience of the world. Was he some kind of ascetic? Or did he shut off the contingent worldly possibilities in such a way that, for example, the execution of the Baptist was unable to divert him? Questions of this kind are unavoidable, as long as we start from the assumption that Jesus expected the imminent coming of the Basileia. His community certainly did this, for they believed he had been exalted to the position of the coming judge of the world, to the position of the Son of Man.

If, however, we do argue psychologically, consistency will require that we raise the question of Jesus' *prayer*. Of course, we can hardly know what sort of mood Jesus was in. But is it not possible to ask objectively with *whom* his prayer was concerned? The object of Jewish prayers was certainly the Basileia. If in this case one prayed for the coming of the Basileia, and so for its coming with regard to oneself, then it is impossible to avoid the conclusion that Jesus prayed for this coming with regard to his hearers or disciples, i.e. with regard to their need. Why should he himself ask for anything different from the Lord's Prayer? Even if he simply said: Thy Kingdom come—then, in view of the 'near expectation' at least in the community, does the question not arise for the historian of whether Jesus' prayer was *not* answered? Can exegesis avoid this tense question? Whatever Jesus may have felt on the cross, the question remains, in view of his execution, of whether his prayer was answered. Can this question remain un-noticed, when we dare even to consider Jesus' possible 'deception' or self-deception?

Yet surely Jesus' proclamation affords an understanding of time based on the 'nevertheless', which is able from the first to provide an answer, because faith *accepted* the word that Jesus gave. Surely the need of the neighbour was from the first the 'primer for the will of God' which Jesus offered.[1] The power of love was no longer a matter of argument, once it had stood its ground against the weakness of anxiety and care. On the strength of this Jesus could be sure of the answer to his prayer, and indeed he had to be. Therefore his expectation of the future necessarily turned into joy in the power of the word; this, for example, he could express in parables. It was not a temporal process but rather the apprehen-sion of the very power of God which now became the content of experience. God's power had appeared as a word which over-powered need. Conversely, sin should therefore no longer be psychologically described as the 'need for recognition'. Instead it is to be defined as misuse of God's power, as sin against God's revelation, as reluctance to accept the word, and as nothing else.

We now turn to the second point, that of the *existential inter-pretation*. It remains within its limits as long as it is only used to bring into relief the *theme* of existing, by selecting this theme from the experience possible for a self-understanding (in the *existentiale*). The existential interpretation therefore asks quite simply what at any time this theme was. For this purpose we hold to the *existen-tialia*, although, of course, not without testing their individual competence. The result is that the *existentialia* are variously arranged, and discovered anew. The criterion for discovering an *existentiale* is the question whether the form of existence which is considered as a possible *existentiale* discloses the world *as* world. In accordance with my *Hermeneutik* I can also say: We find *existentialia* wherever an understanding between men is disclosed, through their having a common world. For here the one easily understands the other, even though they might fight to the death. This is the only way that 'conceptions' are possible and exchange-able. Through these conceptions experience of the world is

[1] Cf. *Hermeneutik*, p. 217.

objectified in such a way that participants can speak with each other about their experiences. But for this reason the conceptions easily obscure those decisions which had always been made in the understanding. If there is any change in the understanding that lies at the root of a common world, i.e. in the understanding which forms a world, then suddenly people no longer understand each other, and the conceptions lose the power which makes them binding for everyone. This, for example, was the way that Cartesian thought broke in and triumphed in modern times. Thereafter the understanding which forms a world turns towards the pure conception,[1] and this is the reason for the critique of reason which immediately arose. It is no accident that mathematical theses were then regarded as the model for the true conception. This process was not really halted by Dilthey's *existentiell* correction. Instead it was necessary to make a *completely* new attempt to base thought on existence. The search for the meaning is no longer adequate. Its place is taken by the understanding about the meaning of *language*; previously one could at most have referred to a language composed of meanings. The return to the personal nature of existence in the I-Thou relationship is also inadequate for the new formulation of the question.

If the '*freedom for the word*' is indeed an *existentiale*, then there exists today not only more than an exterior inducement to give earnest thought to this *existentiale*: the area and limits of existential interpretation are also for the first time precisely defined. As a result theology can make its own contribution to existential interpretation, without having to limit the procedure to theology. The question of what someone *has to say* is thereby removed from psychology and restored instead to the experience of existence, as the distinguishing mark of the conscious or unconscious self-understanding. We shall then no longer resist the established fact that real faith prays. We have instead to ask methodically why this is the case, in view of the special stress which the texts lay on this phenomenon. There is no *existentiell* phenomenon which may remain outside the existential enquiry into the theme of existing. It is not the method that decides *which* phenomena are to be included for this purpose, but rather the text, which is to be interpreted on the basis of the theme of an existence. That is probably

---

[1] *Hermeneutik*, p. 136. Understanding = Einverständnis.

why the text exists. It says something that, without it, could no longer still be ascertained.

Why does the Church need a text at all? It is the Church which has given us the New Testament and has transmitted it. It has not just transmitted it, but has also given it. How did it come upon this process?

The New Testament itself makes it quite clear that its intention is conservative; i.e. it is concerned not to lose the old in the new, but to remain in an historically given context. The reason for this lies not in a particularly well-developed historical consciousness, but in difficulties which characterize faith. Faith must remain faith, without being able to remain faith *by itself*. This is why the community of faith is tempted to replace in the future the missing stability of faith with neatly interlocking *ideas* about faith. On the other hand, the unavoidable forces opposed to faith were always a stimulus to further genuine reflection on the nature of faith. The New Testament serves both tendencies. Once it was there, it assured the proper place to the historical problem lying ahead of it, and therefore to an 'existentiell' theme.

If Jesus had lived longer, the longer he lived the more acutely he would have been faced by the same problem as the New Testament, i.e. as the Gospels and in particular Matthew. This problem concerns not the origin but the consequences of faith. There is no faith without consequences; no faith which in this sense is 'unsuccessful'. Evidence for this is provided by the causal connexion in every event, by the tension between past and future which never remains unresolved. Since Jesus, the future itself—the miracle of God which changes everything—is apprehended through faith. Therefore there is now the greatest conceivable tension between the future and the past; and it is this tension which simply calls man to faith. It is not permissible to object to this by saying that world history simply passed by these companions of Jesus. This just appears to be the case, when we look only at political history and in a very shortsighted way. In fact, Jesus' execution sharpened this tension to an unsurpassable extent.[1]

---

[1] Between ourselves: What does faith believe in? Does it not always believe in a word? Does it not simply have dealings with *the* word which, because it demands faith, therefore bestows faith. Is the wish father to the thought? Absurd! That would not be faith at all. It is important to note that with faith it is not, as with thought, a

Bultmann warns me against slipping back into psychology.[1] But, like him, I am concerned with *overcoming* psychology; that is, with the basis on which it can be overcome at all. The very terms 'near expectation' and 'need for recognition' indicate psychological themes. One must certainly admit that other more significant things lie behind them, because it was only after Jesus' execution that the phenomenon of faith properly came to light and so became conceptually comprehensible. Bultmann, too, speaks of 'Easter faith'. This term is a special burden to the discussion. Must we not, on the contrary, also pose the other question of whether Jesus' execution forced the declarations of faith in Paul's own case into an antithesis, which for its part was only provisionally useful? This antithesis, of course, led to a deepening of the understanding of the 'justification' of faith, which had been asserted even before Paul in connexion with the baptismal language. In fact, it must be asserted that neither Jesus' execution nor the confession of his exaltation or resurrection actually matter for faith, unless these concrete events (Jesus' cross and the confession of his exaltation or resurrection) have forced faith to meditate on what is *peculiar* to it as faith. This is the basis on which, in the discussion on faith, psychology can and must be overcome.

One of the consequences of faith is that it makes the believer glad. But another of the consequences is that faith *must* always be disappointed, for otherwise the transcendence of its object— God's coming, God's power and intervention—would be reduced to the this-worldly sphere of the controllable, and faith would thereby be destroyed by itself. We should not speak at all about refining the 'soul'.[2] Instead it is a case of existence itself becoming transparent. What becomes transparent? In brief, the very thing which had been the main point from the beginning and which was so even for Jesus himself: that the being (*Sein*) of man appears as the

***

question of the content of faith, but of the freedom *for* faith. Faith believes that word which *binds* me directly to faith. Faith believes gladly. Otherwise there is no faith at all. Therefore it is a question of the tension with which faith deals. The special feature of Jesus' proclamation is that this tension in Jesus' word regarding the rule of God simply sets and keeps everything in motion. Thus I say: In Jesus (and in Paul) the radius of faith is determined by *those whom he addressed*, whom he called to faith. Cf. G. Ebeling, *Das Wesen des christlichen Glaubens*, 1959 (ET, *The Nature of Faith*, 1961); E. Fuchs, *Zum hermeneutischen Problem in der Theologie*, 1959, p. 296.

[1] 'Allgemeine Wahrheit und christliche Verkündigung', *ZTK* 54, 1957, p. 254.
[2] E. Frank, quoted by Bultmann, *History and Eschatology*, p. 153.

word which is able to gather everyone together round one thing, round our *relation to* God's coming. This entered language in the similitude of the mustard seed, and it is the theme of existence of those believers.

Bultmann has called this matter the 'unity of power and demand'.[1] That may suffice as a provisional formulation for the unity of indicative and imperative in Paul. But as an interpretation of the context in which faith lives, this formulation was a fateful step backwards. It now appeared as if the believer were the one who *acted*, who saw himself called to 'final' decision, facing decision in the 'final' hour. This formulation had, of course, to clash with Heidegger's philosophically framed 'anticipation of death'. It could hope for confirmation in Luther's *'ad nihilum redigi'*. But Luther's manner of expression, his paradox, was formed or occasioned by the nominalist conception of God as *potentia absoluta*. The solitariness of the individual which Bultmann, with an eye on Kierkegaard's interpretation of guilt and Heidegger's interpretation of conscience, chose as the plane for his view of decision (as self-surrender), is, in fact, only a psychologically motivated exceptional case of the guilty conscience. However, if for Jesus' hearers sin consisted of the choice of *need*, because the man who despaired of history held on to need as his criterion for the interpretation of history or for his self-understanding, then all the circumstances are changed. The word itself now became the power which Jesus opposed to need, and the question was—or is— whether I choose *need* or the *word* as the criterion for the self-understanding or the interpretation of history. *This* decision leads to faith, if the *word* is chosen. History must be content with the fact that the word of faith is handed on, even though history resists this with catastrophes. What matters now is the *course* of the word in history; i.e. the question, *which word makes its way past the catastrophes of history*.[2] This is the word which, *within* history, admits

---

[1] *Theologie des Neuen Testaments,* 3rd ed., 1958, p. 338; ET, *Theology of the New Testament* I, London, 1952, p. 336.

[2] Whoever misunderstands the sentence by thinking that this furthers cowardice would be better simply to put down his New Testament. On the other hand, it is valid to ask what the constancy of faith consists of. The answer is that it consists in the victory of faith's joy. The certainty of hope lies here, the certainty which, for example, can—with Bultmann—term a sentence like that in II Cor. 5.2 the criterion by which hope is known. The victory of joy and the sighing of the afflicted include rather than exclude each other. This is why faith *abides* by the word and takes courage

only faith; the word, therefore, which is distinguished only by being able to continue, to be transmitted, without perishing in history. This is the word which is itself able to arouse faith. The nature of this word is described, not by paradox, but by the 'freedom for the word'. The 'nevertheless' of faith asserts precisely that word which arouses faith, because it bestows freedom from history without *wanting* to put an end to history. Jesus possessed the freedom to say the word in such a way that, in spite of the fate of Jesus and his disciples, we are able to hold fast to it, and therefore ourselves to pass it on. If it were not for this, then in the interests of truth we would have to oppose the assertion of the New Testament and of the Church that he was God's communication to *us*. If we recognize that Jesus' word is concerned with the freedom in which we who are in history so travel through history that our way takes us past this freedom, then he *was* God's communication to us, even to us. For then we, too, believe that, precisely because of our need which arises through history, we are to be involved in God's coming. This consolation, this word which is God's 'yes' to us, has been made and offered to us *in* history from the lips of Jesus. This is why it can also be said that the nature of this word, which opens the way to faith, stems from the *nature* of love; love which can never again turn back once it has become an event.

The interpretation of Jesus' person must therefore try with Paul to penetrate behind the Pauline antithesis of grace and works to the unity of word and love (cf. II Cor. 4.4). But was that not already the way the understanding of faith developed within the New Testament? With the aid of the 'freedom for the word' *existentiale*, the existential interpretation directs us, in the case of faith in the word, into the *nature of love*. In history love always binds us to a word, because it *gives* its word to us. Once that is

---

again. However, we have the duty of seeing to it that preaching does not become extinct. The text, i.e. the New Testament, helps us in this. Faith is bound historically to Jesus and through Jesus, and this is perpetuated in the historically given text. Therefore the exegete must not assert that faith is independent of his work. It is not as easy as that. If we spoil the text, we involve faith in extreme danger. If however, in the interests of the text, we are assistants of preaching, it is clear that for Jesus' sake the expositor of the text also has the task of holding fast to God in that present in which God *wants* us to hold to him. This, of course, would also apply to an exegete who confined himself to philology. But who confines himself in this way? The text demands more.

clear there is, in fact, no further need to ask if Jesus 'knew' everything in this form. He certainly stood in the tradition of the Old Testament. The decisive point is whether we understand now that he himself loved, because he staked everything on the word, which was and is the word of love. What a person who loves does under such circumstances is something that interpretation can only produce from experience. Our own part is important here. It seems to me that those who love in faith understand that prayer is necessary, and they understand also that a great deal depends on *what* one prays for. We are then referred back to our own word, to the word that we ourselves are able to give to each other. And this word will have to be first of all a word of faith, for in love, because of the need of history, what is *always* at stake is love itself (I John 4.15). Christian faith believes in Jesus because, as a result of our own weakness, the power of love *time and again* becomes questionable for us (I John 3.20). Why should it be that faith does not live simply by its own 'nevertheless' to experience, but instead holds fast to the historical Jesus as the event of love? This question is decided only by means of the power of the word itself. The fact *that* Jesus is believed in, and *that* he therefore remains the word of love, depends not on us but purely on love remaining steadfast, so as to vouchsafe to us, in the tension between past and future, the way which God goes with us.

Interpretation thereby finally comes to the concept of God himself. Is the God whom Jesus spoke of simply the power which, *as* love, imparts to us its way. Are we true to the texts, can we remain true to them, if we assert that faith says 'yes' to this God, *because* in such faith man understands himself to be affirmed? We shall then have to demand of an exegesis which insists on facts that it makes the fact of faith comprehensible purely in terms of the context appropriate to it. The conceptual framework which is appropriate for this regards the 'freedom for the word' as its decisive standpoint. The similitude of the mustard seed stemmed from this freedom.

VI

JESUS' UNDERSTANDING OF TIME[1]
1960

1. CRITERIA OF JESUS' PROCLAMATION

THIS lecture is concerned with the question of what Jesus had to say about God.

If in what follows we speak of 'Jesus' proclamation', this does not mean that we have to imagine Jesus' proclamation in terms of our sermons. The term 'Jesus' proclamation' is simply a collective term for everything that Jesus had to say about God. We look for the material of this proclamation in the Synoptic Gospels (Matthew, Mark, and Luke). Using the method of form-criticism, we keep to those layers of the synoptic tradition which are accessible to us, and, along with Bultmann in his *History of the Synoptic Tradition,* we assume that the oldest layer, apart from the core of passion narrative, made a collection of individual sayings, parables and miracle narratives. The so-called logia source (Q), which Matthew and Luke each use independently but which otherwise has not been preserved for us, belongs to the oldest layer of the tradition accessible in a literary form, although in some individual cases we can penetrate behind Q. The word 'layer' is therefore to be taken with a pinch of salt. If it is true that Q consciously included in its collection sayings which even then no one considered as genuine sayings of Jesus, this is an additional reason for not trying at all costs to construct Jesus' proclamation from 'genuine' sayings of Jesus. We do not need to have it pointed out to us that the historical Jesus was closely bound to his environment, and we assert that religious movements, just like other sociologically comprehensible movements, by no means need to

---

[1] From the lecture of the Winter Semester 1959/60 in Berlin. The introductory section on the saying about the ravens was made available in a slightly altered form to the Evangelische Verlaganstalt, Berlin, for their collected volume *Der historische Jesus und der kerygmatische Christus.* The final section leads beyond the lecture and links it with the next essay in this book.

go back to 'original' conceptions. Even if an individual becomes the representative of an historical group, this still does not mean that we can deduce that this group has him as its founder. Historical groups are not 'founded' at all, nor indeed was Christianity 'instituted'. But because we want to know what Jesus had to say about God, we examine the oldest tradition which still has a connexion with his words, with a view to the thoughts which dominate it. But this is not an enquiry into the sum of various possible conceptions of God. The object of the quest is to find out what, according to Jesus, is to be thought of God. *Our theme is this phrase 'what is to be thought'.* We thus look first of all for the *criteria*[1] of Jesus' proclamation.

(i) *The saying about the ravens* (Luke 12.24 par. Matt. 6.26).

(a) Literary context:[2] The saying belongs to Q. There it stands in the narrower context of the collection of sayings in Matt. 6.25–33 par. Luke 12.22b–31. Matthew offers this collection along with the amplifications in v. 34a and b; Luke 12.22a and 12.32 are also amplifications. Matthew obviously supplements (πρῶτον and καὶ τὴν δικαιοσύνην in v. 33) and polishes (μὴ οὖν μεριμνήσητε λέγοντες in v. 31, instead of [καὶ ὑμεῖς] μὴ ζητεῖτε in Luke 12.29). Matt. 6.31f par. Luke 12.29f is therefore to be regarded even in Q as an addition and doublet to the similarly conspicuous Matt. 6.25a par. Luke 12.22b. The question form of v. 25b shows that this verse in Matthew belongs to 25a. Luke has given it greater emphasis as the transition to what follows, and perhaps for this reason has made it the foundation. If we take into account that Matt. 6.27 par. Luke 12.25 appears to be an insertion between Matt. 6.26 par. Luke 12.24 and Matt. 6.28bf par. Luke 12.27f, which conditions the interpolation in Matt. 6.28a par. Luke 12.26 (Matthew has changed the verb in 28b), then it is clear that originally the two comparisons, completed by a conclusion 'a minore ad maius', belonged together; i.e. Matt. 6.26 par. Luke 12.24 and Matt. 6.28b–30 par. Luke 12.27f. The saying about the ravens therefore belongs to a double saying.

---

[1] If the bird is recognized by the feathers, the tree by the fruit, and so on, it is advisable to ask by what we recognize Jesus' proclamation. This harmless matter is what is meant by the word 'criterion', irrespective of what historical consequences may be involved in such a question.

[2] Bultmann, *Tradition*, pp. 84f, 92, 109; ET, pp. 80ff, 88, 106; *Jesus*, pp. 135ff; ET, pp. 115ff.

(*b*) As Matthew polishes more stylishly than Luke, Luke's rendering merits precedence. Q has already provided additions (cf. in Luke vv. 22b, 25, 29 and 31a). But the λέγω δὲ ὑμῖν in Matt. 6.29 par. Luke 12.27b and the address ὀλιγόπιστοι at the end belong to the composition of the double saying. Whether it is a genuine saying of Jesus is nevertheless undecided. The phrase '(but) I say to you' is no criterion of authenticity, as the analysis of the whole complex shows (Matt. 6.25 and par.).[1]

Therefore the text we have to interpret is as follows:

> (Luke 12.24) Consider the ravens:
> They neither sow nor reap,
> They have neither storehouse nor barn;
> and yet God feeds them.
> Of how much more value are you than the birds!
> (27) Consider the 'lilies':
> They neither spin nor weave.
> Yet I tell you:
> Even Solomon in all his glory
> was not arrayed like one of these.
> (28) But if God so clothes the grass of the field,
> which today is, and tomorrow is thrown into the oven,
> how much more will he clothe you,
> O men of little faith!

(*c*) We must agree with Bultmann when he notes that the

---

[1] Cf. as a further example Matt. 5.39; so Bultmann, *Tradition*, p. 95; ET, p. 91. Bornkamm's defence of 'but I say to you' is not convincing (*Jesus von Nazareth*, 1956, p. 91; ET, *Jesus of Nazareth*, 1960, p. 99). The 'Amen' which appears frequently before that phrase is also most certainly conceivable on the lips of a Christian bearer of revelation, i.e. in the early community, if indeed Matthew alone offers thirty examples (Bornkamm, p. 187 n. 7; ET, p. 205 n. 7). The same objection applies to E. Käsemann, *ZTK* 51, 1954, pp. 148ff (ET, *Essays on New Testament Themes*, p. 43). Käsemann makes Jesus *de facto* into an historical theologian of the turn of the aeons, when he writes of the logion Matt. 11.12f par., esp. v. 13 (in the sequence Luke 16.16): 'Who but Jesus himself can look back in this way over the completed Old Testament epoch of salvation, not degrading the Baptist to the position of a mere forerunner as the whole Christian community and the whole New Testament were to do, but drawing him to his side and—an enormity to later Christian ears—presenting him as the initiator of the new aeon? But who then is this, who does justice to the Baptist and yet claims for himself a mission higher than that entrusted to John?' This is dogmatics! Käsemann then continues: 'Evidently, he who brings with his Gospel the kingdom itself; a kingdom which can yet be obstructed and snatched away, for the very reason that it appears in the defenceless form of the Gospel.' On the other hand, I agree with the sentence which follows: 'It was the belief of Jesus that, in his word, the *basileia* was coming to his hearers. But the sentence requires hermeneutical reflection on the 'word' as a language-event; i.e. it must be considered on the basis of the event of language, and in the way that Jesus understood this.

'eschatological frame' is lacking in this double saying, as it is, for example, in Matt. 6.19–21 (the logia about the gathering of treasure).[1] There are no formal marks of an authentic saying of Jesus. Bultmann will also be right when, in the case of sayings like Matt. 10.29–31 par. (comparison with the sparrows and the hairs of the head which are numbered) or Matt 5.45 and also Luke 12.29f par. Matt. 6.31f (your father knows that you need sustenance), he places these on the basis of their content next to the double saying about the ravens and the lilies. As far as the ravens are concerned, Ps. 147.9 also says: 'He gives to the beasts their food, and to the young ravens which cry to him.' The thought that God cares for all has numerous rabbinic parallels.[2] The special emphasis of the double saying is, of course, concealed by the fact that Matthew in particular, but also Q, makes a special point of combating the need to care. The double saying, on the other hand, intends above all else to arouse faith. In this it follows the saying about the 'mustard-seed faith', which is also handed down in Q. (Matt. 17.20 par. Luke 17.6). In contradistinction to the saying about mustard-seed faith, the faith demanded in the double saying in Luke 12.24, 27f is certainly not related to an eschatological situation.

(*d*) The comparison with God's solicitude for lower animals like the ravens and for common plants like the lilies highlights God's solicitude for his own image, man, and thus provides aid for the despairing 'men of little faith'. Bultmann speaks of a 'belief in providence'[3] to which the double saying bears witness. However, as in particular the comparison with Solomon's proverbial raiment indicates, the double saying means to do away with all care by referring to God's action, which not only provides what is most needful, but which is in general miraculous. Bultmann[4] points out that Jesus had no knowledge of 'the question of the justice of God' (and Bornkamm follows Bultmann here[5]). (It would, in fact, be inevitable where only the '*minima*' are prayed for.) Sayings which reflect a 'resigned view of man and the world' are indeed also handed down from Jesus; e.g. Matt. 8.20; 6.27;

---

[1] Bultmann, *Tradition*, p. 109; ET, p. 104.
[2] Strack-Billerbeck, *Kommentar zum Neuen Testament* I, pp. 435–7. Matthew's rendering 'birds of the air', in place of the 'ravens' in Luke, seems to be an assimilation of scriptural usage or a case of mitigation, since ravens were despised.
[3] *Jesus*, pp. 135ff; ET, pp. 115ff.
[4] *Ibid.*, pp. 139ff, 143ff; ET, pp. 119ff, 121ff.
[5] *Jesus von Nazareth*, p. 73; ET, p. 80.

34b; Mark 4.25; 8.36 and 37.[1] We then state cautiously: In the tradition ascribed to Jesus, both the optimistic sayings (like our double saying) and also the pessimistic ones bear the marks rather of the popular piety of Jewish wisdom than of eschatology. Just how these sayings are related to the eschatological 'proclamation' of Jesus must meanwhile remain an open question. If they are, in fact, connected with Jesus' proclamation, one thing can be taken from them: the decision about faith must take place in faith itself.[2] For in these sayings God's working is related to the *present*. *Faith* is demanded for this. Faith is therefore accessible only as an event.

(*e*) We have now also acquired a criterion for Jesus' proclamation, assuming that the circle of these wisdom sayings is in general appropriate to Jesus' proclamation—and the tradition does indeed assume this. The criterion can be put in the form of a question: To what extent was Jesus' eschatological proclamation at all concerned with faith? In another form: *Are faith and eschatology compatible with each other?* It is noteworthy that the relatively concise tradition attributes to Jesus words of wisdom which are even opposed to each other. Do faith and eschatology actually *demand* each other? Since the living 'faith in providence' relates to the present, the question is narrowed down to this point: How are *present* and *future* related in Jesus' faith? May it be that Jesus has knowledge of a future which binds faith more than ever to the present? Then Jesus' proclamation would actually have created the situation in which this proclamation becomes comprehensible. What, then, are the consequences for this situation? Should we be content with the information that the much-talked-of 'near expectation' did not allow the problem of theodicy to arise? But even Jesus' brief activity could scarcely prevent questions like the question of theodicy, i.e. the question of what God allows, if Jesus was from the beginning bound by psychologically limited expectations. Or did Jesus abide by a more profoundly determined eschatology? What would *its* criterion be? This is the next question which we have to ask of Jesus' proclamation, or rather of the tradition ascribed to him. We mean to clarify this question by reference to Matt. 5.25f par. Luke 12.57–59.

---

[1] *Jesus*, p. 143; ET, p. 121.
[2] Gerhard Ebeling has made this clear in his book *Das Wesen des christlichen Glaubens* (ET, *The Nature of Faith*).

(ii) *The warning about timely settlement* (Luke 12.57–59 par. Matt. 5.25f).

(*a*) The *literary context*[1] shows that the saying is an independent similitude, handed down in Q. According to Bultmann, it is a 'typical example of a similitude developed from an "image" '. There is a lack either of comparative conjunctions or of an application.[2]

Matt. 7.9f may be quoted as an example of what is to be regarded as an 'image' which, because of its parallelism, is not yet composed in the unified form of a similitude. The similitudes of the servant and the master (Luke 17.7–10) and of the thief (Luke 12.39f par. Matt. 24.43f) are developed from 'images'; on the other hand, those of the treasure (Matt. 13.44) and of the pearl (Matt. 13.45f) are developed from comparisons.[3]

As far as the 'timely settlement' is concerned, the text in Luke does not completely correspond to Q's version, for v. 57 is a typical Lucan connecting construction, 'in order to link vv. 58f with vv. 54–56'.[4] In the same way Luke transposed the Jewish trial procedure into Roman terms.[5] However, Luke has preserved the eschatological meaning of the parable more clearly, as is shown by the context in which he hands it on (vv. 35–59). Matthew, on the other hand, gives the similitude a more pronounced hortatory emphasis, by linking it on to 5.23f. While Matt. 5.21f assumes that the brother in v. 22 is guilty, and uses him as the provoking occasion of my own fault, vv. 23f, on the other hand, assume that the brother is the one who has something against me. Verses 25f now refer to the disagreeable situation in which, in the face of judgment, I have to be the one who is condemned. It therefore issues a positive admonition to reconciliation, that is, to timely settlement before it is too late. If we consider the peculiarity of that form of judgment (even in a favourable case, the outcome of the process is uncertain), then the 'image' as such makes use of the constantly repeated warning against litigation. The inexorable nature of the judgment, which is questioned only by way of exception in Luke 18.4a, is brought home as strongly as possible in Luke 12.59 par. Matt. 5.26 (λέγω σοι, par. ἀμὴν λέγω σοι—Matthew

---

[1] *Tradition*, pp. 185f, also 101, 103, 160; ET, pp. 172, also 96, 99, 149.
[2] *Ibid.*, p. 185; ET, p. 172.
[3] *Ibid.*, p. 186; ET, p. 173.
[4] *Ibid.*, p. 95; ET, p. 91.
[5] J. Jeremias, *Die Gleichnisse Jesu*, p. 28 n. 2; ET, p. 31 n. 45.

makes it stronger). For Luke thinks of God as a judge, and God cannot be any less strict a judge than the earthly one (cf. Luke 16.31). It is clear from the reference to the fire of Gehenna in v. 22b that Matthew also thinks of God as a judge. In Luke's case this idea stems also from 12.56 on the one hand, and on the other hand from the demand for *metanoia*, for complete 'conversion' (13.1–5; cf. also Luke 12.47f and 12.39f; 13.1–5 is special material). All sayings which have in view the genuine Jewish idea of reward[1] are related—e.g. Matt. 13.12 par. Mark 4.25 and Luke 8.18; or Matt. 25.29 par. Luke 19.26; also Mark 4.24; cf. here Matt. 7.2 par. Luke 6.38. These sayings assume that '*having*' involves obligations; in other words, that it has consequences. This applies also to 'having time'—before it is too late. Does this mean that in the present we have control over the future? Or conversely does the present, according to its nature, already correspond to the future? If, as the idea of reward intends, it is necessary at least to distinguish between present and future, then the future is not simply an extension of the present. In this case the future is not tacked on to the present; the present is instead the precursor of the future. This precursory characteristic of the present prevents the formal reduction of the present simply to the concept of a point in time. It forces us indeed to start out from the *concrete* present, since our relation to the future is decided in the present. Reward and recompense now belong together. But the exhortatory theme of recompense also belongs expressly to eschatology, as is shown by Matt. 25.29 par. Luke 19.26; cf. Mark 4.25 par. (the close of the parable of the talents). This becomes fully evident in the parable of the unmerciful servant, Matt. 18.23–35 (special material), and in the description of the last judgment, Matt. 25.31–46 (special material). In Matt. 18.23ff the *scopus* is that God calls a person to account when he abuses his compassionate gift (God's compassion is always a gift). What is this gift in the similitude in Luke 12.58f par. Matt. 5.25f? Clearly it is the final time before the judgment; that is, the present. This is precisely the meaning of the warning which immediately precedes the similitude in Luke (vv. 54–56). It is a reprimand to those who understand the signs of the present so well in other ways, in the case of the weather, for example, but

---

[1] For the idea of reward in the New Testament cf. G. Bornkamm, *Gesammelte Aufsätze* II, 1959, pp. 69–92 (= *EvTh* 7, 1946, pp. 143ff).

take no notice of the καιρὸς οὗτος—the present itself—although it
is of this that Jesus is speaking. For our enquiry it is therefore
unimportant whether or not the evangelists or even Q intend the
similitude in Matt. 5.25f to apply to the fact of the delay in the
parousia.[1] Does it, then, depend on whether 'something can be
sensed'[2] 'of the moment of acute imminent expectation'? On the
other hand, Jeremias appears to be right in protesting against
Luther's rendering of the μήποτε in Luke (v. 58) as 'lest *here-
after*'.[3] For the important thing in the 'image' is not a reflection
about the length of the way, but the inexorable nature of the judgment. The same is true in I Thess. 5.2f, Luke 12.35–46 par. or
Matt. 25. What is therefore demanded is correct dealings with the
gift of the given time (Matt. 18.23–35). This time is simply the
concrete present. The one question is what possibilities exist for
our dealings with the present, when the present carries eschatological obligations. The present must then correspond to the in-
exorableness of God's judgment. But how? Can the present *itself*
be understood eschatologically, no matter what one may 'sense'?

(*b*) Matt. 25.31–46 (special material) is specially significant for
the Jewish interpretation. The passage has already been Chris-
tianized by the insertion of the Son of Man in v. 31 in place of the
original term 'king'.[4] Bultmann has shown that the 'moral of this
section is not specifically Christian', for man is meant to act like
God, who clothes the naked, and so on (Isa. 58.7).[5] Is this not the
reason why the passage lacks that particular 'acute eschatological
consciousness, with its combined gladness and gravity in the face
of decision', in which Bultmann finds the expression of 'Jesus'
historical self-consciousness'?[6] Bultmann bases this on passages
like Luke 6.20f par.; 10.23f par. (blessed eyewitnesses); Matt.

[1] For the complex of the delay in the parousia, cf. E. Grässer, *Das Problem der
Parousieverzögerung in der synoptischen Evangelien und in der Apostelgeschichte* (BZNW 22),
1957. Grässer will perhaps include me among those who render the 'near expectation'
'harmless' (pp. 12ff). Although I often agree with him, I must nevertheless ask him
if he himself has done justice to the phenomenon of 'faith'. Of course, I do not dispute
that, seen psychologically, the near expectation was the 'form' of Jesus' hope, or of
the hope of his environment (p. 16).
[2] Grässer, p. 192.
[3] Jeremias, *op. cit.*, p. 129 n. 2. ET, p. 126 n. 3.
[4] Bultmann, *Tradition*, p. 162; ET, p. 151. Similarly Ph. Vielhauer, 'Gottesreich
und Menschensohn in der Verkündigung Jesu', in *Festschrift für G. Dehn*, 1957,
pp. 57f.
[5] *Tradition*, pp. 130f; ET, pp. 124f.
[6] *Ibid.*, p. 135; ET, p. 128.

11.5f par.; and also Luke 11.31f (comparison with Solomon and Jonah); 12.54–56; 6.46 (Matt. 7.21—do what he says). What decision is, then, demanded, if we are concerned with an eschatologically viewed present? Gladness and gravity can certainly not be lacking, if we are aware of the fact that by means of the present God grants the time for decision; that is to say, the time for radical obedience. For along with the decision the very 'being' (*Sein*) of man takes place as something new; in other words, it is governed by the promise. As a result 'man is relieved of a grievous burden'.[1] However, moods of this kind only provide us with a hermeneutical *index*, not the matter itself. This also applies to the demand for obedience. The demand for obedience simply means that in the intended situation we are able to do something, which otherwise we would perhaps not have accomplished. We are therefore directed to ourselves, by virtue of our coming freely to a decision. What do we decide for? For the present. Not just in the present. For which present? For the eschatologically viewed present. What does this mean in view of the above-mentioned hermeneutical definitions of gladness, gravity and a free obedience? There is one thing it cannot mean: ignoring the present. For freedom can only be experienced *as* presence, assuming that the being (*Sein*) of man (or as Bultmann also says, the *whole* man) is to be free.[2] That 'near expectation' which even Bultmann attributes to Jesus, does not penetrate to the fact of the matter, certainly not in the sense that the near expectation could exhaust the fact of the matter. Near expectation is meaningful for the gravity of the person who witnesses man being excessively deprived. This might apply to the speaker in Luke 6.20f or Luke 11.31f. Near expectation is meaningful as joy for those who suffer and who will soon be delivered; this might be the assumption in Luke 10.23f and also 21.28—I just cite examples. But in both instances, that of gravity and that of joy, man is still only *passively* involved. An active relationship between the person concerned and the person of Jesus is therefore secondary.[3] But if a person is to be *completely* involved, then, like Jesus, he must take part *actively* as himself—for example, in the way that the commandment of love requires (Mark 12.28–34 par.). Actually,

---

[1] *Jesus,* pp. 72, also 68–71; ET, pp. 64 (61–64).
[2] *Ibid.,* p. 69; ET, p. 62.
[3] Cf. *Tradition,* p. 161; ET, p. 150.

in his book on *Jesus*, Bultmann takes his bearings from the commandment of love.[1] What is at stake here is shown firstly by the
illustrative narrative of the good Samaritan in Luke 10.29–37, and
secondly by the concluding sentence of Matt. 5.48 (par.; changed
in Luke 6.36). In Matt. 5.48 the 'whole' man is 'perfect'; that is to
say, he is undividedly summoned to himself. As a result, he is
unreservedly sure of himself, just as the heavenly father (as the
giver) is unreservedly sure of himself.[2] The element of certainty is
thematically introduced in Matt. 19.21 by means of the question
in v. 20: what do I still lack? In Matt. 5.48 it has to be drawn out
of the meaning of the relationship between God and Israel which
is already fulfilled, or which is to be fulfilled: the free man makes
his response to the 'being' (*Dasein*) of the heavenly father *for all*
through the freedom which he lays hold of because it now belongs
to him. The opposite of this kind of freedom is that fate-like compulsion which involves my being inexorably surrendered to someone else and so bound to him. It is like the man brought to judgment in the 'image' part of our text (Luke 12.58 par. Matt. 5.25).
Freedom and compulsion are now radically opposed to each
other. In the material part freedom had to be on a *higher* plane than
in the 'image'; that is, no longer bound to one particular pattern
of conduct (the need of time). It had to consist of the fact that I
no longer meet my neighbour as my adversary; that is, as one who
has cause for accusation, because I have not met him at all. (In
I Peter 5.8 the 'adversary' is the devil, who is the accuser; but in
Luke 18.3 he is the defendant. The word was a technical term for
this.)

The appeal of the text would be meaningless if it did not
assume that meeting was possible, and spoke on this basis. This
applies even to the 'image' ('on the way'). If we want to do justice
to the text, we must turn it round; i.e. penetrate behind the point
in time of the 'image', so that it is not still an open question how
we would have to act in the role, for example, of those who are
already condemned and due to atone (cf., e.g., I Cor. 7.20–24; but
also Matt. 5.38–42 par.). We ask what the position is, supposing
we have *more freedom* for meeting than the text represents? The

[1] *Op. cit.*, pp. 79ff, 95ff; ET, pp. 70ff, 82ff.
[2] Cf. my study 'Die volkommene Gewissheit', in *Zur Frage nach dem historischen
Jesus*, 1960, pp. 126–36.

'image', which of necessity speaks concretely, conceals the far greater riches of the 'matter'. Even in the 'image' freedom is freedom for meeting. But it is this in view of the resultant possibility that the opposite is to be excluded; that is, the failure to meet, or just the desire to stand by one's rights *and* submit to judgment. This can, of course, be expressed simply as the urging of reconciliation. But the depth of the parable is only plumbed when it is seen that the text, *as a parable* (Luke 12.58: ὡς), presses home its point with the aid of a known situation of compulsion where freedom is lost. This is done through a concrete example, and therefore by concentrating on one thing. The point it makes is *that* presence is freedom for meeting. Just because the parable speaks indirectly, and is thereby differentiated from the portrayal of judgment before God in Matt. 25.31ff (cf. there vv. 35–45), it says directly that the present is the decisive time for the freedom for meeting. In the same way as a debtor, whenever it is too late for any other solution, should ponder the fact that he will be forced to pay right to the 'last', so inversely the man who is here addressed should ponder upon his freedom, as long as it is still not too late. Because I ponder in the present, such reflections direct me to the present, *because* it is still not too late. In reflection I, in fact, overcome myself, but this is a victory in favour of the present, which is the only possibility of freedom. Thus I become open for true meeting.[1]

The question is whether the overcoming of the self which thus arises can be adequately described in terms of the contrast, which Bultmann stresses, to the 'natural will and its claims' (as if no one wanted to pay?);[2] or whether the thematic basis for the parable is not rather man's despair in face of the finite. However, the 'concrete situation in life', which Bultmann rightly stresses, is still decisive.[3] If we refuse to follow Bultmann's antithesis, at most one experience of life contends with another. In any case the parable fits in with Jesus' radical demand for love of the neighbour. But if the parable is viewed only in terms of its 'image', there is the temptation to say with Jeremias: 'Yield then, make a settlement while there is still time. If you do not succeed in doing

---

[1] Bultmann, *Jesus*, p. 97, cf. with p. 77; ET, pp. 84 and 68.
[2] *Ibid.,* p. 94; ET, p. 82.
[3] *Ibid.,* p. 97; ET, p. 84.

so, the worst may happen to you.'[1] The unjust steward had something like this in mind when he resorted to deception (Luke 16.1–8). The parable would then, in fact, be a 'crisis parable'; that is, a parable applying only to judgment.[2] But this classification obliterates the point of view that the eschatological decision can only consist of fully *free* obedience, as Bultmann has shown (see above). The *tertium comparationis* is not an analogous end, but a free new beginning ('on the way'), which stands in *contrast* to the inexorable end. The 'image' demonstrates only indirectly, in a desperate individual case, what freedom is. Bultmann overlooks this also, because he elicits from the parable only a warning about the heavenly judge.[3] The present would then only be a sphere which one had to leave as quickly as possible. It would just be a time of transition, simply preparation. What, in fact, is demanded is that I look the present itself in the face, and face up to it through overcoming my legitimate anxiety. Then I no longer act under compulsion, like the man in the 'image'. This is the only meaning that does justice to the whole context, both to Matt. 5 and also to the command of love. It is the same in Luke 12. These demands do not just appeal to time; they give or bestow time. The important thing is not to flee from oneself any longer. The text means everyone to accept the present in its limitation, in order to acquire full freedom through the very limiting of the present. This is then the present seen eschatologically. It is eschatologically seen, not because I await something in the near future, but because I am directed to it *from outside* by a word like this parable; by virtue of the fact that I am told: '*Only* in your present can you and will you be free. *Your* business is the present, not the future.' For now the one who cares for the outcome is no longer man, who would have just cause to be afraid, but God who through the word refers us to our present.

In Jesus' proclamation the present itself is in the form that Q presents to us—and in this the evangelists have followed Q. It is the *criterion* of the kind of future which must be distinguished from the present, *because* God has *withheld* the future. In Matt. 5.25f par. Luke 12.58f man and the present belong together, as do God and

---

[1] Jeremias, *op. cit.*, p. 130; ET, p. 126.
[2] Jeremias, *op. cit.*, pp. 130f; ET, pp. 126ff.
[3] *Tradition*, p. 186; ET, p. 172.

the future. Does this distinction between present and future still apply in Jesus' proclamation? Will this kind of investigation enable us to work out Jesus' 'proclamation' in such a way that we then subsequently acquire criteria of authenticity in regard to its material content? The methodology of an existential examination of the texts, of our examination of their intercourse with time,[1] would then be made fruitful through concrete reference to the texts themselves.

Like Bultmann, we therefore try to gain a total view of Jesus' proclamation. We must thereby keep in mind that in the first place we can recover only indirectly and in an objectifying way what Jesus meant to say about God, because with the help of existential examination of the texts our intention is to find historically indisputable statements. This attempt is by no means unimportant, even if Jesus' proclamation were 'address' only for a short time. However, if it is true that Jesus' proclamation was address and expressly remained this (which is the opinion of the evangelists)— Jesus' proclamation should have contained an element which provided the motivation for the address. Today's exegetical dispute centres on the question of whether this motivation was the so-called near expectation, or indeed its defence. I wish to show that this conception is not adequate for Jesus' proclamation. Jesus himself had something else in view. This is the sole reason for our still being able to gain a sufficiently clear view of his proclamation. A dogmatic system which judges on traditional lines can then say: Jesus' address did not exhaust itself in an appeal, but was rather a *gift*. *Our* question is: what did Jesus give in his proclamation? What did he give along with it?—assuming we are *not* simply to say, with Mark 10.45, that he gave himself. We therefore examine the justification of the dogmatic answer.

2. REPENTANCE

(i) What was the starting-point of Jesus' proclamation? If we follow Mark and Matthew, Jesus began, like the Baptist, with the call to penitence. This is not self-evident, nor is it certain. What can be said with more certainty is that the Christian community linked together the call to penitence and baptismal proclamation.

[1] Cf. the relevant studies in my *Hermeneutik*, pp. 157 and 145.

This is indicated by Peter's Pentecost address (Acts 2.38), which really should be characteristic of the Lucan period, even though it is constructed on a basis of older material. But a similar pointer is provided by the fact that the Synoptic Gospels, following the example of Mark, make Jesus' baptism by John the presupposition for his appearance, thereby thinking certainly of Christian baptism. The Holy Spirit must make the beginning, before the 'new' can take place. Penitence, therefore, on the *basis* of the efficacy of the Holy Spirit? Why not? The later version of the matter—that spirit comes from Spirit, as in baptism and faith—can very well be a reproduction of the original content. However, the Gospel of Mark, and indeed Q also, distinguish between the *time* of the Spirit and the time before it, the time of Jesus' appearance. This is shown, for example, by the saying about sin against the Holy Spirit (Mark 3.28f; the phrase 'Truly, I say to you' is clearly an element of composition, and therefore by no means a sign of the genuineness of an historical saying of Jesus). This does not mean that the early community's understanding of the Spirit, or the Spirit itself, was the special preserve of the early community. Mark certainly maintained that Jesus' resurrection was the condition for the understanding of the disciples (9.10; cf. with v. 9). It is remarkable that the Gospel does not tell of the post-Easter gift of the Spirit to the disciples. But according to Paul the Spirit, as the Spirit of the Son, is sent into our hearts (Gal. 4.6). This same view lies behind the tradition of Acts 2.33 (in my opinion 2.17–21 was the scriptural proof that originally belonged to this; the parts of the speech have to be rearranged, in order to discover its tradition). A further consideration is that in Mark's description of Easter Peter is pushed to the side, quite contrary to the intention of the evangelist in the present closing section (before the inauthentic conclusion in vv. 9ff), whereas in 16.7 a promise is directed specially to him. Therefore, contrary to the unsubstantiated assertions that the Gospel closed with the event of the parousia of the exalted Jesus—an event no longer recountable but nevertheless really to be expected—it can be established with a probability verging on certainty that Mark's Gospel must originally have closed with the appearance of the exalted Jesus in Galilee; and that there the confessor Peter and the disciples (as in John 20.22) received from Jesus the Spirit which had still been withheld from them in Mark

9.2–8. The passage Matt. 16.17–19, which Bultmann thinks is missing after Mark 8.29, was quite possibly part of this narrative.[1] The transfer of the receiving of the Spirit to Jerusalem may well have made this conclusion to Mark's Gospel impossible, with the result that it was eliminated. All this just shows that originally the Spirit was not to be considered dependent on the resurrection of Jesus, but rather that the Spirit and the kerygma declaring Jesus' resurrection were at variance with each other. If we consider it reasonable to include the saying about the blasphemy against the Spirit among the post-Easter early Christian *theologumena*, then, in view of a saying as old as Matt. 12.28 par. Luke 11.20, we shall have to allow that Jesus' appearance began with the Spirit, and so admit an indirect historical justification to Mark's representation (that Jesus was the bearer of the Spirit since his baptism). Therefore at the beginning there was a *positivum*. We shall have to give due attention to this in the enquiry about repentance.

(ii) At one point in his book on *Jesus*, Bultmann remarks: 'Surely even Jesus' call to penitence is to be understood as an act of love?'[2] This far-ranging but easily misunderstood sentence is not developed in Bultmann's book, because he has already established 'for man' an 'either-or of love and hate'.[3] This either-or is based on the fact that *self-love* is the bearing of the natural man, because of the phrase: love your neighbour 'as yourself' (Mark 12.31 par.).[4] Man must offer in love 'the sacrifice of his own will for the good of the other', if he wants to be obedient to God.[5] The commandment of love shows that love, as Jesus means it, is to be thought of not as a feeling but as an attitude of the will.[6] In the case of Jesus, as in the Old Testament, the will to love the neighbour is motivated by the will to love God and therefore by the will of God. In the double command to love God and love the

---

[1] *Tradition*, p. 277; ET, p. 258. I can by no means agree with the thesis of W. Marxsen (*Der Evangelist Markus*, Forschungen zur Religion und Literatur des AT und NT 67, 1956), which follows E. Lohmeyer: that the conclusion of this Gospel, after 16.8, should have been the parousia itself, which was expected within the present of the evangelist. I think instead that Conzelmann has correctly recognized the christological coherence of the Gospel (*ZTK* 54, 1957, p. 295).

[2] *Op. cit.*, p. 102; ET, p. 88.

[3] *Ibid.*, p. 101; ET, p. 87.

[4] *Ibid.*, p. 99; ET, p. 86.

[5] *Ibid.*, p. 101; ET, p. 87. Cf. also p. 87, ET, p. 76: Jesus 'requires only the strength for sacrifice'; and pp. 63ff, ET, pp. 57ff, under the heading 'obedience'.

[6] *Ibid.*, p. 102; ET, p. 88.

neighbour this second command is motivated by the first.[1] In short, God demands obedience.[2] Love would then be obedience to God with a view to one's neighbour (cf. Luke 10.29–37: the good Samaritan). In the either-or of the demand for obedience the 'old' man escapes from himself, from being at his own disposal in the state of self-love. We could say that he moves backwards under the lordship of another, 'in any case under God's lordship; but it is the lordship either of a jealous God of judgment or of the God of compassion', because through the decision he makes in face of God's commandment of love, man becomes either a sinner or one who is justified.[3] No one has control over this future, because the decision *must* be made—this is precisely the meaning of decision, this central concept in Bultmann's theology. This kind of *real* future will give a man a character which he does *not yet* have: 'This is the meaning of the "now", that it contains the necessity of decision, by virtue of its leading into a future.'[4] Apart from God there can be no good outcome.

But have we really captured the meaning of the present, of the 'now', if the present is to lead into a future and therefore is only to be a *transition*? Moreover, is it a correct premise to claim that the 'natural' everyday man has control of the future as a result of his self-love? We must, then, ask the reverse question, whether it is not the decision of the man who submits to God's will which, with the help of the overcoming of the self and the overcoming of self-love, all the more allows 'control' of the future? As a result we no longer see how faith is distinguished from the subtlety of an obedience of this kind; in short, how faith is distinguished from purposely *calculated* righteousness by works (cf. James 2.21–26). When I really submit to a commandment, in the sense that I begin to live for my neighbour irrespective of all feelings of sympathy, then the question of myself no longer interests me; nor am I interested in the question of the characteristic of my conduct, namely obedience. What does concern me is the concrete question of what I can do for my neighbour and what not. Jesus can simply say to a rich man: Come, follow me (Mark 10.21 par.). It is highly improbable that the people with whom he ate sold everything

[1] *Ibid.*, pp. 98f; ET, pp. 85f.
[2] *Ibid.*, p. 98; ET, p. 85.
[3] *Ibid.*, p. 112; ET, p. 96.
[4] *Ibid.*, p. 112; ET, p. 97.

afterwards, or that he urged this sort of thing on them. The real difficulty lies not in my will, nor even in the future, but outside, on the boundaries of the present. The illustrative narrative of the good Samaritan sounds very pretty, because as a story it not only enlightens but also, by virtue of its happy ending, gives satisfaction (Luke 10.35). But the case at once appears different if the man who fell among thieves dies on the way. What can I still do for him then? I can only look after his burial and perhaps make a contribution to the police. The limit of our ability then involves questioning the demand for penitence. If this demand is placed in the centre, is it at all meaningful? Is the commandment really only concerned to overcome some kind of foolish self-love? Or is the real issue not some other contrast? Even the category of 'contrast' may be misleading. We do not need to take our bearings from Kierkegaard. To create clarity, we shall compare various demands for penitence.

(iii) There is a natural tendency to pursue our intention with the help of the key-word μετανοεῖν or μετάνοια.

The word occurs in the synoptic presentation of the appearance of the Baptist, and in Mark and Matthew it has a place in the first saying of Jesus (μετάνοια: Mark 1.4; Matt. 3.11; also 3.8 par. Luke 3.8—fruit, or fruits worthy of repentance; μετανοεῖν: Matt. 3.2; Mark 1.15; Matt. 4.17). On the other hand, it does not appear in the Sermon on the Mount. This is very striking. Norden has shown[1] that μετανοεῖν, which has also an undertone of remorse (as in some of the few and late Septuagint occurrences), appears in Greek too seldom to allow references to be made which would explain the synoptic linguistic usage. In the previously cited synoptic passages the verb means to do penance, not only to change one's mind in all freedom (Wrede has stressed this).[2] In his commentary on the Gospel of Mark[3] Wellhausen referred to the Aramaic-Hebraic *šûb* or *tûb*. In fact, the rabbis speak of penance as *tᵉšûbā*.[4] The Qumran sect clearly only used the word for the return to the Torah, but they understood this as conversion to the sect.[5] It is significant that the concept of the rule of God, which is

---

[1] *Agnostos Theos,* 1923, pp. 137ff.

[2] 'μετάνοια Sinnesänderung', ZNW 1, 1900, pp. 66ff.

[3] *Das Evangelium Marci,* 1903, p. 8.

[4] G. Schrenk, *TWNT* IV, pp. 991ff.

[5] H. Braun, *Spätjüdisch-häretischer und frühchristlicher Radikalismus* I (Beiträge zur historischen Theologie 24. i), 1957, p. 25, 5, cf. p. 91, 2: The Damascus sect calls itself 'The Community of the Return'; Braun in ZTK 50, 1953, pp. 243–58.

closely linked with penance in the synoptic version of the sayings
of Jesus and of the Baptist, is lacking in the texts of the sect,[1] in
spite of their near expectation of the end of the world. All that
remains is the appeal to the demand of the ancient prophets. They
preached the return to Yahweh as the abandoning of all disobedience, or of cultic-ritual superficial obedience. This is the return to
ḥesed and *daʿath ʾᵉlōhīm*; it is indeed the acceptance of what belongs
to us, of the trust entrusted to us, that is, of the defenceless. They
are in our hand and are entrusted to us, because Yahweh himself
has also acted in this way, however widely he may draw this circle
(Amos 4.6, 8, 9, 10, 11; Hos. 6.1–3 and 4–6; Isa. 58.4b; Zech.
7.5b–6; 7.7ff; Joel 2.3 and 2.12; Isa. 22.12f; the old Isaiah calls
his son symbolically *šᵉār yāšūb*, 7.3; cf. with 10.20f;—this is God's
ḥesed[2]). In linguistic usage μετανοεῖν and the words ἐπιστρέφειν
or ἐπιστρέφεσθαι which are nearer to the Hebrew *šūb*, are ultimately
almost synonymous as expressions for conversion.[3] Cf. Acts 3.19;
26.20. The one result of a lexicographical examination is this:
μετάνοια has its place at the beginning of a definite turning towards
God (act as God acts); conversely this kind of beginning is expressed by the demand for μετάνοια. So we must say *each time*
how the relationship to God which is expressed in this demand is
understood. In the Letter to the Hebrews it is considered unique,
for the so-called second repentance is excluded as contrary to
reason (6.4–6, and the example of Esau, 12.17). In the *Shepherd of
Hermas* (*Vis.* 2.2.3ff; *Mand.* 4.3.4ff; 4.1.8) a second repentance is
conceded (as a confirmation of the first). So the question is whether
we should do penance once and for all, or only because we have
just sinned (cf. I John 2.1 and 5.14ff with 1.8f; also *Didache* 15.3;
I *Clement* 57.1). Both at the beginning of the Synoptic Gospels and
in Acts 2.38 the New Testament starting-point is the definitely
once and for all valid 'turning' in the Baptist's preaching, that is,
in the Baptist's repentance-baptism. (The concept does not
appear in the Johannine writings, apart from the negatively
applied quotation of Isa. 6.9f in John 12.40; it is therefore in-
tentionally left out.) The Baptist's repentance-baptism, like Christian baptism, is formally a βάπτισμα μετανοίας εἰς ἄφεσιν ἁμαρτιῶν

---

[1] Braun II, p. 46, 1.
[2] Cf. E. Würthwein, *TWNT* IV, pp. 978f, 981–3.
[3] *TWNT* IV, pp. 994. 25ff.

(Mark 1.4). It is a confession of sin (Mark 1.5 par. Matt. 3.6). In relation to Jesus' proclamation, one other incidence of the key-word in Luke is to be considered: 15.7, 10; but it is missing in the Q-parallel in Matt. 18.13. The remaining occurrences all point to Christian linguistic usage, though this certainly seems to be modelled on a Jewish usage (e.g. Luke 10.3 par. Matt. 11.21, i.e. Q).

It can be said that the demand for conversion, or for a 'turning' or reversal, was typical of the early Christian mission in both its Jewish and Hellenistic spheres, for this belonged along with baptism. But it is clearly not possible to say the same of Jesus' proclamation. It is at most the second part of Matt. 4.17 which seems to be significant for Jesus—'for the kingdom of heaven is at hand'. However, even this assumption is questionable, because the proclamation of the *nearness* of the Basileia more probably belongs to the Baptist and the early community. The problem of the delay of the parousia arose from this proclamation. We find no trace of this problem in Jesus, when we read without prejudice passages such as Luke 11.20 par. Matt. 12.28; Luke 6.20f par. Matt. 5.3ff. These passages assume the efficacy of the Basileia, but not the question of its relationship within time to the present. We must therefore deal carefully both with the call: 'repent', and also with the concept of the Basileia. Mistrust about the one word brings with it mistrust about the other, for it is hardly possible to deny the close association of the two in view of their first synoptic appearance. Matthew was probably the first to link the key-word Basileia (he prefers to say 'kingdom of heaven') with several of the parables (13.44, 45 ? 18.23; 20.1; 22.2; 25.1).[1] We must ask whether for Matthew the coming Basileia (or else the fact that it has arrived and is present in Jesus, 20.28) has become a thesis which he is defending. The basis of this thesis is not then primarily something like a delay in the parousia, but the kerygma itself. Of course, the kerygma, in the form of the Easter message, originally pointed to Jesus' parousia, assuming that the recollections of the appearances of the exalted Jesus which Paul recounts really had an eschatological meaning. All this shows that it is hardly possible to argue in these terms with regard to Jesus himself. Even the distinction between a beginning and its continuation is precarious, because it assumes a definite, though it may be very small, distance

[1] Bultmann, *Theologie des neuen Testaments*, 1958, 3rd ed., pp. 7f; ET, I, p. 9.

between the beginning and the continuation, that is, between Jesus and the Basileia. It is questionable whether a temporal problem exists here at all. The '*proton pseudos*' of our present research situation might well consist of the fact that from the outset we accommodate the *nature* of the Basileia within a secondary temporal context of phenomena. But there is a difference between the time in which a person moves—whether something passes into the future or arrives from the future—and a time which is defined and imprinted by a definite content and thus always already 'filled' (this applies also to Gal. 4.4). Therefore I cannot be content with Bultmann's presentation of the eschatological proclamation of Jesus.[1] It is worth trying to see if some of the parables have more to say. Just as Matthew's already-mentioned preference for the concept Basileia indicates the need for caution, so also caution is required with regard to Luke. For in his own material Luke gives preference to the *metanoia* point of view (15.7, 10; also 16.30 and 13.3, 5), while at other times (as in Acts) he joins together *metanoia* and the forgiveness of sins (Luke 24.47, cf. 3.3; cf. also the expression 'to be converted to the kerygma', in reference to Jonah, Luke 11.32 par. Matt. 12.41 in Q; Acts speaks of a conversion to the Lord). Apart from these conceptual definitions of *metanoia* and the Basileia, what do we discover from the matter itself? With this question in mind we now turn to the parables, for they are not conceptually tied either to the Basileia or to *metanoia*, assuming that we are not guided by the theology of Matthew.

(iv) If we have to agree with Bultmann, then my exposition[2] of the similitude of the treasure in the field, Matt. 13.44, is mistaken. I must go into the problem here. The similitude of the pearl merchant is to be taken into consideration at the same time (Matt. 13.45f). If Bultmann is right in submitting these to his view of the either-or of the decision to make a sacrifice, then they are both to be treated in terms of the key-word *metanoia*. The starting-point for the understanding of these similitudes would then be his view of the action of most men. For 'most men cling to earthly goods and cares; and when the time for decision comes, they fail—as the parable of the banquet shows (Luke 14.15–24). A man must make up his mind what he wants, what degree of effort he is

[1] *Theologie*, §1.
[2] See p. 94 above.

capable of, just as the means for building a tower or waging a war must first be estimated (Luke 14.28–32). But for the rule of God one must be ready for any sacrifice—like the farmer who finds a treasure and gives all he has to get possession of it, or like the merchant who sells everything in order to acquire the one precious pearl (Matt. 13.44–46).'[1] It is, of course, consistent for Bultmann to sum all this up with the gory saying in Mark 9.43, 47 (or Matt. 5.29f):

> If your hand leads you astray, cut it off.
> It is better for you to enter into life maimed
> than with two hands to go to hell.
> If your eye leads you astray, pluck it out.
> It is better for you to enter into the rule of God with one eye,
> than with two eyes to be thrown into hell.

But the rigorism is astonishing only in theory. In practice it can only be termed foolish, for a person, for example, to castrate himself, as Origen did (Matt. 19.12—here also there is the Matthean addition: for the kingdom of heaven's sake). Even the saying in Luke 14.26 par. Matt. 10.37, which comes from Q (a so-called 'I-saying'), like Matthew's next verse in Q (about taking up one's cross; cf. Mark 8.34 par. Matt. 16.24 and Luke 9.23), is more probably characteristic of a community situation, at a time when persecution allowed no other alternative. Besides, the saying in Mark 9.43, 47 is undoubtedly intended to be taken as an image. If it is taken verbally, it is not, in fact, concerned radically with everything. By contrast, the saying in Matt. 6.22f par. (Q) is aware that the eye is the mirror of the passions. What, then, would be the use of having only one eye? In the same way, the preceding saying in Matt. 5.27f is also a radically considered saying. Yet it is apparent here that this radicalism is intended *hermeneutically*, because it gives rise to a question: to whom do you say this? Even Bultmann adds the following comment on Mark 9.43, 47: 'This renunciation toward the world, this "unworldliness", is not to be thought of as asceticism, but as simple readiness for God's demand. For the positive thing that corresponds to this renunciation, the thing, that is, which constitutes readiness for God's rule, is the fulfilment of God's will, as Jesus makes evident in combating Jewish legalism.'[2] A distinction will therefore have to be made between

---

[1] *Theologie*, pp. 9f; ET, pp. 10f.   [2] *Theologie*, p. 10; ET, p. 11.

the visible representation of God's demand and the demand itself. So we have also to distinguish between the form of the antithetical statement and its true, independent meaning, assuming that Jesus considers God's demand can be fulfilled. This is the case even in terms of Bultmann's interpretation. Indeed, the question is whether Jesus does not directly assume the fulfilment of the demand, with the result that the very fact of the demand being made has the effect of a judgment. Those who love are relieved of judgment by the saying in Matt. 5.27f, though no allowances are made. Those who really love do not even think of adultery. In the exposition of Matt. 5.21–48, or 17–48, we should not be misled by the comparative in v. 20 ($\pi\lambda\epsilon\hat{\iota}o\nu$). It is not simply a case of a new more exacting code, an intensified Torah, being set in contrast to the old Decalogue. It is a new *word* that is announced. For the time of Jesus is a *new time*, which has arrived in contrast to the time of old. This is true whether or not Matthew thought of Jesus as the new Moses of the final age.[1] The new word has its own new origin in God. Therefore its most significant expression appears in the parables.

(v) We are not by-passing form-criticism, but we do guard against its sociological interest, and therefore against the temptation to draw conclusions about the content from the form—in the sense of constructing 'ideal types' (Max Weber) relating to the situation and the author. It is as 'style-criticism' that form-criticism proves to be most fruitful. Bultmann is right in saying, for example, that the similitudes are derived either from a comparison or an 'image'.[2] The similitude of the timely settlement (Luke 12.58f par. Matt. 5.25f), already cited, is derived from an 'image' (on the way to the judge), and the similitudes about the treasure in the field and the pearl merchant from a comparison.[3] In all cases there is, of course, a logical comparison, for it is with 'similitudes' that we are concerned; the image simply gives the comparison a stronger emphasis. In so far as Jesus' similitudes have a tendency towards a pictorial form, the thought stems in all cases from an event or scene. This scene is certainly typical, that is to say it makes use of a typical proceeding—as long as it is a question of real similitudes and not of 'parables' which

[1] Cf. E. Käsemann in *ZTK* 51, 1954, pp. 134f; ET, *Essays on New Testament Themes*, pp. 26f.
[2] *Tradition*, p. 186; ET, p. 172; cf. p. 184; ET, p. 170.
[3] Cf. previous note.

portray an individual case. The question of whether the sphere in which the *tertium comparationis* is portrayed is directly or indirectly significant for the material part also, must be answered in the affirmative. But at this point the utmost caution is required, because the limits which are drawn for the comparison are only those appropriate to the image part. The hearers were hardly pearl merchants, nor were they stewards acting in a calculating fashion like the man in Luke 16.1–8a. Neverthelses, they lived in a world in which examples like this were to hand. To this extent the hearers were addressed in their own sphere. On each occasion the similitudes exemplify some particular action, as it would suggest itself, in the appropriate situation of the image, to a perceptive person or even just on the basis of experience. But in the material part there is *no* other available experience corresponding to this every-day experience, because the fulfilling of God's will does not leave the world as it is, but changes it, just as all true love changes the world.

The explanation of the parable of the sower in Mark 4.13–20 par. Matt. 13.18–23, Luke 8.11–15 is therefore misleading, even though it is not a question of an allegory. The easily suggested application *e contrario* (Luke 12.56) must also be treated with caution—it would still be the transference to the material part of the experience exemplified in the image part. Nevertheless, we still have to look for the *tertium comparationis*. This must be quite logical; that is to say, it must itself express a conclusion drawn from the exemplary experience of the image part. The logical application then appears in two forms: firstly with regard to the image part, which yields up the *tertium comparationis*; and secondly with regard to the material part, the understanding of which is enriched by means of the *tertium comparationis*. The image part is itself an *application* of the *tertium comparationis*, which, in fact, has the material part as its basis. This is the reason why we can work back from the image part to the material part. If we call the application B, and the *tertium comparationis* A, then the relation A : B is the same as A : B^1—when B^1 is what we are looking for, that is, the material part. Examples are provided by the treasure in the field, and the pearl merchant. In both these cases A is the great gain in relation to the great stake, and B is the example of the husbandman or the merchant. What will the material part be,

assuming that the issue here is the relation between a great gain
and a great stake? In my opinion what dominates here on both
sides is a certainty which is sure of its object and action. This
certainty is now just another expression for the *tertium comparationis*.
Moreover, it is portrayed in the joy of the man who finds the
treasure: and for joy (instead of *his* joy, as the text says) he goes
and sells everything he has and buys that field (which is defined
and distinguished by the discovery). When at this point Bultmann
thinks of sacrifice, he is carrying over into the material part the
phrase 'sells everything he has'. But it is necessary to be able to
distinguish clearly between the material part B^1 and the image
part B, otherwise the punch is taken out of the *tertium comparationis*. (Besides, how else could Matthew, who so often gives
warning of judgment, have thought clearly of the Basileia? Surely
the strict Matthew would have recognized the morally doubtful
part of the proceeding, the defrauding of the previous owner.)
Indeed, we can now ask if it would not be more correct to regard
these two similitudes as examples of similitudes derived not from a
comparison but from an image (or proverb?). Then (in this regard)
Matthew's introduction to them is misleading. We should therefore in the first place exclude from them the rigorist tone which
they acquire in Bultmann. But we also exclude from the material
part the special experience which is indicated in my formulation: 'great stake—great gain'; and we hold fast simply to the
logical scheme of the consequent experience which is sustained
by a certainty. What does the certainty stem from? The consequent
experience, into which the certainty naturally fits, corresponds here
to a thought of reward. This thought does not wish simply to
obtain 'deserts'. It is aware of the coercive power of the kind of
succession which comes to rest only in what follows. It is like an
earlier thing producing a later, like a good tree bringing forth
fruit, while a bad one yields none or only a little (Matt. 7.16–20 or
Luke 6.43f; Q), or like the morning indicating the day's weather
(Luke 12.54f). Certainty does not just stem from acquaintance with
a premise which we gain from that premise; it stems from acquaintance with the consequence which we gain from the consequence.
The people in the image part know what is to be done, because
they wish to taste the pleasure of the consequence which they know
and therefore expect. And the hearers? If the difference between

the material part and the image part is not formal but material, then the decisive point might well be that the hearers need do precisely nothing—indeed, that they should do nothing, if they wish to be sure of the gain or consequence. Highly paradoxical—but only for us.

For Jesus does not let his hearers guess riddles. They already know what he has to say about God, that he means to speak about God. But he does not make them subservient. He impresses on them what is true and needful for their salvation, what must therefore be said to them because none of them is able to say it for himself. Here it is no longer a question of general truths. The *form* of proclamation cannot therefore be made up of general truth—hence the similitude, with its pictorial way of thinking.

If we consider what man would have to say to himself in view of the phrase 'Death is so permanent', as Thornton Wilder does in his play *Our Town*, then in place of the possibility that I myself am quite unable to say to myself anything essential, the point can be made that there is a lack of better insight, for example, into a life limited by the present. I can quite possibly tell myself truths like those which lie behind that phrase and play. Indeed, Wilder means me to do this. He means to help me avoid being diverted by hotch-potch from what is essential for us all. He guards against this diversion by using some hotchpotch himself. Conversely I can well understand what it is that I cannot say to myself or give to myself, what instead I must have said or given to me; for example, the love of someone else to me and for me, his trustworthiness and fidelity, and so on, even if it is only a monetary gift. All gifts are distinguished from robbery not by their inexplicable nature but by the one condition which robbery cannot fulfil; no one can himself take a gift. By means of his word, Jesus points to a gift which concerns man as the recipient. However, he describes this situation in terms of a fortunate discovery, which brings a person to his feet and activates him. In all this Jesus acts quite logically, though with the aid of a paradox. Everything remains comprehensible. The *conduct* of the finder really belongs to the setting. Only the discovery and its consequences are decisive: in other words, the fact that the discovery 'completely' lays hold of the person. There is a contrast between those who are described as running and acting and the people who are really intended, who need do nothing more for their discovery. But this is paradoxical only inasmuch as the image, according to its outward appearance, says the opposite of what is meant: that is to say, it expresses activity instead of rest. However, this is only an aesthetic paradox, for, as we now see, Jesus is in this way pointing out the *difference* between the image and the truth. The hearers understand this easily, because they know whom Jesus deems worthy of his company and whom not. The paradox is therefore concerned with art: it is an artistic medium. In reality Jesus draws the hearer over to his side by means of the artistic medium, so that the hearer may think together with Jesus. Is this not the way of true love? Love does not just blurt out. Instead it provides in advance the sphere in which meeting takes place, assuming that love has become an event. Paradox and image make up the quiet invitation to the hearer to set off with Jesus. This is Jesus' '*language*', irrespective of whether or not he formulated this or that parable. Its advance provision is the mark by which it is recognized. Jesus does not allow what he says to be outbid by what has been said. In his case the thought is just the medium for the word, not its end, in the same way that the wood of a tree serves the interests of the bark and not the bark the interests of the wood, even though the forester could rightly say that his wood has grown particularly well thanks to the bark. The word of love is able to formulate the thought which it uses more delicately than any kind of teaching might do. Love does not toy with its word, but its word does toy with the thought.

It is remarkable that Bultmann does *not* take paradox into account in the case of the parables. It is as if the parables were simply extensions of the truth expressed by then—in a sense, exterior aspects of truth. This would make sense only if the image were either to make clearer something that was too small for our eyes, or if it were to scale down to a comprehensible level something that was unbearably immense for our spirit or heart. The parables would then be either enlargements or reductions of the material part. This would make the *tertium comparationis* the main thing. This is illuminating in the case of moral truths or of principles of experience analogous to them, which are normally handed on in the form of a proverb. It must be admitted that, in fact, the *tertium comparationis* is meant to express a judgment, and that the image or comparison confirms the soundness of the judgment: great stake—great gain, and so on. But assuming that paradox is indeed a stylistic form which is applied in Jesus' parables, we would be mistaking even its aesthetic character if we were to rest content with appealing to paradox simply as 'contrast' (Jeremias). Even so it is the underlining of the contrast in certain parables which draws attention to the stylistic form of the paradox. The paradox refers purely to the comparison between the two parts, not to anything within the image part or the material part. This means that no parable is indispensable, although forgetting an appropriate parable would perhaps have its penalty. However, the 'real matter' will suggest both the comparison and also, with its aid, the image. Assuming that the treasure was a valuable *discovery*, then the real matter means more than ever something *valuable*. If Jesus' intention was to speak about God, he pointed to something so valuable on God's part, that the closest conceivable relation had to exist between what he pointed to with regard to God and what he intended to say by means of the image. It was this relation which, for example, made the 'finder' certain and happy. But if Jesus, like the Old Testament, started from the point of God's giving and love, in other words, from the fulfilled will of God which God himself fulfils and applies, then the most certain and firm relation between God and the man for whom God acts can only consist of the fact that on man's side it is a 'non-action' which corresponds to the action of God—because God has already acted. This is the 'discovery' which is meant by the similitude of the treasure in the field. In fact, finding is itself primarily 'non-action'—not a work or a deed, but an event that happens to me. Is it an overstatement to suppose that the Torah of the Old Testament, in Amos and Hosea at least, means just this? Did Paul not reject justification by works simply because it had become superfluous (Rom. 3.28)?

We have no intention of referring prematurely to the key-word Basileia in regard to God's action. First we shall cite other parables, in order to make a further test of our point of view for exposition.

3. THE REVERSAL OF THE SITUATION
(JESUS' UNDERSTANDING OF TIME)

Following on what has just been said, the next stage is to look back from the firmness of the relationship between God and man in Jesus' parables to the concept of faith in the Old Testament. Since Jesus does not use the word 'faith' technically, the Old Testament understanding of faith—that is, the firmness of the relation between God and man—is to be accepted as self-evident in his case.[1] In the New Testament, too, faith is to be taken as a firm unwavering faith. This is why Abraham becomes a model and example and precursor of faith. A new question can only be concerned with the possibility of the firmness peculiar to the faith of the Old Testament and Jesus being of value to new kerygmatic formulations. If this was not a case of joining together two things of the same value, a theology had to arise which pursued this problem. But in this case the object of discussion is the kerygma itself, not a problem concerned with a world-view like that of the delayed parousia. I merely outline this complex of questions, so as to ward off prejudgments and stimulate proper questions. If we are on the right path with our analysis penetrating to the parables, we regain firm ground under foot, and hence the prospect of being able at a later stage to solve questions, including those just touched on, which are still by no means adequately explained.

The parables in Mark 4 and parallels will now be discussed.

(i) We have previously said that in the similitudes of the treasure in the field and the pearl-merchant the main issue is certainty; a great stake can be sure of a great gain, the beginning can be sure of its outcome or consequence in the situation indicated. As an alternative, and in closer agreement with Bultmann, we can now say that in the case of something costly all or nothing is at stake; in other words, that the main issue is an 'either-or'. Even so, these parables by no means portray an externally viewed situation. They move *within the context* which by their examples they delineate; that is to say, within *human existence*. Existence is to be understood not primarily on the basis of its will or passions or anxiety, but on the basis of its constant 'being-alongside-another'. It is not what I desire but what I have, and hence the difference between having and not having, between what is to be had and what is not to be had—it is this which determines the being (*Sein*) of man and also the tension of this being, which is to be settled by man himself. That is the only reason why everyone is from the outset open to

---

[1] Cf. G. Ebeling, 'Jesus und Glaube', in *ZTK* 55, 1958, pp. 70–79; ET, *Word and Faith*, 1963, pp. 206ff.

association; this association is also, for example, the presupposition of the so-called royal rule in Matt. 7.12 par. Luke 6.31 (Q). Only if we were to understand the two parables in a specifically eccle-siastical way could we say that they demand a 'sacrifice' (which would, in fact, really be cancelled by the sacrifice of Jesus Christ). In the case of a person who faces the demand for a repetition of his decision of faith, the thing that matters is that he must give up whatever might allow the exchange of a genuine security for a false security. What applies to him primarily is the warning that he is not to misuse faith as an instrument of security. For he must know that God has acted for him, in order to draw him to God's side. Matthew may well have found a warning of this kind ex-pressed especially in the parables of the tares among the seed and of the fish-net (13.24–30 or 36–43; 47–50). The same applies in Mark, with reference to the similitude of the seed which grows by itself, assuming that the advice 'leave it to grow' is given, as in H. Conzelmann's formulation of the tares among the seed (Mark 4.26–29).[1] We exclude considerations of this kind (deeming them to belong to a later period) and assume in the case of Jesus himself, as indeed we must, only the kind of situations which were signi-ficant for those addressed at the beginning of the Sermon on the Mount (i.e. Matt. 5.3–6 or 9). We are then well advised to use as the basis of exposition only the *setting* described in the parable within a self-contained context. The aim is to elicit from this setting the *tertium comparationis*. This is what I meant when I wrote[2] that 'Jesus' communication of truth' was concerned with 'existence properly becoming an event, not with "having" but with "being" (*Sein*)'; certainly with 'decision' as Bultmann stresses, but with decision in favour of 'Jesus' understanding of time'. If I contrast 'being' (*Sein*) with a 'having' (*Haben*), then what I mean is the difference of our existence which is to be settled in being and as being, the state of rest to which all its tensions apply; there-fore an authentic, in contrast to an inauthentic, 'having'. For if I believe, I have God. If faith is right, it would be asking too much of any other state of rest to expect it to have decided human existence. This is why Heidegger's book *Sein und Zeit* is anchored in the questionableness of human existence. If we examine Jesus'

[1] *ZTK* 54, 1957, p. 285.
[2] *Hermeneutik*, p. 224.

understanding of time in terms of this condition, it can be expected that this understanding of time will turn out to be different from the time of authentic existence which Heidegger investigates philosophically. In Heidegger time must keep to the plane of its questionableness, because it knows it can only follow close behind existence. But it will be clear that the parables are, in fact, the product of Jesus' understanding of time, as soon as we simply take note of the maxim illustrated in the similitude (e.g. leave it to grow). This maxim demands a 'reversal of the circumstances or situation, perceptible in relation to the course of time'.[1] Why?

(ii) The seed which by itself grows into harvest (Mark 4.26–29)[2] depicts the process in the way it appears when we view the beginning in terms of the end, when we measure the growing plant by its final form; that is, when we look with the eyes of the farmer. But a transformation of the object is thereby completed. The farmer sows the seed; later he sees the bud sprouting, the stalk standing, and then the head, at first empty, then full, and finally it produces for him the fruit he wanted. Then he puts in the sickle (as the realistic phrase says, Joel 3.13), because the harvest is come. The realism of the whole presentation tempts us first of all to follow the irresistible process of growth from the moment of sowing to the time of the harvest, to 'go with the time', so to speak. We are then aware that the seed is constantly growing while the farmer sleeps and rises, night after night, day after day. But by means of this remark about the life of the farmer the similitude also follows quite the opposite direction. It stresses that the earth 'automatically' brings forth fruit by itself (v. 28), and it is the same earth to which the seed was entrusted (v. 26). All this can be awaited once the first thing, the sowing, has been done. We must indeed wait for it. The process which produces the time of the harvest is entrusted to another power, to the earth. The whole course can and must be awaited, because the earth lets time work for the farmer (in Matt. 5.45 there is an analogous point of view). Since the earth lets time work for him, the farmer meanwhile gains time; that is, during the growth right up to the time of the harvest, which will then bring with it its own time. Various times are distinguished not just in succession, but also in relation to each other, because

---

[1] *Ibid.*
[2] For the same text cf. p. 180 below.

literally everything has and should have its own time: the sowing, the earth or the growth, the harvest; and meanwhile the farmer, too, who after the sowing is freed for other business. The fact that the farmer has become free is certainly not specifically mentioned in the text, for it simply talks of sleeping and rising. But this viewpoint is self-evident and should indeed be noted, because from a logical point of view it is complementary to the *stress* on the activity of the earth, which is not self-evident. It is this activity which relieves the farmer of work between sowing and harvest. We should therefore stress firstly the activity of the earth and only then the seed's growing by itself. The earth gives the farmer time because it unburdens him. He knows this. The *tertium comparationis* may then be formulated thus: *Everything has its time.* This is a good Jewish thought (Eccles. 3.1 and elsewhere).

A viewpoint like this naturally clears away cares about a delay in the parousia of the exalted Lord. If everything has its time, Christians will also be able to wait. This applies the more if the Easter kerygma, conceived in terms of salvation-history, divulges the new time of the Spirit—certainly the Gospel of Mark means to contribute to this view. Therefore the literary Gospel in particular needs time, that is, time for its dissemination (Mark 13.10). But this application of the parable is not the only possible one. In just the same way we may assume in the case of Jesus' own proclamation that he meant to release his hearers from every care about the future, in order to lead them anew into this kind of freedom in the present. The objection that they still found nothing but their old torment in the present is of no avail (cf. Matt. 6.34b). He who is certain of the future in the same positive way as the farmer in the parable is certain of the harvest after the sowing will have come to terms with the present, because of having found satisfaction in the chief matter, that is, care about the future. When the parable is seen for what it is, it points the way to a courageous distinction between present and future, because everything has its own time. The course of time, which is considered *certain*, involves a change and *reversal* of the situation. Sowing or care was previously, as present, just a transition to the future. Now, as a parable, this bestows the full present, freed from all care—the present in being (*Sein*), based on freedom for the other enterprise which had previously been excluded by the context of care.

(iii) The freedom for a new unburdened enterprise (the seed which grows by itself) provides a contrast to the 'need-to-do-nothing-more' (the treasure in the field). But there is no real contradiction here. The two fit together into a unity. Indeed, we must say that they are the same thing. In this respect the similitude of the seed which grows by itself differs from *the parable of the tares among the corn*, which follows it in the synopsis (Matt. 13.24–30). This remains true even if we ignore the allegorical application of the parable to the advent of the Son of Man, which involves the judgment of the world (Matt. 13.36–43). The householder certainly reacts to the distressing news of the sowing of tares by the 'enemy' (v.28; cf. v. 25). A point of correspondence to the similitude of the seed which grows by itself is provided by the fact that he insists all the more on waiting for the future time of harvest. But his patience is due to a consideration of the still greater damage which the servants would be bound to do by weeding out the tares (v. 29), and this accords solely with consciously later reflection which satisfies the ecclesiastical situation (v. 28a). Its assertion involves a *threat* (v. 30). Thus the parable confirms in its own way the understanding of time contained in the similitude of the seed which grows by itself, and this is presumably Jesus' understanding of time. But it itself is a later ecclesiastical addition, applied to the new situation which had meanwhile arisen *between* the beginning and the end. It is concerned with disturbances or obstacles to growth, and so it curtails the freedom of view of the similitude of the seed which grows by itself. By using this special material, Matthew therefore consciously goes beyond Mark. For Mark could hardly have wished to make use of this parable. We can ask if it did not originate along with its explanation, and if it was not just as significant for Matthew as the similarly threatening parable of the unmerciful servant (18.23–35). This parable replaces the Lucan illustrative narrative about the rich man and poor Lazarus, and also the narrative about the rich farmer (Luke 16.19–31; 12.16–21). Conversely the similitude of the seed which grows by itself does not go far enough for Matthew. In my opinion the two evangelists have each consciously chosen from the tradition a passage which suits their purpose. This means that Mark may have consciously reduced the tradition, in just the same way that Matthew complied with the tendency of the tradition to adapt itself to new circumstances. In any case the similitude of the seed which grows by itself should not be devalued because it fits so well into the christology of Mark's Gospel—if indeed in the Easter pericope Mark consciously removes the Lord from any direct encounter, and on the other hand by means of the messianic secret means to create in the person of Jesus *alone* a new sphere of the Spirit of the Lord, bounded by the beginning in Jesus' baptism and the end in his parousia. It is within this sphere that the literary Gospel is to be disseminated. Mark rejoices in the knowledge that there is time. But Matthew combines this time with warnings against dissenters and he goes beyond Mark (Mark 12.1–12) in using the persecution of the gospel by Israel as an illustration of the inexorable judgment of God on Israel (even Matt. 5.17–20).

(iv) It is different in the case of the similitudes of the mustard-seed and the leaven, Mark 4.30–32 par. and Matt. 13.33 par. Luke 13.20f. Both are in Q, but that of the leaven is missing in Mark. The linking formula in the introduction to the similitude of the leaven and its absence in Mark provide a formal reason for the contention that the two together do not form a double similitude.[1] It seems that this conclusion can be confirmed by the exposition.[2]

I begin with the *similitude of the mustard-seed*. Matthew has combined Mark's text with Luke's (= Q; Luke 13.18f) and has thereby tightened up the Marcan text. The decisive point is that a contrast is presented between the imperceptible beginning and the end which towers above everything (the mustard-seed, and the mustard bush which is over six feet high). There is no reflection on the process of growth, and therefore a development within the Basileia is not considered at all. It seems to me that for this very reason the Basileia is in this case closely bound up with the similitude. This is not to say that the intention is to explain the Basileia. In what context is the tiny beginning meant to be decisive? In the image part the context is clearly the process of the small mustard-seed becoming a magnificent tree. What is it in the case of the material part? If we are not to think of the Basileia, then Bultmann's considerations would apply: is it meant to comfort or to warn?[3] If we do not allow ourselves to be influenced by the *similitude* of the

[1] Bultmann, *Tradition*, p. 186; ET, p. 172.
[2] Cf. p. 90 above.
[3] *Tradition*, p. 217; ET, p. 200.

leaven, and instead keep the two similitudes apart (and the formal reasons mentioned above are evidence for this), then we shall accept that of the mustard-seed as the more important, on the basis of its total synoptic emphasis; and, like Mark and Q, we shall assess it firstly in terms of the concept of God's Basileia. In Jesus' proclamation the *Basileia* can only be understood eschatologically. This is clearly enough vouched for by the future references in the beatitudes at the beginning of the Sermon on the Mount (or the Lucan Sermon on the Plain); and also by eschatological logia such as Luke 17.20f—assuming that the *actual wording* of the Baptist's proclamation is not similarly cited as proof.

For the Baptist's proclamation, see Matt. 3.2—this sentence is missing in Q. Luke 3.7–9 par. Matt. 3.7–10 (Q) offers no substitute and is in any case doubtful tradition. However, the baptism of John stands securely in the tradition. We can never definitely decide whether he proclaimed one who would come, i.e. the Son of Man, or the coming of God in the Basileia. But he certainly extended his demand for baptism to *everyone*. This means that he gave it an eschatological basis. By virtue of the fact that Jesus submitted to his baptism, they *both* base their understanding on an eschatological context. We cannot deny that the tradition was right in maintaining the close historical connexion between Jesus and the Baptist, although it then had to take great pains to distinguish between them.

The eschatologically understood Basileia undoubtedly relates to the future, to the future coming of God. But according to the oldest passages in Q this future is operative only through its signs, only in the form of Jesus' offensive presence (Matt. 11.6 par. Luke 7.23; cf. Mark 3.23–27 and parallels in Q; also Matt. 12.28 par. Luke 11.20). These signs are not the beginning of the Basileia itself. The Basileia does not come in instalments, nor does it come secretly or only indirectly. Otherwise the eschatological chapter 13 of Mark, with its appeal to the Danielic Son of Man who will come on the clouds of heaven, would have no significance at all for Jesus' thought. But this is very unlikely, even in the case of the Baptist.[1] If, on the other hand, the Basileia were only to appear

---

[1] I fail to be convinced that the early community were the first to speak of the Son of Man, and that he was not already conceived as an individual, e.g. in II (4) Esdras.

here or there, while this might not contradict the declaration in Matt. 11.5f and 12.28, it certainly would contradict Luke 17.21, and in any case it would still not dispose of the concept of the 'sign', σημεῖον (cf. Matt. 12.38–42 par. Luke 11.29–32 with Luke 12.54–56 par. Matt. 16.2f; also Luke 11.29 with its parallel Matt. 12.39, or Mark 8.12 taken on its own; the isolated saying in Luke 11.16 may also be mentioned). What is the position? In Jesus' eyes, was there a 'sign' or was there none? If it is said of Jesus that a 'greater' than God's great miracle-worker Jonah is 'here' (or has happened), the 'sign' must be so strong that every questioner is ashamed of having asked. Jesus did not hide his light under a bushel, Mark 4.21 (cf. the parallels). As a result, he gave *offence*. This is evidently not unlike the offence which Paul, who had 'nothing' to show, was able to arouse in Corinth (II Cor. 12.11; I Cor. 2.2). What are a few exorcisms, in comparison with God's Basileia itself? The sayings in Matt. 12.28 par. and Mark 3.23ff could hardly have originally been part of a discussion. (The concept of the Basileia can easily present a thesis for our research, but certainly not for Jesus himself.)

If the Basileia was linked with the image used in the similitude of the mustard-seed, we can only consider it as the miraculous phenomenon at the *end*. It is significant that this phenomenon is underlined by means of an eschatologically intended allusion (Mark 4.32b points to Dan. 4.9, 18; Ezek. 17.22f; 31.6). There is no question of a self-developing growth. The tiny beginning must therefore be something outside the Basileia. It is certainly a 'sign', in the same sense as the offensive person of Jesus was (Matt. 11.6 par.). This 'beginning' is in the present. In this parable, too, we must think of present and future in a close connexion; but at the same time this connexion enables a clear distinction to be made between present and future. I have written that in the case of the beginning it was the entirety, or the visible success, that mattered.[1] This viewpoint applies sooner to the *similitude of the leaven,* although in the image there its paradox is less strongly indicated. We shall therefore distinguish between the two similitudes with regard to their content also, though this does not involve a devaluation of that of the leaven. Mark at least means to avoid any misunderstanding that could point *too soon* to a visible success. According to

---

[1] *Hermeneutik,* p. 223.

Mark's interpretation, what Jesus explains only to the disciples is the connexion between present and future which is based on the difference between them, that is, the conditioning of the present by what will *necessarily* follow after it. This is to be understood messianically; it refers purely to Jesus; and it will be visible to everyone only after Easter, through the working of the Spirit (Mark 13.7; compare this with the theory of the secret in Mark 4.10–12, 33f, and 9.1; 13.1 on the one hand; but on the other hand with 9.9–12a, 13, the prophecies of suffering in 8.31, etc., and Peter's confession in 8.27–30). In Mark's Gospel the epiphany of Jesus, which is unbearable for the faithless world, has to remain secret in spite of the miracle stories (the transfiguration scene in Mark 9.2–8 is an illustrative model for this epiphany; the miracle stories do their best to suppress it). The announcement of Easter in Mark 8.31 is therefore not yet understood (8.32f; 9.32; cf. 9.10), nor is it even understood by the sons of Zebedee (Mark 10.35–40). For Mark the *pro nobis* in 10.45 must first be fulfilled. This conception of Mark underlines the fact that, in the case of the similitudes of the mustard-seed in his Gospel, only a *hidden* relation between the present and the future can come in question. It is a relation which is not evident to everyone, but only to the twelve; and even in their case it is evident only after later reflection on Jesus' appearance, prophecy, and community with them. The viewpoint of Church history and allegory creeps into the similitude here, and it settles a problem that is not mastered in Q: within the Church one starts from the particular relation between present and future which, both before and after the Easter revelation, was given to the Church solely in the person of Jesus, but which now continued to be given with the help of the Spirit. This was the only way they thought they could maintain the firmness of faith. The familiar question of why Mark's Gospel uses so little discourse material is explained by a criticism of Mark in relation to Q: for Mark the Easter revelation says more than the entire discourse material in Q. For Jesus' person had bound the past to the future and had afforded a certain share in the Spirit to his own (Mark 3.28f, in contrast to all relationships of a sociological or historical kind; 3.31–35).

But this Marcan thesis cannot be appropriate to Jesus' own proclamation, because although Jesus' proclamation quite of itself illuminates his own person, it was in the first place a free word spoken to his hearers and not to an intimate circle. This emerges from the collection of quite varied sayings and material in Q, and also from the beatitudes in Luke 6.20f par., even though no single beatitude can be traced back with certainty to Jesus. I can also say: it emerges from the criticism of Mark in relation to Q, for Matthew and Luke for their part have corrected the Marcan conception by including material from Q. We shall therefore do well to avoid attributing from the outset a secret meaning to Jesus' parables. This would, in fact, contradict the linguistic function of their image nature. However, this same image nature ensures that not everyone who has heard the parable will be in agreement. We must instead be able inwardly to adhere to the parable and to participate in it. In the case of the *similitude of the mustard-seed,* the hearer had to be able, because of its contrast, to relate everything to himself; and this 'everything' means the immense difference between beginning and end, present and future. This is the *one* thing to which the similitude points—the relation *to* the miracle at the end, *to* the rule of God—however terrifying the picture of this end might be. Otherwise what would become of the risk and the decision? Did God not choose the weak and the foolish? Did Paul himself really misunderstand the beatitudes (I Cor. 1.25)? If Jesus meant to portray in advance the aim or miraculous working of the rule of God, then he *had* to make it clear that the slight and poor and weak were the object of the rule of God. The risk, however, lay not in the image, but in the application of the image. Every pious Jew knew that God clothed the naked. But to say that this faith produced a firm relation to the *rule of God* was bold and daring and a slap in the face for the ruling liturgical opinion. If Jesus reinforces this proclamation still further by means of similitudes like this provocative one of the mustard-seed, he is not just illustrating something huge; he is issuing a *summons* for the *Basileia.* His proclamation does not create some *theologically* new connexion with the rule of God; it creates an *'existentiell'* state which transfers those who are called to God's side. The Basileia will benefit those who are called, as if they were already those birds in the branches of the mighty tree. At the same time they are comparable to the mustard-seed which at present is practically nothing when it is held in the hand. This is a miracle, the miracle of God's action. Jesus is concerned with precisely this miracle.

We therefore have to distinguish from each other *two miracles*, the miracle of the calling and the miracle of God's coming itself. One conditions the other. *This is Jesus' understanding of time.* For present and future are now related to each other in the same way as the miracle of the calling and the miracle of God's coming itself. As a thought, even this connexion is nothing new for the Jew; Paul thought in just this way (Rom. 4.17, and the example of Abraham). The new factor lies purely in the *event* of a proclamation of this kind, and therefore in its unconditional nature: Jesus' word applied unreservedly to whoever accepted it (cf. Luke 11.28; 8.21 = Mark 3.35, etc.). The sentence must indeed be reversed, because Jesus' proclamation was itself a firm bond: the person to whom Jesus' word unreservedly applies is meant to hear it and to hold to the fact that in the parable he is specially and unsurpassably intended and *addressed*. The parable appeals by its simplicity. It is itself a gift—*the word that gives, because it gives itself*. The result is that God lets himself be taken at his word, just as the Syrophoenician woman did in relation to Jesus (Mark 7.28 par. Matt. 15.27). I call this a 'language-event'.[1] In this way the whole is involved at the beginning. The *similitude of the leaven* has the same meaning, once we understand that a miraculous event is to be elucidated, in which one thing brings the other after it. This similitude (Matt. 13.33 par.—note the exaggerated quantity of meal) elucidates the firm connexion of the two miracles, of the calling and of the Basileia itself. It would be an allegory only if we wanted to compare Jesus personally with the leaven and the mustard-seed. But we would then have had to understand why Jesus took the place of his word which issues the summons for the Basileia, why therefore he intervened between the two miracles. Meanwhile we do not yet take this next step, which links up with the nature of the word as a gift.

(v) We turn instead to an assessment of the *parable of the*

---

[1] Cf. p. 207 below. Translator's note: *Sprache:* Fuchs is specially interested in the problem of *Sprache.* The rendering 'language' is on balance preferable to 'speech'. However, it should be noted that Fuchs is concerned with language in relation to existence, and therefore not in the sense of linguistics. For this reason the adjective 'linguistic' has been avoided as much as possible in the translation of compounds. Hence 'language-event' for '*Sprachereignis*'. '*Zur Sprache kommen* (*bringen*)' is rendered 'to enter (bring into) language'. Alternatives such as 'to come (bring) to expression' fail to do justice to the intention of the German. What matters most is not that something is defined, but that it enters the sphere of existing. For example, love becomes an event through entering language. Cf. also pp. 213ff. below.

sower (Mark 4.1–8 par.). The fact that an explanation is added on to the end of the parable (4.13–20 par.) again indicates the need for caution. It is notable that the parable remains entirely within the sphere of the natural process. As in the case of the similitude of the leaven, it is only the abundant result that is emphasized. The losses involved in sowing are stressed only in the explanation. The threatening tone of the explanation is unmistakable (cf. the explanation attached to the parable of the tares among the wheat). We can admit that it is perhaps only the restriction which the parable suffers because of the threatening tone of the explanation that is allegorical. As has been said, the parable itself avoids these emphases. The image simply says that the sower, with his comparatively random enterprise, achieves his object just because he sows. The abundant harvest will reward him. There is at first nothing at all extraordinary in this. However the emphasis rests more strongly on the sower himself, and not on the seed. The success of the seed is seen from the sower's point of view, and he pays no attention to the losses (the similitude of the seed which grows by itself could therefore follow afterwards). When Jesus told the parable he may well have thought not just of the audience and the firm faith expected of them, but also of his own activity, of his proclamation. This would make it clear to the audience that neither their faith nor his proclamation succumb to any objection. This is the point of distinction between the material part and the image part. The explanation had therefore by-passed the natural first stage of understanding by emphasizing new circumstances as objections, though they were, of course, rejected. Accordingly the tradition added in the following section the parable of the tares among the wheat (Matt. 13.24–30). As we have seen, this easily runs counter to the similitude of the seed which grows by itself. Why should Jesus have emphasized the firmness of his proclamation? If he did not head straight for conflict—and the considered manner of what he said is evidence against this—but still appeared only long enough to make reflection on what he said unavoidable —and the fact that he had pupils or disciples is evidence for this— then he *had* to emphasize the firmness of his proclamation, so as not to expose the authority for it to misunderstanding. Thus we must assume that discussions with questioners and opponents took place in Jesus' company. But in addition to this there is a much more important fact. If we consider Matt. 11.6 par. and also Mark 8.38 par., passages expressing the *offence* involved in Jesus' appearance,[1] we quickly see that even those who were called, that is the disciples, had necessarily to contribute to the sharpening of all the circumstances of life. Those who had been made free for the present were now opposed to others who did not co-operate. The gathering of the called, even though they were not yet brought together into a community, directly involved division and separation (cf. Mark 3.31–35). This severing was all the more incisive, inasmuch as the good were not simply separated from the evil (that could only have been fair to the evil). If indeed the *present* received its true 'character' only through the calling for the future, then all who *refused* to hear came forcibly into conflict with the present. This was a *reversal of the situation*, resulting simply from the power of the proclamation and of faith. Hence the warnings in Luke 12.54–56, but also the reward of the blessed eyewitnesses in Luke 10.23f (Q). In this connexion the parable of the sower strikes the note of certainty.

However, we must now ask if these considerations are adequate with regard to those who, as a *consequence* of their faith, necessarily came into conflict with their environment?

4. THE FREEDOM OF THE CALLED

(i) What has emerged is that neither the Basileia itself nor repentance make up the content of Jesus' proclamation, of what Jesus said; instead it is the miracle—the miracle of the calling in the present, which corresponds to the miracle of God's coming in the future. How does the freedom for the present which is given with the calling take place in the present? Is there a new demand connected with this event? Jesus' proclamation certainly contains demands, inasmuch as he does not abolish the Decalogue, although he tolerates no casuistry. Indeed, in his view casuistry would be the abolition of the Decalogue, because God demands for himself man's heart and his innermost will (cf. Mark 7.15 par., and the exposition of this passage in the context; see also Matt. 12.34 and

---

[1] I see no sound reason for doubting the authenticity of the logion which is the basis of Mark 8.38, precisely because of the altered terminology in the parallels (confession or disavowal).

Luke 6.45 par. Matt. 12.35; Q). This is also the meaning of the whole complex in Matt. 5.21–48. Woe to those who stifle essential matters in the law! (Matt. 23.23 par.; Q). Casuistry demands from the present not too much but too little (cf. Matt. 5.20). Real obedience must be free obedience—*my* will. Kant also enjoined this. Good action, in fact, allows no dallying; it is only the evil man who hesitates. For the good is always simple, because it need fear no consequences. The only thing that has to be considered is whether action should and can be taken at all. Was Yahweh not *the one who acts*? Did sin not arise at the point where man wanted to act in place of Yahweh—when, as it seemed to Elijah, Yahweh delayed? According to this view, God's *demand* can relate solely to the present. If God's will is to call to salvation in the present, there can be no more explicit obedience in the present than that the call should be heard and accepted. But the calling gives freedom. What does freedom consist of, if the Decalogue still applies? What does God's demand look like?

(ii) Freedom reveals itself only to the called. It can therefore mean impossibly unrestrained arbitrariness, for it is the freedom of those who have been called for the miracle of God's coming, of those who have been drawn over to God's side. The *freedom* of the called is not confined to the present, but it is indeed limited and confined by the present. For the present is undoubtedly distinguished from the future, that is, from the miracle of God's coming itself. This means that the call also has its own time. But the present thereby gains a meaning which is all the more clear and independent. Here there is further confirmation of the fact that the present is by no means simply the transition to the future of God's coming, to the Basileia. Instead it 'corresponds' to this future. It is only this correspondence, and not a transition, which lends weight to the phrase 'on the way' in Matt. 5.25—quite apart from the word 'quickly' which Matthew probably inserted in the text himself. Inasmuch as the present is limited by the calling in a salutary way, the hearer who is thus reached is freed from himself, as one who is poor or bereaved or deprived of justice. He now stands in a new relation to everything, with the result that demands can again be made of him, even the demand to love his enemy (Matt. 5.43f par. Luke 6.27f; Q). On the other hand, the saying in Luke 6.12 par. Matt. 5.46f which comes from Q can hardly be attributed to

Jesus, if it implies contempt for the publicans. Its thought would not be based on the calling, unless Luke has indeed handed on the better version. A contrast is provided by Luke 18.9–14, a passage which we might hesitate to attribute to Jesus only because he was often a guest of the publicans. (Cf. Matt. 11.19 par. Luke 7.34, a very old saying in Q which preserves historical material in the form of defamation by opponents.)

As a result of the present being limited in this way, the person who is called sees the more clearly that the position of his neighbour is his own limitation. His own and better situation will serve as a standard for him (cf. Mark 2.19a). In the exposition of this new present situation we should not be misled by the traditional *legal* form of the commandment of love. If, through the calling, God's will has appeared on the scene as love, then this love itself becomes the thing which encircles and supports the situation and governs its content. As a result there appears all the more plainly what can be done and what not, in short, what *is* to be done. Out of this situation there then arise real and practicable demands or instructions, which are delimited by the new situation itself and which everyone can and should be able to conclude for himself. Whoever speaks of 'a person who is loved by God' should certainly make it clear that only a person who is aware of being *called* by God is able to make full use of the new freedom. It is then also self-evident that one forgives another, without even needing an express community regulation (cf. Matt. 18.21f with Luke 17.4, a community regulation; Matt. 6.14f is also formulated as a community regulation, as indeed is the fifth request of the Lord's Prayer itself). When love fills the heart there is no thought of adultery (Matt. 5.27f), however incalculable the heart may be. Similarly it is self-evident that in this kind of situation hatred cannot raise its head (Matt. 5.21f, 23f). But if, since they are in a legal form, these sayings are understood legally, we are then treating them as a part of the criticism levelled at the Church, even though, as in the case of Matthew, it is a *loving* criticism. However, that is still not their original meaning.

(iii) The freedom of the called brooks no restriction, just *because* it is tied only to the limited character of the present. Hence all community regulations turn out to be secondary; for example, those listed in Matt. 18.15–20, and also all restrictive legal precepts such as the prohibition of divorce and the exception to this in Matt. 5.31f par. The same applies to the pericope about the prohibitions of swearing in Matt. 5.33–37 par. Matt. 23.16–22, though this is in any case suspect because of the parallel in James 5.12. We shall therefore regard with suspicion the legal form of all the 'antitheses' in Matt. 5, and not just Matthew's presentation of them. The same objection applies to the prophetic form of the invective in Matt. 23 par. Luke 20.45ff or 11.39ff (Q). As has already been said, form-critical analysis must not lead us astray by inducing us ultimately to draw conclusions about the content which are based on the form. This of necessity leads to a double construction of an ideal type, which represents a prophet Jesus and a rabbi Jesus. Ernst Käsemann has noted this correctly.[1] A model of this kind was only possible as a result of the variety of charisma in the early Christian community. In place of the concrete leadership of Jesus, the community had to let everything depend on the working of the Spirit on itself. However, the Spirit does not impose uniformity. It adapts itself to the particular gifts appropriate to individuals, with the result that Paul has later to refer back to what all have in common (I Cor. 12.12–27). There can be no talk of Jesus first of all having to force his hearers back ethically and morally into the confines of a contrite heart or conscience, so as to be able to make clear to them that the person of the individual who is in irremediable distress could receive a new being (*Sein*) through the word of forgiveness. This being would then still only be believed. It would be restricted just to the proclamation. In short, it would have to remain the theological equivalent of a mathematical point. Once transubstantiation has been removed from the sacrament, it should not be allowed promptly to slip back into the word! We are concerned not with the issue of whether an appeal can be addressed to us; not with the whole man but wholly with man; with being (*Sein*) which is based on an event, not with the event of being (which is suspense, or a moment of rest contained within movement, and could therefore only be spoken of dialectically). Besides, the action of forgiveness is recorded, for example in the miracle story about the healing of the sick of the palsy (Mark 2.5b–10), in just the same way as the Christian formula is in other instances—'Your faith has made you

[1] *ZTK* 51, 1954, pp. 145ff; ET, *Essays on New Testament Themes*, pp. 37ff.

well' (Matt. 9.22; Mark 5.34; Luke 8.48; 7.50; 17.19; Mark 10.52; Luke 18.42). This is not to mention the power of the keys granted to Peter or the community after Easter (Matt. 16.17–19; 18.15–18; also John 20.23). Cf. also the request 'Lord, save us' or 'me' (Matt. 8.25; 14.30). Jesus did not forgive sins, but he called sinners, and therefore fearlessly and gladly ate and drank with them (cf. both Matt. 11.19 par. and also Mark 2.15 par.).

(iv) However, as should now be fully evident, if freedom neither extends the present into the boundless, nor legalizes it, but simply leaves it to be limited, then freedom leads unavoidably to conflict *within* the limited present. This happens as soon as others decline the call, as apparently Jesus' own family did at first (Mark 3.31–35), or when they regard it as a threat to their own situation and take steps to defend themselves, as the Jewish authorities clearly did. Dispute certainly arose (Matt. 11.12; 10.26 are passages which, among others, show this clearly enough). In face of rejection, Jesus had on the one hand to act in a detached way, because he could not allow 'language', which had miracle for its content, to be torn apart by discussion. On the other hand, he had to offer resistance, because the calling to freedom brooks no restriction of freedom itself. The Jewish Christian tradition presents Jesus in too simple a way, as the shepherd and guardian of the lost sheep of the house of Israel (e.g. Matt. 15.24; 18.12f; Q). If we follow the tradition in placing the invective sayings at the end, because Jesus did not force his followers into conflict (Matt. 23, Q), then the only remaining expression of Jesus' resistance is the apologia for his miraculous deeds (Mark 3.21, 23b–27 par.; Q; also Matt. 12.28 par. Luke 11.20). But *this* classification could be based on the misunderstanding that it was Jesus' miraculous deeds which had given rise to the offence. Where the issue is that of sabbath healings, this misunderstanding is indeed remedied. However, what should have given rise to the offence was not Jesus' miraculous deeds, but his word, his call, his calling for the Basileia (in Matt. 11.5f par., v. 5 par. conceals the real matter, but Mark 8.38 par. makes the offence clear).

(v) Assuming that there were conflicts with the Jewish surroundings and influential people quite some time before the crucifixion—and indeed the execution of the Baptist had already been a conflict of this kind—the question then inevitably arises of how Jesus dealt with the temptations which followed from this for his disciples. The temptations were not the result of a 'time-lag', because God's coming had been delayed. As the parables show, Jesus never questioned the trustworthiness of God's action. It was the situation which arose from Jesus' crucifixion which of necessity made the 'parousia' itself an issue for the disciples. This issue may already have played a part in the riot involved in the cleansing of the temple. That is uncertain. The Easter visions of Peter, then of other leading disciples, and finally also of the five hundred brethren (I Cor. 15.6), certainly assume varying times and places, and were by no means simply confined to Jerusalem. From these we may draw conclusions about the enthusiast susceptibility of some disciples, above all of those who like Peter had been disciples of the Baptist. If even Paul had apocalyptic visions, then Jesus was surely also capable of them. But before Jesus is assigned psycho-logically to a grouping of this kind, we should consider whether and how Jesus resisted those temptations which were from the outset unavoidable in his surroundings. For the calling in the present inevitably gave rise to opposition. If freedom is the ability to love, this freedom constantly has its outworking also as *judg-ment*. In reality there is no more severe judgment than love. Love results in driving all others to oppose the bearers of love. How did Jesus deal with this opposition?

We mean to treat this question in a new section. It should first be noted that all references in the texts which point to a gospel free of law correspond too closely to the experience of the com-munity and its problems to allow them to be traced back directly to Jesus. Examples are provided by the narrative about the faith of the pagan centurion (Matt. 8.5–13 par. Luke 7.1–10; Q); also the narrative about the woman who was a sinner (Luke 7.36–50), in which the much older parable about the two debtors has been inserted (vv. 41–43); also, pointing in the other direction, the pericope about the Syrophoenician woman (Mark 7.24–30 par. Matt. 15.21–28). It is not as if God had withdrawn his word from the community after Jesus' death. In view of our interest in the matter of Jesus, it would be quite unacceptable to our historical consciousness if we were to feel induced, along with the evan-gelists, to trace all the synoptic exhortations to faith back to the historical Jesus. The evangelists themselves do not do this naïvely, but rather within the framework of their kerygmatic theology. Indeed we shall have to learn that the genuine *action* of faith was able to achieve clear consciousness of itself really only in the community after Jesus' death (cf. John 16.6). For this reason the *concept* of faith was dispensable for Jesus, and this applies especially if we are to agree with Bultmann in understanding faith as the decision for obedience in face of the *proclamation*. Jesus issued a call, the community a proclamation. Strictly speaking this is the formulation we should adopt, especially as the synoptic terminology of proclamation clearly belongs not to the language of Jesus but to the language of the community, and thus bears a missionary stamp.

5. JESUS' CARE

(i) It seems extremely rash to speak about Jesus' care, considering that care is forbidden in the tradition in Matt. 6.25–34 (Q). But this passage has already been permeated by the interest of the community, which in time of persecution demanded the greatest possible resolution and the least possible material ties (Matt. 5.10–12 par. Luke 6.22f; Q; Matt. 10.34–36 par. Luke 12.51–53; Q; Matt. 10.17–24; Mark 13.9–13 par.; Luke 14.26f par. Matt. 10.37f; Q). For this reason we must also treat with caution all the apparently reliable sayings about 'discipleship'; that is, sayings which spring from a maximum distinction between future and present (Mark 8.34 par. Matt. 16.24 and Luke 9.23 ($\kappa\alpha\theta'$ $\dot{\eta}\mu\acute{\epsilon}\rho\alpha\nu$); cf. Mark 10.21 par.; 10.29f par.; also Matt. 19.28 par. Luke 22.28–30; Q; Luke 9.59a, 60b par. Matt. 8.22a; Q framework; Matt. 8.19f par. Luke 9.57f; Q; similarly Luke 9.62, with the addition $\tau\hat{\eta}$ $\beta\alpha\sigma\iota\lambda\epsilon\acute{\iota}\alpha$ $\tau\sigma\upsilon$ $\theta\epsilon\sigma\hat{\upsilon}$). All the Gospels lay the greatest of emphasis on resolution, and even on discipleship which is ready for death. Of course! What else is left in time of persecution? This is by no means a hard-hearted reflection. Rather is it an indictment, because there are rogues and traitors. But this point of view conceals the real position in Jesus' surroundings. Jesus was neither a missionary nor a Jewish insurgent. (Nothing against missions and missionaries who, when they are good, all pay dearly for those who are not. But we are concerned here with an historical reflection from which in the long run the missionary himself is meant to benefit.) Jesus' invective does not stem from fanatical zeal; it is the logical consequence of the miracle of the calling in face of its despisers (Luke 11.39–51 par. Matt. 23; Q). God says 'no' to 'this' generation, which wants to remain evil, adulterous, perverse, stubborn, and unbelieving (cf. Mark 13.30 with Matt. 11.16f. par.; Q; 12.45b; 23.36 par.; Q; 12.39 par.; Q; 16.4 par.; Q; 17.17 par.; Mark 8.12b par.; Q; Luke follows Q in favouring the formula 'this generation'). In spite of Mark 10.30 par. Luke 18.30, and in contrast to the Lucan description of the Basileia in Luke 18.29, God's 'no' is better not interpreted on the basis of the apocalyptic presentation of the dualistic two-aeon doctrine. Instead it should be interpreted on the basis of Jesus' understanding of the will of God, because it is concerned with a contrast *within* the present itself; and this present is confined or limited by God's future, that is, by the Basileia (Luke 16.8b: Mark 4.10–12; cf. Matt. 13.10–15 in contrast to the blessed eyewitnesses in Matt. 13.16f par.; Q).

For the dualistic two-aeon doctrine, cf. W. Bousset,[1] who cites from II (4) Esd. 7.50 or 8.1: 'The Highest has created not one aeon but two', etc. The expression αἰὼν μέλλων appears only in Matt. 12.32, αἰὼν ἐρχόμενος in Mark 10.30 par. Luke 18.30, and αἰὼν ἐκεῖνος in Luke 20.35, where it interprets the traditional 'resurrection of the dead'. The Matthaean expression συντέλεια τοῦ αἰῶνος, which is confined to Matt. 13.19f, 49; 24.3; 28.20 (cf. also liturgically Heb. 9.26), has reference only to the end of the world and not to the two-aeon doctrine. The popular expression 'turn of the aeons' should be used very sparingly. It does not give sufficient emphasis to the early Christian intermediate position of the Spirit. As positivistic exegetes have a special preference for it, it should be expressly noted that the term does not appear at all in the New Testament, and therefore cannot be 'quoted'.

(ii) It is not the case that Jesus' sayings were conditioned by the individuality of the called. They include the poor, the mourners, and those persecuted as in war (cf. Matt. 5.41 along with Matt. 5.11f par. Luke 6.22f; Q). The narratives of the calling which have become normal already correspond to the pattern of the conception of the Lord: by means of his calling, the Lord gives an order which must be obeyed (Mark 2.14, etc.). Luke emphasizes the radical

---

[1] *Die Religion des Judentums im hellenistischen Zeitalter,* 3rd ed., 1926, 243-6; quotation from p. 245.

nature of obedience (5.28, also 19.8), while Q is more threatening (Matt. 19.28 par. Luke 22.29f); and Matthew's Church seems to complain: 'What then shall we have?' (19.27b).

The original situation is contained simply in the miracle that the present has been limited by God's (future) coming. Whoever lets this be said is called; cf. Luke 17.20f. In so far as present and future are compared, there is only one consequence of this situation; it is described in Mark 8.35 par. Luke 17.33, and Matt. 10.39 (Q) (without the additions in the verses following Luke 17.33):

> Whoever seeks to gain his life (ψυχή)
> will lose it,
> but whoever loses his life
> will preserve it.

Life (ψυχή) corresponds here to what makes man a man, and therefore to his lifetime rather than to the will (cf. Mark 8.36f par.; Luke 12.16–20). The will must instead be subordinate to the lifetime, which is the factor not at our disposal; this, in fact, means it must be subordinate to the calling, that is, the calling to accept the limited present. This is why Mark places in front of this saying from Q the confessional saying about discipleship in 8.34b par. (Luke adds the word 'daily', 9.23). The succeeding wisdom-saying in Mark 8.36f par. is a reminder, like the parable in Luke 12.16–20, of the uniqueness of the present, though certainly it does not expressly mention the motif of God's coming. In the community this motif was actually diminished, because, with the help of the ambiguous conception of the Son of Man (cf. Mark 2.27f), the community then placed God's coming in relation to the fact of Jesus already having come. The struggle in the present (which was our starting-point; see section (i) above) was interpreted by Jesus himself as a struggle for the present. It is a struggle which the called settle *within themselves* and in relation to themselves, Mark 7.15 par. On the other hand, the resentful wage the struggle against the called (cf. Matt. 15.12–14 and 10.17–25, along with a passage like Mark 8.34 par.). Bultmann speaks of Jesus' 'conflict-sayings' (e.g. Mark 7.15).[1] It is questionable if sayings of this kind are correctly classified when they are compared with the so-called 'debating-sayings' and assessed historically as their precursors

---

[1] *Tradition,* p. 158; ET, p. 147.

(these 'debating-sayings' are contained in disputes based on scriptural argument,[1] like Mark 2.25f; 7.6–8; 10.3–9; 12.23–25, 26f, 29–33, 35–37). It seems to me that they are spoken in the interests of the called and for their protection. As a result the unequivocal nature of the calling is established, because the calling, which is a demand and not a command, corresponds to the will of God itself (Matt. 5.21–48 par.; Q). Whoever has God's will on his side—this is the intention of Mark 8.35 also—*is* protected, even though he is a disturbing influence in the world (cf. Matt. 5.13–16 par.; Q). Luke 12.32, which is a later saying, still preserves this same idea.

(iii) God's 'yes' is indeed also his 'no'. But this identity of God's will does not lead to a dialectic of the new existence in the present. On the contrary, God's 'yes', in the form of his 'no', defines the present as a present on God's side. It is therefore the advance working of God's coming. The substance of the great parables in Matthew's and Luke's special material is in accordance with this definition of the present. This is evident from the parable of the unmerciful servant in Matt. 18.23–25, which may be interpreted as a companion to the parable of the labourers in the vineyard in Matt. 20.1–16a.

(a) The parable of the unmerciful servant (Matt. 18.23–25)

1. The parable issues a threat to the servant who, because of a triviality, flies at the throat of his fellow servant, even though he himself has experienced a very considerable act of mercy from his master. This special section is peculiar to Matthew and it is clear that he views it in connexion with the obligation of unlimited forgiveness previously laid on Peter, and according to 16.18f on the Church (18.21f par. Luke 17.4; Q; a community regulation). However, the obligation to forgive stands for its part in close relation to the obligation of the community set out in 18.15–18. This demands that infringements of commandments should be settled within the community (18.15: 'but if your brother sins ...'). Lapses of this kind can be very considerable. No boundary is drawn here.

After the admonition to unlimited forgiveness, the threatening parable lays down the exclusion of the sinner from community life (cf. v. 34 along with vv. 17 and 18). The application in v. 35 only

[1] *Ibid.,* p. 157; ET, p. 146.

appears to refer back to v. 22, and it by no means abrogates the duty of exclusion in v. 17. Only the prudent and penitent are to be completely forgiven, however severe this may turn out to be. It is impossible to suppress misgivings, even though this regulation appears to be imposing. Certainly Matthew is interested above all in drawing the community together to itself, as vv. 19f show; he has this in mind also when he concludes his Gospel, 28.20. But the very authority to act possessed by individual members of the community, when combined with the prayer association in vv. 19f, can become unrestrained. It will then inevitably have to be checked by an institutional restraint. For the individual might not always have the total view which he really must have if he is to be authorized in the sense of the community rule, and thus enabled to make an appeal to a brother about his sin, even though it is only in the presence of the two concerned.

2. Nevertheless there are two essential thoughts contained in the parable itself. If we ignore its application (in v. 35), it is then clear that the small misdemeanour or transgression which is driven home to the fellow servant by the one who had experienced great mercy after great transgression, only, in fact, appears 'small' in the image part. If, however, we think of God's mercy, even the greatest transgression on earth will signify little in relation to this mercy. The application has this meaning in view. But apart from the application the parable also has a *threatening* tone. The concluding vv. 32–34 overstep the limit of the image, for something new appears which is seldom the case in daily life: the pitiless man, who had himself experienced mercy, is severely punished and the previous act of mercy annulled. This means that God does not stand for the misuse of his kindness (cf. Gal. 6.7a). In fact, it is obvious that the one who has a right to kindness will not allow this right to be abused or derided through unintended consequences of the kindness (cf. also Rom. 12.19). But this thought contains a reflection which hardly does justice to the dignity of the kindness itself—would it not watch over its honour in silence?—and which contradicts rather than confirms Matt. 5.45. In actual fact the parable does not have in view Jesus' precise distinction between present and future. Instead it *complains* about the misuse of the divine kindness. Therefore it does not contribute to our understanding of Jesus' care.

(b) The Parable of the Labourers in the Vineyard, Matt. 20.1–16a.[1]

1. In Matthew the parable stands within a context which protects marriage and the family. The intention is to warn about the danger of money, which is so necessary for the family, and to point to the heavenly reward (19.27–30), which is inevitably preceded by suffering (the third prophecy of suffering, 20.17–19; the Sons of Zebedee, 20.25–28; the two blind men, 20.29–34—in Mark it is just Bartimaeus, 10.46–52). The parable is the climax of Matthew's Gospel. In Matthew it sets the seal on the community of grace, through the knowledge of him who came so that those who were last in the world might be first in the Basileia and might have a full sufficiency. Bornkamm has rightly placed it in the context of the 'idea of reward in the New Testament'.[2] He places this parable beside the one in Luke 17.7–10: we should not act for reward, but God knows and wills the consequences.[3] Luther catches the point of the difference when he says: 'Si dignitatem spectes, nullum est meritum, nulla merces. But: si sequelam spectes, nihil est, sive bonum sive malum, quod non suam mercedem habeat.'[4] The idea of merit is therefore to be excluded, as it is in Luke 17.7–10. This is correct, but not adequate.

2. In the exposition of the parable itself the details should not be too rigidly adhered to. The two applications should also be disregarded, both that in v. 16b (= 22.14), which is questionable on grounds of text criticism, and that in v. 16a (= 19.30), for they are both individual sayings. In spite of Jeremias's objection, the reversal of the order before and after v. 8 is a dramatic device.[5] For the section that follows on from v. 8 is a set scene, which gives the limelight not to the last and the first but to the lord of the vineyard. The intention is that the first who then come at the end should be the audience for what the lord has to say, so that the lord can be clearly distinguished from them all. We are meant to see into the heart of the lord (v. 15). However, this is only possible because the lord has made his kindness manifest in what he has done. The 'same reward' for varying periods of work demonstrates

---

[1] Cf. pp. 32ff above.
[2] Cf. 'Der Lohngedanke in neuen Testament', see p. 32 n. 2 above. Also Bornkamm, *Jesus von Nazareth*, 2nd ed., 1957, pp. 126ff; ET, pp. 137ff.
[3] Art. cit., *Gesammelte Aufsätze* II, p. 89.
[4] *Ibid.;* WA 18.693, 18f and 694, 5f.
[5] *Die Gleichnisse Jesu*, p. 21 (following Jülicher); ET, pp. 24f.

the unvarying superiority of the lord. The intention is that we should come to know the lord as a result of the superiority of his kindness. The audience—that is, the first who have apparently been slighted—have an opportunity to do this; for they feel wronged and must therefore be the first to have the excellence of the event drawn to their attention. There is therefore something to be comprehended here, which the unmerciful servant did not comprehend, even though it is so easy: it is that kindness bestows freedom (from need), not just on the person concerned, but on every understanding community. Since kindness has no wish to be misunderstood, it can also give in secret (Matt. 6.2–4). But if God has made his kindness visible, then it was because he wanted to make himself *understandable* for us. This is the *tertium comparationis* in Matt. 20.1–15. This thought is to be attributed to Jesus, because Jesus continually strove to speak and act in such a way that he made God himself—'your (heavenly) father'—understandable; cf., e.g., Matt. 5.45, 48 par. Luke 6.36; Q; Matt. 6.32 par. Luke 12.30; Q; Matt. 7.11 par. Luke 11.13; Q. This is after all the meaning of Jesus' addresses which use images, whether they are parables or just logia. Everyone who is called to the Basileia is meant to have God on his side, with the result that he is drawn over on to God's side and learns to see everything with God's eyes. He then understands God, as a child understands his father (cf. Matt. 18.2f par.). Jesus' *care* is concerned solely with this event of God's intelligibility. What he intends is not some relationship to God, but *concrete* knowledge of God. This knowledge is directed to God, because and as God has *now* given knowledge of himself. Did Jesus' own conduct in relation to his surroundings not provide the unequivocal example of God's will in the present?—of the salutary distinction between God and man? (Matt. 11.25f par. Luke 10.21; Q.)

3. Jesus affords protection to his own, by allowing them to take part in his own knowledge of God and thereby strengthening them. God's working may remain hidden to the world. The rules of piety in Matt. 6.1–18 assume this. Our giving, praying and fasting should not press into the open, nor have they any inclination to do so. But God himself now wills to appear openly. This is why Jesus also appears openly (Matt. 11.6). The called should not and cannot conceal the fact of their calling through Jesus (cf. Matt.

10.26f par. Luke 12.2f; Q). God will accompany them (cf. Matt. 10.29–31 par. Luke 12.6f; Q; also Matt. 10.20f). Certainly no one can escape from the world; but God enters in even through the eye of a needle (Mark 10.25, 27 par.). Knowledge of God begins not with the beating of drums but, as in the 'ideal' scene with Mary and Martha (Luke 10.38–42), with the unpretentious word of love. This word is expressed in the miracle of the calling of those who did not expect it (cf. Matt. 25.37–39) and therefore it gives a future where there was no prospect of a future (Matt. 5.7–9). By this future everyone will recognize what had begun (cf. Matt. 7.16–20 par. Luke 6.43f; Q). Indeed, they will see *that* a beginning had been made. Knowledge of God *begins* with the distinction between present and future (Matt. 13). It induced Jesus to assert God's future will through his own word in the present. This word has its effect on the hearers and their situation. Jesus gives God's secret to them through his own word. Knowledge of God therefore by all means *concludes* with the coming of God himself. For God remains unchangeably true to himself (Matt. 5.45, 48). Therefore true knowledge of God comes to an end just as little as love itself does, although both have their own time.

Surely the whole burden of the world must rest on the person who knows this and brings it about. Jesus' care should also have been the reason for his torment.

6. JESUS

(i) Jesus' indubitable certainty of God, which the issue of his authority already underlined indirectly (cf. also Mark 1.27 par., along with Matt. 7.29; Mark 1.22 par. Luke 4.32), should not—as an outward appearance or the like—become for us a self-evident conception. There was nothing self-evident about it, nor could there be. For certainty of God must be concrete knowledge of God, which has in view not only God's 'yes' but also God's 'no'. Who could so comply with this knowledge of judgment and grace that he would be able to travel God's way with all men? No one can do this, for it means going in two different directions at the one time. For this reason Jesus had to go his own way alone. However, he is not yet thereby distinguished from all other men. What distinguished him was the burden that lay upon his word, by virtue of the fact that it was not only unable to save everyone, but also that it made the world so dangerous for those who adhered to him. Wherever God appears the powers that endanger man rise up the more. God's 'finger' obviously accentuated what was offensive in Jesus' appearance (Luke 11.20 par.). What could happen to keep Jesus' call unequivocally what it was—the word to men who really needed God? The presentations of the evangelists have elevated Jesus in order to protect his working, although they each endeavoured to make known their own theology and not to avoid the responsibility for it: *Matthew*, by keeping in suspense the relation of the Church to Israel; *Mark*, by retaining the relation of faith to the historical Jesus; *Luke*, by making the time of the Church dependent on the past, in which Jesus had died for all. How has *Jesus himself* provided for his word? Jesus has provided for his word by surrendering himself completely to his word. This should not be confused with the situation of martyrdom, which is close at hand in the Synoptic Gospels. In spite of Mark 8.34–37, and in view of Mark 8.38 and parallels, *self-surrender* is *not* the category of the believer or of faith, but simply and exclusively the category of Jesus. For only Jesus possessed the freedom for this, assuming that his own—human and completely contemporary—word was indeed the word of calling for the Basileia. Then he simply had the task of creating faith (Mark 9.24).

(ii) The New Testament has attributed sinlessness to Jesus (Heb. 4.15; but cf. also 9.28). So in Mark he alone forgives sins (Mark 2.10) and performs miracles, because he alone has the Spirit. However, this dogmatic consequence should not be prematurely linked with the quest of the historical Jesus, for as long as we investigate historically, Jesus may not be divorced from his situation. Jesus' freedom was ambiguous. He had at least to be compared with the Baptist. It seems that Jesus compared himself with the Baptist when, according to one tradition, he termed him as the greatest of all those born of women and assessed him as Elijah, with whom the Basileia was to begin (cf. Mark 9.12a, 13; 6.14f; 8.28 with Matt. 11.11a, 14 and with the ἀπὸ τότε in Luke 16.16 as well as Luke 7.28). According to Luke 7.30 the pharisees and lawyers rejected the Baptist, but Jesus accepted him. He submitted to baptism by John, and after his death he took his place.

As a result other disciples of the Baptist, like Simon (Peter), came to him (cf. John 1.35–42). In its form in Matt. 11.12, the saying about 'taking by storm' could refer to the death of the Baptist; cf. also Matt. 17.13.

Assuming we do *not* eliminate the future Son of Man from the context of the sayings of the historical Jesus (Luke 12.8f par. and Mark 8.38), the conclusion is not that Jesus considered himself to be the Son of Man who would come or had come, but that, on the basis of the appearance of the Baptist (as the new Elijah), he considered that the time of calling for the Basileia had come. This time is then, in fact, for Jesus the last hour of the world, and so of the 'evil' generation. Yet at the same time it is, as a result of the appearance of Jesus, though not the first hour of the Basileia, certainly the first hour of freedom for the called. Thus Jesus' present is a *time between the times*—a chronologically impossible time. As a result, interpretation is tempted to snatch at the now popular comparison with the mathematical point. But the comparison founders, because it is dialectical. Logically it still depends on a conception of the continuity of time; thus it promotes Jesus' present to a reflection about it, instead of leaving this present by itself. The logically powerful point in Jesus' procedure is simply to be admitted: Jesus lays claim to his time as the present before God's coming, in such a way that he contrasts it to every other time. He must then also contrast himself to all others, for example, to Elijah, Moses, Jonah, Solomon. He does this by comparing himself to the coming Son of Man, without directly identifying himself with him; however, this coming one can only confirm him (Mark 8.38; Luke 12.8f). This last thing seems to me to be the sole consequence of which Jesus, as it were, makes theoretical use. His situation is singular, unique, like the miracle which he serves with his calling. In Jesus' understanding of time the last thing is not the temporal sequence of the two miracles, of the calling and of the coming of God, but rather their *difference—the knowledge of God itself*. This lets Jesus express the intention of God's coming as the calling to freedom, with the result that God's 'yes' outbids his 'no'. Only the free can be on God's side; only they can see into God's heart. But if the hour of this freedom has come, if it is realized in Jesus' call, then Jesus himself has also his own freedom, by virtue of holding fast to his call to freedom. Nothing more depends on him, if everything depends on his call, and if he has issued this call. His word *was* then the *time-word* and nothing else.

(iii) What is really the nature of love? The question becomes answerable when we make up our minds about what matters in a question about the nature of a thing. The *saying about the tree and its fruit* may serve as an example for this. The often-misused phrase— 'you will know them by their fruits' (Matt. 7.16a, 20)—is familiar to us in an already metaphorical application (v. 20). The same applies to the phrase about a good tree bringing forth good fruits and a bad tree evil fruits; Matt. 7.17. We are led nearer to the saying by the pointed words: 'Are grapes gathered from thorns, or figs from thistles?' (Matt. 7.16b). The saying itself originally meant that we recognize by the fruit what kind of tree it is, because we name the tree after the fruit and therefore recognize it by the fruit. This is what is meant in Matt. 7.16a. If we want to recognize the nature, we must know the effect. Examples from nature do not suffice for the question about the nature of love, since for us at least the things of nature mostly remain dumb, whereas love speaks. However, language is not simply the effect of love. What does love speak? It gives its word—it promises. For the lover promises himself to the beloved and thus gives himself to the beloved through his word.[1] The wish of the lover is that the beloved should take him at his word. But love needs *time* for this. Without this expenditure of time, its promise would have no meaning. The longer love lasts, the more beautiful it becomes. Its nature is the duration, its effect the gift of time. Love gives time as a gift. It is claimed when the time that it gives is claimed. Love can therefore wait. Thus the word that it gives corresponds to the time that it gives. Love has time. As it presents its time through its word, the time of love will be understood as the time for love only through the correct word. Whoever knows its time knows its word, and vice versa. The time of love as the time for love does not fit into any other kind of continuity, for it has its own continuity. Love insists on its own time, and is far removed from being referred to other times. Jesus' understanding of time is of this kind. It can be reached only in his word, because his word was a *word of love*. Therefore his time was also independent from every other time.

[1] Gogarten in particular pointed to this.

Hence his situation was unique. But his time remained comprehensible. For Jesus distinguished between the present and the future, just as love distinguishes between the present and the future, because it gives time by promising its word. Therefore the time of love consists of the difference between present and future.[1] In this difference the past is abolished. This is why Jesus could adopt words of wisdom like the saying about the ravens and the lilies of the field, and could also say words like those about the sunshine and the rain upon just and unjust. Such words are in his case words of love, in which the past is abolished. He has demonstrated this in his finest parable; indeed, his sayings in general mean to be understood as words of love. This is their 'sign of authenticity', at least within the synoptic tradition.

(iv) *The parable of the prodigal sons*, Luke 15.11–32. The parable can be explained in the context of the chapter, that is, on the basis of vv. 7–10, which are after all supported by Q (Matt. 18.14). However, this is not necessary. The parable itself says enough.

The younger of the two sons receives the love of the father on his homecoming, although he in no way any longer deserves it. He does not take advantage of the compassionate father; he holds bravely to his confession of guilt, to which he had previously won through (v. 21, cf. v. 18). Meanwhile the elder son, who claims to have served the father faithfully (v. 29), hears the significant words: 'All that is mine is yours' (v. 31). He is meant to understand: also your recovered brother! In the eyes of the evangelist such statements are also directed as an accusation against resentful Israel (v. 1f). But they also help us guess what Jesus thought. The parable certainly reminds us of a saying like Luke 17.33 or Mark 8.35: Whoever seeks to gain his life, etc. The image part again does not shrink from what normally is almost offensive: What am I working for day after day, when this scoundrel returns and gets the fatted calf? It is clear that Jesus does not justify the one or the other of the sons. It is the father who is meant. Under our circumstances, fathers who act in this way (in a motherly way?) would probably be the object of criticism, just as the father in the parable was criticized. But there are events which revolutionize everything. Usually this is so in the case of the evil person, for then

[1] Cf. my *Hermeneutik*, p. 200.

there is destruction, just as the younger son destroyed his life. But this time what is revolutionary happens in the case of the good person, of the superior person, who can by no means earn criticism, because he *knows* what he can do. The revolution is just as self-evident as the simple (though not unconditionally good) word with which a servant, in answer to his question, explains exactly to the elder son what is going on: your brother has come, and your father has killed the fatted calf, because he has him safe back again. The father comes to the son and entreats him. Then follows the torrent of words from the (long since) deeply wounded brother. It is shameful. It is also hopeless, more hopeless than the other case of scoundrels like the younger brother coming back home more or less fit and being able to be kindly received. 'Normal' circumstances are to be adduced against both cases. Jesus knows this, too. Nevertheless he shames us with his parable. Of what weight are 'normal' circumstances in comparison with the one event in which love reveals its depth and greatness. 'Normal' circumstances are indeed tolerable. We must be thankful for them, assuming they exist. But they do not create life. Here, on the other hand, it says at the end: 'This your brother was dead, and is alive (again); he was lost, and is found (again).' We only find what is lost if we are lucky. But Jesus means to say: you are found, *because* you are lucky. The parable speaks of the miracle of finding; we can also say of the miracle of recovery (cf. John 3.4 with Mark 10.27 par.). When love becomes the great event everything becomes new. Then love decides about us; indeed, it is then apparent that it has long since decided (Matt. 11.27 par. Luke 10.22; Q). But for this to happen love must become an event. This happens solely through its incontrovertible word. Whoever receives the *verdict* of love through its promise—and this is proclaimed only to the beloved—has reason to rejoice. For love sets free. It is greater than us. It is the beginning. It is God. It alone has the right to address us as ourselves, because it does what it says, because it arouses us when it speaks, because its word is its deed, in which it has always already given itself. Through it we are set free, because we are meant to claim another completely. This is why Jesus placed himself at our disposal, because we were meant to have his word completely—the word that he gave because he believed that God will honour it. Because he believed that God would honour his word, Jesus cast himself completely into the present—and was crucified. That was his self-surrender.[1]

(v) Have I already said too much in these last sentences? If it is true that love is not an idea but an event, which either takes place or passes us by, then for all those who are used, either themselves to steer the course of temporal connexions, or at least to have a hand on the steering, love must appear like a kind of sickness of history. It is not the evil but the good which, in love, brings the incalculable into the world. It may perhaps be possible to confine death largely within firm bounds, but this cannot be done with love. In the form of *eros*, it even makes use of our body. Non-erotic love, which completely forgets the self, is still more passionate, though more conscious of its goal and unyielding. Death cannot affect it, as Paul knew. This is by no means to say that those who love die more easily than the others. But when the death of a lover becomes the cry of love (not just the sigh), because a man has to die for the sake of love, then love triumphs over death, by virtue of the fact that the death of the lover itself becomes the word of love, the clear voice of an inviolable assertion. Death cannot possibly reduce love to silence; indeed, when love allows it, death has to become the voice and 'mirror'[2] of love. *Had* Jesus himself, after his execution and indeed as a result of it, to become the word of love? Luke (24.26) is of the opinion, and not only he. It is indeed self-evident that Jesus had to become the word of love for the *disciples*. The question is instead whether, as the word of love, he was also the word of God. He was believed in as the word of God soon after his execution, and he was this not only for the little company who had known him and who could tell others of

---

[1] The passage about Jesus' prayer on pp. 62ff above fits in at this point. Our position today arouses the question of whether, in connexion with form-criticism, we can still say with Adolf Schlatter that the three deeds of Jesus which form his history are that he fashioned his own message from the message of the Baptist, that he therefore called the community to the divine kingdom, and that he took the Cross upon him; and that the understanding of these points enables us to grasp the marvellous riches of his word together with its unifying factor (Preface to *Geschichte des Christus*, 2nd ed., 1923). It seems to me that the 'unifying factor' of Jesus' word, which Schlatter rightly sought, is to be grasped in Jesus' understanding of time. If we really perceive him, we must free ourselves not only of form-criticism but also, in our own thought, of all biblicist and positivist historicism. Form-criticism and hermeneutics thus certainly combine in working towards the goal that Schlatter had in mind. Only the outworking of the hermeneutical problem frees us from an unfortunate 'Epigone fate', i.e. from being sentenced to the stylistic waste of endlessly repetitive academic labours.

[2] *Hermeneutik*, p. 108.

him, but also for the whole world, as the Hellenistic Church finally believed. The question is not decided for the 'historian' by virtue of the fact that the miracle of the resurrection of Jesus was spoken of in the Christian confession. The question is instead intensified by this confession. Is a third miracle consistent with the two other miracles already distinguished by Jesus?—with the miracle of God's coming and the miracle of the calling for this coming; with the simple distinction between present and future, the present being the time of the called or of those who are to be called, and the future being the time of God, for which man should do nothing at all and indeed can do nothing, with the result that calling means being free for the present within the bounds of the present? We mean to stand firm against this question.

Present is indeed always present, of course not for everyone, but for those particular people who share a present with each other. This is the present which they together may call their present, their time. It is the thing which they consider limits them all, the one perhaps in sorrows, the other in joys, depending on what the circumstances impart. For his 'own', Jesus' death put an end to the particular present which gave them a common boundary along with Jesus, because in it they had expected God's coming as future. In that present they were themselves free, because they had been summoned by Jesus as free men. This was now past for them. Now they had to decide whether they for their part were in a position to accept Jesus' call. The first sending out of the disciples in Mark's Gospel is, in a sense, the model of this situation (Mark 6.6–12 par.). Their return does not indicate a failure (nor does the return of the seventy in Luke 10.17). But it is a return to Jesus (Mark 6.30). The meaning of this is underlined in Luke 10.20: the firmness of faith, which had been practised by Jesus and portrayed in the parables, had now to stand the test in view of Jesus' death. Out of Jesus' call, which we understood as calling, there arose the proclamation of the early Church, which made Jesus the 'object' of a new language and, when it wanted, could understand Jesus himself as that pearl or mustard-seed, etc. The confession of Jesus' resurrection became the all-decisive statement for this change in the situation. This statement was combined at a very early stage with the narrative of Jesus' crucifixion, since the confession of Jesus' resurrection was always a confession of the crucified Jesus.

Paul explained this unity in his theology; so did the Fourth Evangelist. Accordingly the historical Jesus was also retained in the confession of the early community, which reached agreement with Paul as the representative of the Hellenistic communities (Gal. 2.1–10). The result of this was the uniting of the tradition about the historical Jesus with the Easter kerygma in the literary Gospel of Mark, a development that reached its conclusion in the two other Synoptic Gospels. Was this process necessary? Had the firmness of faith stood the test in it? If we assess the process in terms of the Pauline (and also Johannine) theology, then as a result of this development faith ran the risk of becoming, so to speak, *too firm*. For the confession of Jesus' resurrection threatened to exclude all questioning, or else reduced it to silence through the decision of the disciples, through their confession of the crucified one as the risen one. There was a threat of the firmness of *faith* being overruled or replaced by the authority of the 'witnesses of the resurrection'—we could almost say, of the apostles. The Church of the apostles then rests on a *ius divinum*, founded on Jesus' resurrection, and allowing no contradiction. Without question the predicate Lord, which is now applied to Jesus, lends strong support to this interpretation. But Jesus' understanding of time was thereby surrendered. For with the 'Lord' God *had* come, with the result that a distinction had to be made between his first and a second advent; seen in terms of Jesus' understanding of time, between a first action of the *future* and a second, but no longer simply between man's present and God's future. Can we surrender Jesus' understanding of time, when we want to retain the historical Jesus? Paul and John saw the question, and as a result strove for the purity of faith itself and tried to bring faith to its concept. What is the result of our efforts to investigate Jesus' understanding of time?

Something very simple. Jesus' death, his cry (Heb. 5.7), was indeed the voice of love. This voice accuses. But by accusing it calls those who can hear all the more loudly, as Luke's version of Peter's Pentecost address knows (Acts 2.36). Now there could be only one question: Does God *hold* to Jesus' word? Is the time which God accords to Jesus' word the time of love or is it not? Is it the time of love or the time of judgment, or is it somehow both together? We know what the answer of the authoritative disciples

turned out to be. What will our answer be? This question will
certainly have to be answered by everyone for himself. But the
criterion which governs whether the question has been correctly
heard consists of this: whether we now properly distinguish
between present and future, between man's freedom for faith and
God's work of love. Jesus has therefore become the word that is
proclaimed, because everyone faces the question of whether Jesus'
call, his appeal, was the event of love, which drew even us over
to the side of love, to God's side. The very *historicity* of Jesus'
word made him himself God's word; because, with a view to Jesus'
understanding of time, only this one question is to be decided:
Did love at that time *call once and for all*? For equally surely, on the
basis of Jesus' call, the future is meant to remain entirely God's
affair. The foolish question of whether Jesus was at that time
deceived about the span of time is then transformed into the
correct and lasting question of whether Jesus was deceived in
believing that the time *for* love had come. But for love itself this
is no question at all. Believers will therefore be lovers, and the
faith of the lovers will endure. Seen from Paul's angle, the early
Christian confessional construction expresses nothing other than
this firmness. Those who mean to call to faith will therefore retain
the historical Jesus by likewise proclaiming the time for love, and
they will make this preaching their business because, although
everyone can understand what love is, no one can say to himself
that he has been called to love. This must be said to him, and he
must believe it, just as surely as it is impossible to have a discussion
about the truth of love. Love can only be an event.

Does *our entire time* therefore depend on this event of love?
Certainly. Love alone makes our time the present. And death? It is
abolished, wherever love is an event. Have we, then, to proclaim
the resurrection of the dead? And before that, the resurrection of
Jesus? Of course. This is self-evident, and has more weight than
any *brutum factum* of the archaeologists, more weight than a misunderstood empty tomb. For love gives up *nothing*. It has time.
This is why the past is abolished in it. Love rejoices in the present,
because it rejoices in the future as future, and relates to the future
both what is its own and those who are its own. Like Jesus, love
risks everything on the word, as long as faith is still necessary, and
it is distinguished from Jesus solely by the fact that it measures the

present in relation to him, as its word. Therefore love does not dispense with perceptibility; instead it provides the very greatest perceptibility, because it sees made manifest in Jesus what love always makes manifest: the event of its word. It knows: all that is mine is yours. It is its joy to distinguish between God and man, because *everything* has its time—God, and therefore also man in the world.

VII

THE THEOLOGY OF THE NEW TESTAMENT
AND THE HISTORICAL JESUS[1]
1960

ANYONE who speaks about a theology of the New Testament must say at the same time that there is no one single theology of the New Testament. The phrase 'theology of the New Testament' is an abbreviated expression for the enquiry about the theology *in* the New Testament. This enquiry can be conducted in two ways. One way is to assess the theological thought of the New Testament in relation to the thought of the Christian Church. The New Testament itself is then assessed in relation to theology. The other alternative is to ask how faith in the New Testament thinks. Then faith in the New Testament is assessed in relation to thought. The two possible ways of posing the question converge on a relationship which obtains between faith and thought. The accents can, therefore, get very significantly out of place. If we consider thought to be the better known, and faith to be lesser known, then we shall ask the New Testament how it relates faith to thinking. If, on the other hand, faith is regarded as the better known, the reverse procedure will apply. For my part, I consider thought to be the better known and faith the lesser known, with the result that I am inclined to ask the New Testament how it relates faith to thought. For thought is available to us at any time, whereas faith is not. There is, of course, the possibility of someone being unable either to think, or to have faith; and I grant that the temptation to present oneself in this deplorable position is by no means small.

If today we again speak of the historical Jesus, it appears as if we were thereby introducing something neutral into our reflection on faith and thought: a third element which belongs neither to faith nor to thought, but to history. An historical stock of facts seems to precede both faith and thought, and therefore to be

[1] Lecture delivered in Heidelberg, Zürich, Stuttgart, and Berlin-Weissensee.

independent of faith and thought. For what is historical has either taken place or will take place. The governing concept of history is then termed event. Faith and thought are also historical inasmuch as they take place. Thus we are able to pose the further question: in what events do faith, thought and the historical Jesus converge? Is it possible at the outset to name such events? I think so. When, for example, in the New Testament the historical Jesus receives titles, and is called the Son of Man or Lord, then something is said about Jesus by means of such titles or names, something which has to do with our faith and which should lead and determine our thought. We are to think of Jesus in such a way as, for example, the title Lord thinks of him; and we are to believe in him accordingly. We should then also confess Jesus openly as Lord, because everyone is meant to come to know him in this way. When someone utters the confession: 'Jesus is Lord!' he is not just getting hold of some kind of name or dignity for Jesus. What he intends to say is that the crucified Jesus makes a claim which everyone must obey if they are not to perish. A phrase of this kind is self-explanatory, yet it is easily misunderstood. In the New Testament Jesus is called Lord, not just in the sense that an order is issued by him, with which we have to comply. What is meant is rather an effective lordship, which results in Jesus really ruling. It is not just a case of our being asked if we will obey a claim of the crucified Jesus; the lordship of Jesus itself expands, becomes operative and reveals its lordliness. Therefore the next question is: Where does this happen? This new question shows that our faith cannot be far advanced if we are still posing questions of this kind. But we can nevertheless at least ask. It is clear that a phrase like the above-mentioned confession 'Jesus is Lord' should itself belong within the sphere of Jesus' lordship. From the point of view of the New Testament confessions of faith themselves, the lordship of Jesus leads us into the sphere of confession and therefore of language. Our language is expanded with the aid of confessional statements about Jesus.

It cannot be denied that the historical Jesus himself attached great importance to language. We shall, therefore, examine the kind of events that include, for example, sayings of the historical Jesus and then confession of him. I call events of this kind 'language-events'; i.e. events that emanate from language and also themselves further affect language. In the New Testament there is a way or path of language which leads from Jesus' word to confession of Jesus. On this path of language one meets with the historical Jesus, faith and thought. We thus enter upon a kind of doctrine of language. This is faith's doctrine of language; as is at once evident, it can also be called a hermeneutic of faith. With this end in view we shall now point out three signposts which are provided in the New Testament; they are sited at John's Gospel, at the Apostle Paul, and finally at one of Jesus' parables. We therefore travel backwards along the path of language that we are seeking. As we want to arrive at the historical Jesus, we link the question which we put to John's Gospel with the question about the content of faith, the question which we put to Paul with the question about the form of faith, and the question about Jesus with the question about the whereabouts of faith. But in each case, thought is our starting-point. The following arrangement emerges:

1. What does faith think in John's Gospel?
2. How does faith think in Paul?
3. Where does faith think in Jesus?

I. WHAT DOES FAITH THINK?

For this section we confine ourselves to John's Gospel. Although the question 'What does faith think?' has a close connexion with the other question 'How does faith think?' it may still be said in advance: Faith thinks what it believes.

This is the meaning in John 6.69 '. . . we have believed and have come to know, that you are the Holy One of God'. In the immediately preceding verses, which presumably belonged to the close of the first half of the Gospel,[1] it had been noted that many disciples had deserted Jesus. On the other hand, the twelve are still all there. To Jesus' question (which still conceals the future) asking whether they also want to leave, Peter answers with a question in reply: 'Lord, to whom shall we go? You have the words of eternal life.' After what follows—Peter's confession of faith which has already been quoted—Jesus answers with the word of grief, that one of them is a devil, although Jesus had chosen them all.

[1] See Bultmann's Commentary at this point (p. 321).

If we compare this striking Johannine confession of faith by Peter with the Easter confession of Thomas: 'My Lord and my God' (20.28), we are obliged to ask whether Peter or Thomas says the more. Yet even Thomas's confession is not without its offence. Blessed are those who, though they have not seen like Thomas, have nevertheless come to faith (20.29). The Johannine confession of Peter does not, in fact, depend on what can be seen, especially as many had left Jesus, but on Jesus' words, because they are words of eternal life. Peter's confession is of the very highest standard. Jesus is the Holy One of God (cf. Mark 1.24). He is this both in the sense that the world receives its deserved judgment when it rejects Jesus, and in the sense that Jesus, as the true high priest, takes responsibility for the world by consecrating himself for all the faithful (17.19), so that he, with the help of the faithful, may provide a last opportunity for the world. The faithful need this kind of consecration for two reasons: because the world is to be given a last chance through them, and because they themselves are threatened by the devil, and therefore are still open to temptation even in their community. Their knowledge of faith is directed to Jesus, for when they really believe they will recognize not just Jesus' suffering but also Jesus' anguish. Faith which remained a private matter would really be inadequate. Jesus' activity is concerned with the fate of the world. Faith, like Jesus himself, must become public and remain faith in full publicity. It is this and what follows from it that is to be considered in faith. Faith must become the confession of faith, which evades no offence.

We said that faith thinks what it believes. ('You have the words of eternal life.' 'You are the Holy One of God.') We can now say: Faith thinks what it confesses. The knowledge of faith comes to light in the confession of faith. It is not as though this knowledge has to lead the way beyond the content of faith. Faith is not a kind of first step on the way of knowledge. The significant thing is Bultmann's phrase, 'Faith is everything'.[1] Why?

An almost incidental observation may lead us further. The gospel is aware of a juxtaposition of faith and taking or accepting or receiving ($\lambda\alpha\mu\beta\acute{a}\nu\epsilon\iota\nu$). When faith and acceptance are denied, the two things are parallel and contemporary to each other; so in John 3.11f; 5.43f. But when, on the other hand, faith exists in a positive

---

[1] R. Bultmann, *Theologie des Neuen Testaments*, p. 426; ET, II, p. 74.

way, what dominates in it is the characteristic of a previous time, due to faith's having been received; the believer has received what he believes. This connexion between faith and having received is definitive even in the prologue and it characterizes the prologue; 1.12, 16; cf. also 3.33. This is connected with the need to say in parallel terms: '. . . and they knew in truth that I *came* from thee, and believed that thou *didst send* me' (17.8).

Faith looks back to Jesus' mission; it looks back on it as a completed happening which has been brought to its conclusion. Therefore, according to John, Jesus' last word on the cross was 'It is completed' (19.30). The famous phrase in the prologue 'and the word became flesh' is therefore also a phrase signifying the complete knowledge of faith, and it has in view Jesus' mission extending into death. Phrases of this kind are at the same time confessions of faith. This applies equally to the theme sentence of John's Gospel: 'For God so loved the world that he gave his only Son, that whoever believes in him should not perish but have everlasting life' (3.16). This is why Jesus says in 11.25f: 'I *am* the resurrection and the life. He who believes in me, though he die, yet shall he live; and whoever lives and believes in me shall never die. Do you believe this?' Martha answers him on behalf of the community. 'Yes, Lord; I certainly believe; you are Christ, the Son of God, who was to come into the world' (11.27). And in John 5.24f we read the words that explain all this. 'Truly, truly, I say to you, he who hears my word and believes him who sent me, has eternal life; he does not come into judgment, but has passed from death to life. Truly, truly, I say to you, the hour is coming and now is, when the *dead* will hear the voice of the Son of God, and those who *have* heard will live.' What death was and what life is, is decided solely by this: whether a person has heard what Jesus says here in the fulfilment of his mission.

The completed mission of the Son gives eternal life to the person who believes in the completion of the Son's mission. Through Jesus' having come, faith has received everything that God willed to give, whereas unbelief squanders everything (3.18). Jesus' miraculous doings add nothing to this matter. They can just confirm it, but they can in no way lead beyond it. Whoever is blind to it will remain blind (cf. 9.41). Faith is everything.

Thus faith thinks what it confesses: that God was present in

Jesus (14.9), since Jesus himself was God's word which wishes to give us life (1.1–18). Faith thinks what it believes: that Jesus was the word of love, which makes every question superfluous because the Father fulfils the Son's request (16.23). Jesus' prayer in John 17 arises from the anguish of love. This hymn of the dying Jesus is the Song of Songs of God's faithfulness. God is faithful because, in the Son, he gives nothing less than himself (John 5.26f). For the Father loves the Son. This most of all is what we are accustomed to forget.

Knowledge of faith is confession of faith, because knowledge of faith is knowledge of God (John 17.3). For John knowledge of God and confession of faith belong inseparably together. Faith has something to say because God has given knowledge of himself in Jesus.

We have so accustomed ourselves to linking faith with hearing that it has become questionable whether faith still has any kind of appearance at all. But it is now clear that the Johannine Jesus is by no means removed from the perceptual. He was not crucified because he remained unrecognized, but because he appeared publicly in complete clarity (11.46ff). But it is still possible to remain blind when faced with him. This does not mean that faith itself becomes a dialectical movement of existence, even though the Johannine theology proceeds dialectically in its train of thought. Faith must instead be certain, confessing faith. Faith *sees* when it thinks. What does it see? *It sees Jesus*. And when it really sees Jesus, then it has seen the Father (14.9). Why? The sole answer is this: Because the Father is at work in Jesus (14.10f). God's working became perceptible in Jesus. This became evident even in Jesus' miracles; they also could lead to faith (14.11b). But as faith itself is to do still greater things (14.12), it cannot be allowed that the demonstration of God's working should be confined to Jesus' miracles. The decisive point is not what is still to be, but what has already happened through Jesus' mission. Jesus' mission itself made God's working amply evident. In what way? Because God's love became evident in Jesus' mission. The perceptibility of love objectifies, in just the same way as anything else that becomes perceptible. But love becomes perceptible through its taking place. The result is that a man can relate it to himself, and even appeal to it (3.16). Further: it is not only possible to appeal to the event of love; this has to be done in order to do justice to the perceptibility of love (13.34f). For the event of love consists of its wish to have someone claim it. When God reveals his love, when indeed he reveals himself as love—and the mission of Jesus says just this—God *intends* to be claimed as love (cf., e.g., 7.37). This is possible for everyone because God has manifested himself as love. In Jesus, God made himself the event of love, by giving to the world in Jesus the 'Logos', *the word* of love.[1] The perceptibility of faith's knowledge of God consists of this. Faith thinks by holding fast to Jesus as the word of love, as the uttered word of God. This is why the Johannine Jesus really just says the one thing all the time: I am what I say, *the word*. And faith confesses: You are the word. Thus Jesus, as the word of God, lifts faith into the realm of love in which God gives eternal life; and the world which is hostile to love sinks in collapse. The only thing that has to die is what is not fitted for love. That is the difference between God and us: we not only live, but also die. But dying can be overcome by us, when we hold firmly to God's word. For God's word keeps watch over everything that belongs to love (10.28). Thou hast words of eternal life. This is why faith confesses Jesus as God's word.

2. HOW DOES FAITH THINK?

For this section we confine ourselves to Paul. Whereas in John's Gospel thought was made dependent on faith, in Paul's case it almost appears as if he were making faith dependent on thought. Certainly the Pauline assertions of faith also centre on christological formulae of faith. But these formulae of faith, in contrast to those characteristic of John, have been almost entirely moulded by the pre-Pauline form of confession, and indeed are expanded by Paul only here and there: Rom. 1.3f; 3.24–26; 4.25; 10.9; also I Cor. 12.3; 15.3–5; II Cor. 4.5, etc. Paul's theology gains so much the more in importance. This theology is indisputably anthropology, reflection on the being (*Sein*) of man, before faith and in faith. It is naturally also possible to say that Paul's theology is exposition of baptism, interpretation of the formulae of faith which are modelled, for the most part, on baptism. However the matter ought not to be watered down by making Paul's

[1] See my article 'Logos', *RGG* IV, cols. 439f.

soteriological interest, which unifies the christology and the anthropology, into the leading motif of his idea of faith. The missionary motif would then be transferred overhastily into the centre of the Pauline theology. This sort of thing can only lead us on to false paths, if we allow the later chapters of Romans, i.e. Rom. 9–11 and 12ff, to mix in with the first half of the letter, which is considered to be much more fundamental; or even if we allow the later part to conflict prematurely with the first. We should not worry about Schlatter's jest that the Reformation exegesis tired itself out with Rom. 5. The Letter to the Ephesians, which stands closer to Paul, was not on Schlatter's side. In any case the Letter to the Romans ought to be assessed in relation to the Letter to the Ephesians, and when in doubt, advice can be taken from the Letter to the Philippians and the Letters to the Corinthians, if one wants to know what appears in the centre of the Pauline theology. This is *the problem of the law*. The Pauline theology circles consciously around this problem. As a result, this theology, when viewed systematically, will indeed have to be conceived as anthropology.

How does faith think in Paul? The familiar passage Gal. 4.8f gives a first indication: 'Formerly, when you did not know God, you were in bondage to beings that by nature are no gods; but now that you have come to know God, or rather to be known by God, how can you turn back again to the weak and beggarly (natural) elements, whose slaves you want to be once more?' There follows a sentence about the introduction among the Galatians of sacred seasons of stars, the intention of which was certainly liturgical; presumably efforts were made for the most effective distribution of the vital power. The mischief came about through the Galatians' failing to bind the Christian freedom in the Spirit firmly to faith, with the result that (by means of appeal to Peter?) they had to erect new safeguards even against the gnosticizing libertinism. Paul now makes great efforts to impress on them anew the text which they had lost from view, namely Christ's cross (cf. 3.1). This is why he writes them a letter about the law. What he then says about the Spirit is only the consequence of what has been said about the law. In the Letter to the Galatians also Christ is the end of the law, because the law (of Moses) remained in power only until the time came when faith was to be revealed, i.e. until Christ came (3.23f). In Christ, on the other hand, all are free for faith, whether they are Jews or Greeks, etc. (3.26–28). Thus they are all Abraham's seed and heirs of the promise, not because they are descended from Abraham, for they are mainly Gentiles, but because they have been called to faith and have received the Spirit of faith (3.29; 4.1–7). This was God's grace for them all (2.21).

Paul therefore certainly thinks in universal terms, but not in terms of universal history. Strictly speaking, it cannot be said that in Gal. 3 he thinks unequivocally in terms of salvation-history. There is a new relation between Abraham's promise and the largely Gentile heirs of this promise. They now, as God's Israel, stand over against an Israel which has remained almost completely faithless (6.16). This new relation breaks the salvation-history scheme of 'promise—fulfilment' which had previously applied to Israel. For Paul everything now depends not on Israel's history but solely on faith, and this is true not only of the heirs, but even of Abraham himself. The *sola fide* turns completely against the structure of the scheme 'faith and works' which, according to James 2.22, dominates the Old Testament; even though Paul revealed the true inner nerve of the Old Testament revelation through his concept of God's righteousness, and drew a contrast with Israel. Paul certainly called the law a *paidagogos*, a taskmaster (3.24f). Yet it should be noted that, although according to Gal. 3 the law threatens with the curse everyone who does not obey it, only the promise which is given solely to faith makes clear that all men are sinners (3.10f). If Paul had not quoted the passages Hab. 2.4 and Gen. 15.6 against the misuse of the law, he could never have used the scriptural proof he wanted (Gal. 3.22). Moreover, it is clear that for Paul kerygmatic statements of the gospel are by no means of lesser importance than scriptural declarations (cf. v. 13); the scriptural declarations have to yield to the kerygmatic assertions.

In Gal. 3, therefore, the thought is not that the fulfilment of the promise was expected, but that the promise should only fall to faith. Certainly both have their 'time', promise and faith. This is the very thing to be learned. Faith, too, is bound to its time 'in Christ', which means that Abraham was only the precursor of faith. But once the gospel had arrived, the exact time for faith arrived for everyone along with it. The law by no means contradicts this. It, too, had its time and is now, just as impartially as ever, an impartial witness of faith. The law certainly punishes evil-doers unflinchingly and thereby directs the whole of scripture towards faith, if salvation for sinners is to be possible. But for this very reason the law and the promise of faith do not conflict with each other. For, in fact, the law damns the evildoer, while faith saves him. Thus both set their seal on the scriptural declaration that God's promise belongs only to faith. When scripture spoke of the seed of the faithful Abraham it meant Christ (3.16); because Christ is proclaimed in order that faith may save, when the time for faith has come.

Therefore: the law stands impartially against the sinner, whereas Christ, as the end of the law, stands on the side of the faithful. Just as the law had its own limited time and only came after a limited time (3.17), so now faith has acquired through the pro-clamation of Christ its own definite time. This time can be under-stood only as time subsequent to the law, just as Abraham had his time long before the law. Not that the one time flowed into the other. Paul lays no stress at all on a continuity of salvation-history; but he does stress the *difference between the times*, as Luther has rightly seen. This is why, in Gal. 4.1–7, the difference in times between the time of the gospel and that of the law, when seen from God's side, can be grasped only qualitatively and so only by means of an image. Before Christ there was no distinction between freemen and slaves, because they are to be compared with minors who have not yet come of age and require supervision. Now this has become different. The one group have received the Spirit of the Son in faith, because God has made them his sons, whereas the others, as Luther comments with regard to Gal. 2.20, have 'foundered' in sin. It may then be said fully in keeping with the Apostle's thought: whereas before Christ all men were to be held together only under supervision, now in Christ they have all truly become one in the Spirit; the comparison in Gal. 4.1–5 is a counter to the declaration of unity in Gal. 3.26–28. Anyone who wants to support an objection by an appeal to scripture is to be referred to Abraham's example, and should consider what was really pro-mised: salvation from faith alone. The titles Abraham's children or Abraham's inheritance are to be rated less highly than this governing concept. This is the same point of view as in Rom. 4 or Rom. 9–11. In this whole theology what is thought depends entirely on how it is thought: evangelically rather than in terms of salvation-history, even though it may seem that formally a succession apparently in terms of salvation-history runs alongside. The search for the continuity and discontinuity of any history completely fails to reach this text; it is instead rejected.

The same argument applies in terms of the conscience. Like the law, the conscience is also impartial. As a result man comes into conflict with himself in his conscience, where his intentions rise up before him, Rom. 2.14f. Paul can thus refer the Corinthians to their own conscience when they want to give judgment on him (II Cor. 5.11: 4.1f). It is not what enters language in the conscience, but certainly the way that it enters language, that is the same in all cases. Paul therefore rejects every other court of judgment (I Cor. 4.2–4). Even the 'Lord' will adhere to nothing else in his searching of the heart (I Cor. 4.5: II Cor. 5.10). Strictly speaking, therefore, man cannot take himself in. He can know what he wanted.

For us the most important aspect of these declarations is that they also remain binding for the faithful. All have need of exhortation. Exhortation is an aid to self-examination. Those who practise it need not suffer chastisement from the Lord in the sacrament (I Cor. 11.31f, 28–30). Like the Apostle, Christians ought to live in 'fear and trembling' for their faith (Phil. 2.12f; I Cor. 2.3). Weakness and strength certainly seem to overlap in faith, for not all are capable of the same thing. Everyone must instead examine himself to see for what kind of task or in what kind of situation he is sure of his faith. The result is that in each person's case faith has to become a measure of his actual ability (Rom. 12.3; 14.22). Nothing that comes from without is in itself reprehensible; sin is simply the thing that has faith in opposition to it (Rom. 14.14, 23). So there is most certainly a difference between weakness and strength. But it is possible only to be happy about faith. Inasmuch as the strength of the faithful consists of Christ's power, then all are certainly weak because they need Christ's power. Those who conform to faith will receive in faith the strength they need, like Abraham or Paul himself (Rom. 4.18–20; II Cor. 12.9f; 6.3–10). In Paul faith always stands in a relation to the Lord. But the Lord is distinguished from the faithful by virtue of being Lord. The Spirit is the Spirit of the Lord and only thus the Spirit of faith. In

Paul, therefore, faith is constantly a fighting, obedient faith which vindicates the lordship of its Lord (Rom. 14.7–9).

What sort of *knowledge of faith* is this ? Without doubt always one of self-examination. The man without a conscience will never be able to make this knowledge of faith his own. Therefore, at least as far as Paul is concerned, Wilhelm Herrmann was right in assuming that moral seriousness was the hermeneutical principle of faith. According to Paul, faith is concerned with everything that we are able to answer for morally, when we lay claim to Christ's power. But this hermeneutical principle of moral responsibility simply leads back to faith again and again. On the road of faith itself our responsibility is made precise, and so the struggle which is laid upon the Christian also becomes concrete. According to Paul faith has to respond first of all to the gospel, i.e. to the proclamation of faith. It has to respond to the message that God in his grace allows man 'to participate in the omnipotence of God', as Gerhard Ebeling puts it. Christ's strength, in which faith puts its trust, is indeed the power of God (Rom. 8.2–17). What ought to be proclaimed is not an idea of God, but God's presence in power as the 'demonstration of the Spirit and of power' (I Cor. 2.4). Along with the time for faith there came the time of this demonstration in Jesus' name; that is, the time of Christ's lordship (Phil. 2.9–11).

The self-examination therefore consists of this: I have to examine myself to see if I am concerned with the demonstration of the Spirit and of *God's* power in my active and passive conduct; i.e. in regard to my neighbour, in all suffering and indeed in all joy. The object is to see if my conduct, my being (*Sein*) coincides with this demonstration. Only then have I understood the grace which is meant to be imparted to us all in Christ. Knowledge of faith is not thus made subordinate to thought, but it is certainly bound to the kind of thought which is self-examination. In the same sense Rom. 8 is bound to Rom. 7. Indeed, the self-examination for its part is bound to the knowledge of faith, because faith is not something that remains individual and hidden, but the testimony and confession that declares to everyone God's power in the present (cf. I Cor. 14.24f as a practical example). It is then self-evident that this power is love, because it never withdraws, but certainly sharpens the conscience.

How does faith think ? Not scrupulously but conscientiously, by testifying to everyone through his own determination that God acts for him. In order to grasp this treasure properly we shall now consider more clearly something else—under what circumstances faith takes place, that is, *where* it thinks.

3. WHERE DOES FAITH THINK?

For this section we confine ourselves to the proclamation of Jesus.

Even in regard to the Pauline theology there was a tendency to say quite simply: Faith thinks *in the world*. Faith thinks conscientiously because, as confessing faith, it thinks with the neighbour's interests in mind. This means that faith thinks with the world's interests in mind, and therefore in the world. It can be said that faith takes place in the world and for the sake of the world. Faith does not lead out of the world, but right into the world. Here, however, a reservation has to be made. For faith is nevertheless not worldly faith. I simply refer to this matter and introduce it here in order to link up the question of where faith thinks with a passage from the proclamation of Jesus.

Jesus' proclamation is, of course, a matter of dispute. It can never be certainly decided whether any indisputably genuine saying of Jesus has been handed on to us. On the other hand, it is possible to deliberate with more prospect of success on the subject of what Jesus' proclamation could have been about. However, we probably evolve too schematic conceptions about this, because we are accustomed to speak of a *proclamation* of Jesus. We then involuntarily look for the themes of a sermon. But if Jesus did not, in fact, *preach* in our sense, or in the sense of the Pauline mission, then he did not have any preaching themes. For example, it is by no means certain, and in my opinion not even likely, that Jesus proclaimed the rule of God, or preached repentance. What have been handed on to us in this connexion are stylized formulations of the early community or of the evangelists (e.g. Mark 1.15; Matt. 4.17). On the other hand, it is practically certain that Jesus also pondered upon the subject of the rule of God. His understanding of the rule of God should then indeed be accessible to us. For Jesus without doubt expressed himself on the subject of the rule of God. The historical analysis of the tradition has been able to make this much likely for us, because by going beyond the christological insertions in this tradition we now see more clearly what stems from the previous era, and therefore what comes into consideration for Jesus' form of thought.

The reason why I now venture upon this kind of doubtfully transmitted passage will become clear to you from the example itself. I choose the similitude of the seed which grows by itself, Mark 4.26–29, and for this reason: because this similitude can be attributed to Jesus only on one special condition.[1]

The similitude occurs only in Mark. Matthew appears to have replaced it with the parable of the tares among the wheat (Matt. 13.24–30). As a result our similitude may in my opinion be reckoned to belong to that part of Mark's Gospel which Matthew knew. The content can be told quickly: A man casts seed into the ground. While he sleeps and rises, day after day, the seed comes up and grows high, without the man taking notice of it. For the earth attends to its work by itself, 'automatically', until the man puts in the sickle because the harvest-time is come (cf. Joel 3.13). It is just the same with the rule of God.

A similitude of this kind is naturally fitting for a community which was anxious because there seemed to be a delay in what they hoped would be the imminent parousia of the 'Son of Man', of the Jesus who had been exalted as Lord. It also fits into the christology of Mark's Gospel, which represents the resurrected Christ continuing to care for the community (16.7), because he had done this previously during his time on earth and right up to his giving of himself. The similitude then says: Cast all your cares on him, for he cares for you (I Peter 5.7). An understanding of this kind need not make the similitude into an allegory, because it would only be an edifying application of the similitude. At most it would only be the concept of the rule of God in the introduction to the similitude that was allegorized, because the community would be concerned with the lordship of Jesus Christ himself. The similitude itself, by means of its scenic compactness, guards against allegorical extensions. This may have prompted Matthew, working from the same understanding, to seize rather on the parable of the tares among the wheat, which is more suited to allegory and which he could

---

[1] For the exposition cf. in particular G. Harder, 'Das Gleichnis von der selbstwachsenden Saat Mark 4.26–29', in *Theologia Viatorum* 1, 1948–9, pp. 51–70. The echo of Joel 4.13 in Mark 4.29 should in my opinion not be overstressed; there is only a partial quotation (cf. Mark 4.32).

despatch on its way along with the corresponding meaning. Matthew's intention is to threaten.

If we ignore applications of this kind, which are, of course, provoked by the 'Joel quotation' in v. 29, what emerges is the simple meaning that the man who has sown need worry about nothing more until the harvest is come. For in the meantime the earth looks after its own. This means that the earth requires from the man only the sowing. Once the sowing is past the earth relieves the sower of all care. He can now do what he wants. Now it is the turn of the earth. For the time being it sets the sower free. This seems to me to be the decisive point. We are concerned here not with a miracle of growth, but with the difference between the further working of the earth and the inactivity of the man after the first act of sowing. Both certainly belong together. The similitude makes use of an experience of nature. The sowing and the harvest each have their time. The sower can depend on this. This is why now, in the present, he is without a care, a free man. The present is, then, indeed a restricted time between sowing and harvest. But this very restriction makes it for the sower into a time of unrestricted freedom.

If we think our way into the similitude like this, an allegory is then suggested which claims the earth as the image of God's working. The meaning could be that God's working relieves man of the complex of care of his time in the world, which so often becomes a torment. The thought is hardly mistaken. It tallies with the sayings about not being anxious in Matt. 6.25ff and its parallels. But there is no need to go so far. It may be that a thought of this kind echoes in the similitude, or it may perhaps be that it contains no original thought at all. For, in the form of a fairly fully narrated image, i.e. of a similitude pictorially composed, it in fact always really acquires its value through the application.

If Jesus told the similitude, he obviously related it only to the present. And if we assume that the similitude was able to pass on Jesus' understanding of the rule of God, it then gains this meaning: The rule of God does not draw a contrast between God's care and action and your cares and action. Instead the rule of God makes you free for yourselves. Certainly, as in Paul, two times are distinguished from each other. But from the beginning attention is directed entirely to the present relation of man to God. Even in this case the rule of God does not bring any direct comfort to the poor and the mourners. This is done rather by the beatitudes at the beginning of the Sermon on the Mount or in the Lucan sayings on the plain (Matt. 5.3ff par. Luke 6.20f). What the rule of God does do is to confine the present to what can be expected of man in the present, *because* God cares for the future in the same way as the earth cares for the growth. The rule of God does not give an unlimited time to man—this gift would be devilish—but it does give a time limited by God—the rich corn farmer, for example, had just as little grasp of this as the introverted rich man obsessed with the commandments (Luke 12.16–20; Mark 10.17–22 par.; Matthew presents him to us as a young man). The word also makes good a claim like this. It demands that the hearer should indeed believe in God's working. But this demand is, in fact, a giving, a gift of the time given to man; and it is bestowed on the very man who otherwise, apart from faith, wastes it.

This kind of thing can certainly only be said if one is *sure* of God's will. But this appears to be an assumption that applied to Jesus. For all those parts of the tradition which come into consideration at all and which can fittingly be attributed to Jesus, provide common agreement for this assumption. This is the only reason why the question of 'full authority' can be posed with regard to Jesus. Indeed, it has to be said that the tradition has preserved this trait of Jesus' thought extremely well, even at the point where it falsely assigns apocalyptic prophecies to him. It is not surprising that, since Jesus was sure of God, he was therefore credited with knowing *everything secret*. It is all the more remarkable that the tradition has nevertheless not harmonized the thoughts attributed to Jesus, but has allowed them to survive alongside each other in their main parts. (Hans Conzelmann has recently shown this in an illuminating way.[1])

If Jesus was sure of God's working and if he asserted this certainty in his words and deeds, then the usual talk about a 'near expectation' and when possible an 'imminent expectation' on Jesus' part is misleading. For this expectation was already a part of tradition, as is clear when we compare Jesus with the Baptist, whose penance-baptism could equally well presuppose something in the nature of a 'near expectation', at least of God's judgment.

---

[1] H. Conzelmann, 'Zur Methode der Leben-Jesu-Forschung', *ZTK* 56, Beiheft 1, 1959, pp. 10f.

The frightened community were the first to fasten again emphatic-
ally on to expectations of this kind. In my opinion the Easter
visions are nothing other than the expression of such expectations.
They were later corrected by thinking of Jesus' cross and resurrection together, above all in the Pauline theology, and finally they
were increasingly overcome in the theology of the evangelists,
even in Mark. On the other hand, in the case of Jesus another care
certainly thrusts to the fore. It is true that our deliberations now
take us into extremely uncertain territory, but we must press on
with our thinking, because we have now reached the point at
which the risk of interpretation really begins.

   If God's working releases the present for man, this indicates,
as has been said, comfort and encouragement for the poor and the
mourners, because they can leave their needs to God, but there
will also be another group of men who have no desire to hear
these words. If the future lies entirely on God's side, then the
present that God releases is no arbitrary endless time, but a
restricted present. This newly offered present will bring with it
contrasts, which arise purely because one section of the audience
resolutely gives heed to Jesus. These contrasts are beyond the
scope of the *ius talionis*, for they arise not from injustice but from
God's justice, because God is believed in as God. This does not
mean that Jesus' exposition of the law—for instance, the dual
law of love (Mark 12.28–34 par.) or the directions expressed in the
antitheses of the Sermon on the Mount (Matt. 5.21ff)—necessarily
acquires an interim character. Jesus trims down God's will just as
little as he does God's grace. This is why Jesus confines man's
action to what can be concretely expected of him. Whoever loves
will quite spontaneously avoid offending, committing adultery, etc.
But all this certainly indicates that, as a result of the heightened
contrast between the willing and the resentful, the need of the
present becomes even greater. The alternative to the inexorable
rejection of an evil and perverse generation will be hope in God
alone. In this case what matters is not so much when God will
intervene, but the immediate survival of this need. Will the num-
bers of those who support the willing be sufficient? This is why
I maintain that the unhistorical chapter 17 of John has, in fact,
captured the situation of the historical Jesus. For this same
reason the christology of the Letter to the Hebrews is probably

superior to that of Paul, although Paul was the greater theologian.

In what situation does faith think? Surely in the kind of situation in which it arises. In what situation does faith arise? Not in the kind of situation in which man is directed to faith and to God, but in that situation in which faith is also able to remain faith. What sort of situation is this? A dogmatic answer is possible: one in which faith takes part in *Jesus' obedience*. This was Paul's answer. But we say, perhaps more clearly and precisely: faith has its abode in the kind of situation in which it takes part in *Jesus' certainty*. This is why Jesus spoke. Through his word Jesus conveyed to his hearers his own individual certainty of God. He therefore portrayed to them in his word the faith that remains faith, until he himself became in his person the lasting portrayal of the faith which God had intended for them.

We asked *where* faith thinks. Now we have to say: Faith thinks in the place where Jesus' word and person become the portrayal of faith. *How* does faith think? Faith thinks as Paul thought, in conscientious self-examination. *What* does faith think? Faith thinks of God, by holding fast to the word of love, which corresponds to Jesus' *certainty of God*. The New Testament testifies to this faith. Is our situation really different? Do we understand the faith to which the New Testament bears witness? Do we understand Jesus' certainty of God? If we say that we lack this certainty, we have then, nevertheless, understood. Even supposing we were to lack Jesus' certainty of God, the historical Jesus would have become clearly present for us, as soon as we had recognized our own situation. It is, therefore, not true to say that faith can be recognized only in faith. Unbelief understands faith as well, and most certainly better than a presumptuous faith does. This is why the exposition of the New Testament is something that can be expected of everyone. It can be carried out in the form of faith's 'doctrine of language'. Now for a further methodological comment about this.

4. FAITH AND THOUGHT

What does faith's hermeneutic or 'doctrine of language' strive after?[1] It appears at first as if I were bluntly offering a programme

---

[1] Cf. my *Hermeneutik*, and my first volume of essays, *Zum hermeneutischen Problem in der Theologie*; also G. Ebeling, *Das Wesen des christlichen Glaubens*, ET, *The Nature of Faith*, and his *Wort und Glaube*, 1960, ET, *Word and Faith*, 1963.

based on the passions or subjectivity as an alternative to the historical-critical method. But this impression is due to ignorance of the historical-critical mode of working. It certainly analyses as methodically as possible. But the refinement of its methods, which we have before us in the form of the assessment of historical probability and right on to the form-historical practice, should not blind us to the passion which motivates even this work. As an alternative we can call it resolution. The historical-critical method is resolved to admit as its working-material only what can be clearly established as given. Its interest in history is entirely conditioned. It confines itself to an interest in the kind of declaration of truth which is able to extract clear conceptions from incontrovertibly established facts. Behind this there stands a deep and justifiable mistrust of historical tradition, indeed of history itself. This method has a thorough knowledge of its limits. It knows that it must always reconstruct afresh, that the interpretation of historical relationships is always a risk, and at its high points it realizes that it is the art of combining the material with the sympathetic understanding of the historian. The interpreter must be able to read between the lines. He understands the past better than it understood itself, because he has a knowledge of subsequent developments. As in every scientific study the result must be a representation of the complex which has been methodically brought into relief. The intention of the historian is certainly not to construct fables—he scorns the novel—but it is to relate reliably how things were.

Fundamentally there can be no objection to this, as long as there are a number of good historians who can correct each other. When criticism preponderates it leads easily to a dispute about the material. This is the position in New Testament study at the present time. It has become uncertain whether, for example, one can still rely at all on genuine 'Jesus tradition'. The stubborn clinging on to the psychology of the so-called 'near expectation', in general the psychological interpretation of eschatology—these are explained not only by an apocalyptic mood of our age, but at least equally by the anxiety that otherwise the last remains will be lost, as they are sayings of Jesus which have probably been given greater prominence. The outcry about the Qumran texts has made the longing for material abundantly clear. Now it is the turn of the Gospel of Thomas. What will have been found tomorrow? The recent history of New Testament study shows that its lexicons certainly grow, but not its theological presentations. Bultmann's theology dominates the field because it is fundamental.[1]

Next to the dispute about material, *dogmatic prejudgments* are the second obstacle. They probably operate more strongly in exegesis than in dogmatics itself, because dogmatics reflects consciously about itself. This is why, in narrative exegesis, there is a justified insistence on a method. This same demand naturally applies to a hermeneutic of faith, which I understand as faith's 'doctrine of language'. This title does not imply that the exegete must be a believer. Nor, of course, is it required that the exegete should not be allowed to bring any faith with him. Faith ought instead to be energetically sought for. Faith is by no means a self-evident matter. But for the New Testament it is the main thing. The quest for faith is central to its exposition; it is not just the *conditio sine qua non* of the understanding of the text. It demands the self-examination of the exegete. But this self-examination should not take place naïvely; it must instead have a place within the method of exposition.

At this point the ways divide. I agree with Bultmann that the exegete must have a relationship to the matter he investigates, i.e. the matter of the texts. Inasmuch as the texts are concerned with faith, he will therefore have to bring with him a 'pre-understanding' of faith, which motivates him. It is possible for this pre-understanding to consist of the knowledge that for us today faith is frightfully lacking. Everyone can understand this. This is the concern of dogmatics, in our time also. Faith means first and foremost dependence on God. It is precisely this that we usually do not do at all. Dogmatics is aware of this. A more precise formulation is provided by Gerhard Ebeling's thesis that faith, according to the New Testament, participates in God's omnipotence. Faith, then, means 'entering upon' God. The immediate effect of such a formulation can certainly be alienation. Faith may at first be still further removed from me. Can I, or should I, then perform miraculous cures? It may be necessary expressly to say something like this about the correct proclamation, when one knows what happens there. However, another consideration

---

[1] It is a counterpart to F. Chr. Baur's *Vorlesungen über neutestamentliche Theologie* (published by his son in 1864).

intervenes first of all. The formulation points to something quite near at hand, because it draws a complete distinction between God's action and my action. I participate in God's omnipotence when I finally really assert God's action to be God's action and no longer mix it up with my action. In this way Gerhard Ebeling defines the situation of faith, the *coram Deo* of Luther and of Paul (II Cor. 2.17). This includes the knowledge that God effects our salvation *sub contrario*, so that we could have God as God, as *incarnatus*; otherwise we perish before him. It is in this sense that Paul speaks of God's wrath, of God's judgment and law which, when correctly understood, drive us to Christ. Another formulation of Ebeling's would still have to be added to what has been said: that the gospel identifies man.[1] The meaning of this formulation is this: God identifies man by means of the gospel in the present.

At the end of my survey it became evident, on the basis of the exposition of the similitude of the seed that grew by itself, that, in a present confined or limited by the future and so by God, God frees man in such a way that man is able freely to accept his present. In this case, therefore, the 'today' is so defined by the 'tomorrow' that the 'today' becomes the criterion of our freedom. This is man's identification by God. If, as Bultmann holds, faith is something like self-surrender, I can agree with this formulation, assuming it is to mean the acceptance of the present as a consequence of the call of Jesus in the present. Hence the texts disclose Jesus' certainty of God as the factor which determines them; and they disclose the need of the present as the object of Jesus' care for his own, as the inner nerve of his words. This need increases and indeed only really appears as a result of faith, and the present is disputed *because* of faith.

The academically decisive question still remains entirely the one about the method I have followed. The answer is simple: it is the method of existential interpretation introduced by Bultmann. As this interpretation considers possibilities of existence, as it wants to know how a person exists when he thinks, I, too, have asked how faith thinks—how a person thinks who knows that his existence is won in faith and lost without faith. In this also I am in agreement

---

[1] G. Ebeling, *Wort und Glaube*, pp. 90–160; ET, pp. 98–161: 'The Christian is man properly identified' (p. 159, n. 213; ET, p. 160, n. 1).

with Bultmann. Like him, I have started out from the 'what' and have at once adhered to the 'how', with the result that the Pauline theology has achieved a special significance for the whole procedure, just as it does for Bultmann. Further to this I have expressly sought the '*existentiell*' situation of thinking faith; i.e. I have enquired where a thing like believing thought takes place, where it becomes an event. Thus in my own way I came upon the event-character of the word—of the word of love—and thereby upon the language-character of human existence, as, for example, it appears in the form of conscience. If I was able to restore to love its own kind of visible nature, there then emerged as a consequence an insight into Jesus' certainty of God. Thus the text, e.g. Mark 4.26–29, was set anew in motion.

Exegesis is always subject to the failing that through its very handling of the text it ties the text down and reduces it to silence, whereas the text ought really to come to light in the exposition. To say that we question the text with regard to its context or its *Sitz im Leben* is no further help, if the exposition either ossifies or dissects this material also. Why, then, do Jesus' words ostensibly say much less than the discourses of the resurrected Christ who, it is said, lives and works through the Spirit? In fact, when armed with these formulae one is all the more off target, because formulae are easy to handle but are themselves dead. The person who speaks about life does not therefore live long, assuming that life is more than the product of words. Every text is an expedient, a necessary aid for the real spoken word. The more life the text acquires, the more markedly does it give way to the context in the interests of which it was written. If the text still survives, i.e. if it is cared for, then this is simply because the context in the interests of which it was written demands this care. This applies specially when the appropriate context is not self-evident as a context in life, but instead needs signposts which delineate it. We should not fancy that we shall still find faith alive after we have killed everything that belongs to it. We want rather to catch live fish. We want to have to do with faith itself. This is why we seek faith by posing the question of how and where it is active when it thinks. The texts answer this question, but they say still more. They say how and where faith speaks.

However, faith has consequences with which it must come to

terms. This is why there are texts which speak of faith by virtue
of the fact that they consider the consequences of faith. Since these
texts take part in this happening, they do not remain unchanged.
They are altered, set in new contexts, enriched and also abbreviated.
This applies most of all to Jesus' sayings. His very fate necessarily
aroused questions which were compared with his sayings. Mark
has already made this comparison. If Jesus' fate was the consequence of his sayings, then Jesus' sayings had later to come to
terms with their own consequences. This and no other is the
process with which the principal question of exposition must
deal. It is not permissible to announce dogmatically that Jesus'
sayings express too little because, seen historically, they say
nothing about Jesus' fate; nor may one as exegete emulate the
evangelists, who simply attribute to Jesus prophecies about his
fate, even though the evangelist may thereby have been theologically in the right. As soon as the evangelist adduces sayings of
Jesus, an examination must be conducted to see with what justification he does this. We have, then, to ask what context Jesus'
sayings really fit into; formulated in a modern way: *at what point
they gather us together*. This is the only sense in which Jesus' call
(or conduct) 'implies' a christology.[1] The question was whether
the present which he insisted upon was a present decisive for all
time, so long as there was a present; whether at a later date also it
would be necessary to distinguish between present and future, as
he had done. Only then were his words an advance portrayal of
lasting faith. Only then could his person, his call, form the basis
of a 'once for all'. But is this not precisely the meaning of the
kerygmatic language of the early Church? This would indicate
that Jesus' words remained kerygmatically useful and needed only
to be guarded from misunderstandings. Why should new sayings
not have been added, to bring Jesus' call into language in a new
way? When Jesus himself was proclaimed, this procedure could, as
in the case of Paul, certainly bring again into language the event
which had already entered language in Jesus' sayings. What was
said was that God takes care of the future, and what was shown
was that we have to accept the present. Just because Jesus accepted
his present there arose in the future a task for those who followed
after. It was the task of having to do this same thing by bringing

---

[1] Cf. Bultmann, *Theologie des Neuen Testaments*, p. 46; ET, I, p. 43.

Jesus' word into language through their own word; and this meant that, because they themselves spoke, they brought the *historical Jesus* into language. Therefore the salvation event began *with* Jesus, because it later continued *without* him. This meant that Jesus remained decisive.

If this is the position of faith in relation to history, then for our understanding also faith is to be found where Jesus himself is. But once we have found it—and the texts seek to help us do this—we shall then have to say in our own words that we are gathered around the historical Jesus. For there is obviously only the one true relationship to God: Jesus' certainty of God. This is faith, for it corresponds to the will of God, with the result that we have not only the right but also the duty of calling God by the name God and so giving him the honour. Then we think as we exist. This is the sphere at which the exposition of the New Testament has arrived, as soon as we give up merely reconstructing and instead allow ourselves to be led by the texts. Here Jesus speaks, because God has called to faith through Jesus.

VIII

TRANSLATION AND PROCLAMATION

A Hermeneutical Lecture[1]

1960

THE practical theologian repeatedly observes that candidates for the ministry tend to stick to a safe wicket in drafting sermons, in so far as they simply attach their text to key clauses of the Church's confession of faith. The plan of the sermon then falls into two strangely contrasting parts, the exegetical part and the sermon itself. The so-called meditation which lies between the two has more or less disappeared, even though it may have been attempted experimentally. What is the reason for this? It is without doubt partly due to 'ecclesiastical' norms, to a harmful, uneasy style in the tradition, of which the candidates are in reality afraid, and to which they therefore hastily submit, so as to be able, somehow or other, to salvage a personal remnant of their existence. But the cardinal error is in the exegesis. It is not carried far enough, and, being prematurely concluded, it therefore remains fragmentary, and naturally does damage to the thinking out of the sermon, that is, to the meditation. The exegete does not know what he really has to do in the exegesis. What ought he to do? Well, the answer is so easy to give and so hard to carry out: he should *translate*. But what does this mean?

I once tried to render a translation in such a way that it could be fitted in to a sermon.[2] The subject is an old hymn, Phil. 2.6–11, which we must hum to ourselves once we have got the ring of the truly eschatological clamour which the cry: Jesus is Lord! releases —and stills. Indeed, our hymns have often laid such stress on inwardness that, for us at least, the power of such a passage is no longer perceptible. They have done this because faith in fact means

---

[1] In reference to two articles by M. Mezger, 'Die Anleitung zur Predigt', *ZTK* 56 1959, pp. 377–97, and 'Die Sprache der Predigt', *Schweizerische Theologische Umschau* 29, 1959, pp. 1–16.

[2] In my *Hermeneutik*, p. 104.

tranquillity. But the tranquillity of faith must not be confused with a vacuum, however true it may be that faith is unassailable. For in the tranquillity of faith, where noise is reduced to silence, a *voice* is heard, the very voice which is of central significance for the texts. This voice is identical with the voice of true preaching. It rings out in Phil. 2.6–11; that is to say, it rings out in the form of that hymn. The fact that faith can sing such a thing is its distinguishing feature, its participation in God.

God's word thus becomes the word of faith. The miracle of faith in the New Testament consists of the fact that faith 'is capable' of God's word; not simply that it can apprehend it, but also that it can say it. Part of a proper sermon is, then, the correct choice of hymns—not an easy matter—and the appropriate prayer, so that it becomes possible to surmount the obstacle of the traditional emphasis of the liturgy. (There is no doubt that the traditional liturgy affords assistance to that previously mentioned flight to the official tradition, although fragments of a once living tradition may, of course, also be preserved in the liturgy. We need only pose the question of whether the liturgy is in agreement at the point where the text for preaching arose.)

Such considerations take us right into the territory of hermeneutics. The very word 'translation' forces us to deliberate on the question of how we should translate. This is the starting-point of all hermeneutics, at least in exegetical theology. The key phrase 'living translation' is a concise description of the endeavour on the part of a hermeneutic which observes the freedom of exegesis, an endeavour within the sphere of our exegetical study which works by historical-critical methods. My own hermeneutical endeavours are concerned in addition with explaining the phenomenon of the 'text' itself; not just the language of the New Testament texts which can be ascertained philologically, but the 'language-event' in these texts, which above all can make them into texts of the proclamation. This is what we shall be discussing in what follows, especially since the practical theologian today often feels neglected by the exegete. But I must begin at the beginning.

I. THE HERMENEUTICAL PRINCIPLE

The prevailing view is that exegesis begins with the question of how one should translate. In the case of the New Testament the reason for this is simply the linguistic strangeness of the texts, since they have been handed down to us in Greek and Latin. As soon as we mention Greek and Latin, we touch on the critical strain which emanated from the new edition of the Greek New Testament issued by Erasmus (1516 or 1519). Luther made use of this, after having originally made use of the links between the Latin of the New Testament and the Old Testament. The very tradition to which we owe the texts is at the same time an obstacle to their understanding. Translation requires dictionaries (which, when they are good, aim beyond purely grammatical points); but translation also requires a critical check on the understanding of the text which has been handed down with it—put more explicitly, on the *usage of the text* which already exists. For the texts, at least the biblical or New Testament texts, are by no means dead. They reach the translator fully alive in the established usage, for example, in the liturgical usage. They are translated, not to bring them to life, but because they are already alive, and are meant to remain alive. But the life which is bound up with them should be one which, at least in principle, neither distorts nor alters the text, but allows it to live itself. The text which has been handed down is already the object of a life distinct from it, just as life is the object of the text, assuming that the text is itself meant to live. From the outset the activity on the part of the translator encounters not a passivity on the part of the text—this is excluded by the fact that the tradition makes use of the texts, e.g. in worship—but the text's own activity. Indeed, the activity of the text obliges the translator to play the role of passive participant; that is to say, the translator is involved in the activity of the text. If the translation is successful, the text would then speak, and not the translator. Only in this case can the demand justifiably be made that texts must always be translated anew in order to prevent their life being paralysed. As far as Protestant understanding is concerned, the characteristic feature of this is preaching which is bound to the text.

Although every preacher is involved in this demand to make a new translation of his text, it appears, according to the experience which we mentioned at the outset, that what happens instead is that the texts are always freshly struck dead. What is the reason for this? We must reply that it is due to the lack of the correct hermeneutical principle. At this stage, however, we must anticipate an important point: this is the statement that every *analysis* of the text *must* in the *first instance* 'strike the text dead'. However, if we may retain this useful image, it is really only that part of the text to which it makes no difference that can be 'struck dead'. I mean by this the outer form of language, which can be repeated at will, as it at present exists in print. It is this part of language which can be repeated at will that we can call its outer form. If we were to take the next step along with Humboldt, we would have to distinguish an 'inner' form from this outer form of language. Of course, this, too, does not lack constancy, in a sentence, for instance. Humboldt is also aiming at something in the nature of a language-event. However, our intention is to avoid his course of investigation, and instead bring into play the 'hermeneutical principle' of translation. If there is any point in speaking of a principle of this kind, it must be in a position to unite the formal aspect of translation with the aspect concerned with the content, in a way that enables the life of the text to appear. This does not mean that the formal aspect of the text—what can be repeated at will—is to be enlivened and newly infused with 'spirit'. On the contrary, the live part of the text, its spirit, must be willing and able to be *expressed* by us, and also for us, in the form of our language.

It must be admitted that every text which is to be translated in this way contains elements which defy translation. Greek is simply not German; Paul spoke a different language from Luther, and so on. The question is whether the translation can still be termed successful, when untranslatable parts are appropriately omitted. Here again we have to distinguish between the outer form of language and the spirit of the text. Certain parts of the outer form, for example a participial construction in the sentence, may well be untranslatable, without the translation violating the spirit which characterizes the sentence. For there were from the outset various possible forms of expression; for example, the syntactic choice of parataxis, or the hypotactic arrangement in the sentence. The spirit which characterizes the sentence does not necessarily disappear, just because the sound, for example of Paul, no longer resounds in the same key in the translation. It may be sufficient if the translation simply creates the sphere which the text meant to create when the spirit spoke in it. By saying this we have also already cited a hermeneutical principle of translation. It is one which joins together the formal aspect of translation and the aspect concerned with content, in such a way that the two together allow the life of the text to come to light: translation should create the same sphere, which the text meant to create when the spirit spoke in it. It was this, for example, which enabled Jews and Greeks to unite.

But surely this principle is still too vague to be of practical assistance to translation. Where did the text mean to create a sphere for the spirit? Both in the world (Humboldt),[1] and in existence (Bultmann). We must take note of the crucial characteristic of the text, in order to avoid getting entangled in ontological difficulties. The text is a linguistic construction. We must free ourselves from the prejudgment by which even Humboldt is bound, namely that language is principally the means of expression for thoughts, concepts, or possibilities of understanding. Then (as Humboldt really intended) we leave intact its character, which is varied and different from all else, even from thought. Thus it can become clear that language, together with what is peculiar to it—namely the word (Humboldt)—not only assists hearing, but subserves hearing. Even if the spirit which prevails in language is separable from language (as, for example, events of nature have no need of language), it is in language alone that those possibilities of the spirit come into operation, which live by hearing, and which therefore reach fulfilment only in word and not principally in thought. Therefore, as a language-construction, the text will want to create a sphere for the *word*. Where? In language itself, if indeed a translation is to be made, if indeed the text repeatedly awaits its translation, because in our case its intention is to be a text of proclamation.

The hermeneutical principle which we are seeking consists in the first instance simply of this, that the translation does not merely pave the way for proclamation, but demands it, makes it possible, and indeed *initiates* it. The proclamation itself then becomes the true translation of the text. But we should not conclude that the text wants to become proclamation, because it was itself once

[1] W. v. Humboldt, *Über die Verschiedenheit des menschlichen Sprachbaues und ihren Einfluss auf die geistige Entwickelung des Menschengeschlechts*, 1836 (cited from Wasmuth's ed. of 1935), e.g. p. 250.

proclamation. At the time of its origin, the text certainly had a part in the proclamation. But this does not mean that the text was necessarily directly proclamation. Theses about the kerygmatic character of the New Testament are better left out of our context. This applies even to the recently recommended abbreviation 'proclamation history', however meaningful it may be in its application (Hermann Diem). The reason why translation makes the text into proclamation must instead be found and maintained in the word itself.

The word of language is a language-event, which we both receive outwardly with the ear, and which we also grasp and receive inwardly, or else reject or ignore. If we wanted just to say that it was language being spoken, and therefore rather a 'speaking-event', we would then be distinguishing the word, as a brute fact, from the thought which it expresses. But we are better to understand the thought itself as a word, and to equate what is heard outwardly with the ear with what is grasped inwardly, without thereby according a primacy of inward understanding to the discernment appropriate to thought. For the true language-event—for example, an offer—shows that, though it sets our thoughts in motion, it is not itself thought. The immediate harmony between what is said and what is grasped is not the result of a process of thought; it takes place at an earlier stage, as event. Events of this kind take place both in our various moods and in our conscience. These two, mood and conscience, must be brought into harmony, if the word 'gets home'. Only then is a word heard, in the sense of the New Testament texts; the word then finds a sphere in language, and as a result the word itself can and will be *repeated*, because the text has now been *translated*.

We have thus to distinguish, at least in principle, between the text and the word, and in such a way that primacy is given to the word.

2. THE PRIMACY OF THE WORD IN THE NEW TESTAMENT

Proclamation means repeating. What? The word, which should and will be proclaimed. Where? In language. How? As a language-construction, in the same way as the text was a language-construction; therefore in clauses, as the inner form of language. Language,

in its outer form, can basically be repeated at will, but is nevertheless unique, if indeed the word leads to the kind of hearing which
unites mood and conscience in the hearer, because the word has
'struck home'. The word which is intended in this proclamation is
therefore a word which is determined by hearing, not merely a
word which can be heard, but one which in its origin has already
been heard.

Translations are spoiled only at this stage. This is not surprising,
since a word which we hear immediately changes into thoughts.
As a result, there is an interchange or substitution of word and
thought, of proposition and doctrine. For example, the justification
of faith is at once transformed in theology into the doctrine of
justification by faith and not by works. But this doctrine must not
take the place of the text, if proclamation is indeed the intention.
The obvious definition of faith as obedience is also inadequate,
because the doctrine itself must demand obedience, that is,
obedient thought (without thereby being *sacrificium intellectus*).
Faith belongs rather to the word. It is primarily a hearing, and the
proclamation which desires faith is ἀκοή, an inducement to hearing.
What of the word? According to Paul, is it not Christ himself? It is
indeed. Does his proclamation then intend to make Christ heard,
to express him as a word? Certainly. In what way is Christ something like a word? In accordance with what we have said, this
question must also be answered on the basis of hearing. How is
Christ heard? Only in the way that he was originally heard. How
did Paul hear him? This is an awkward question, since the
tradition, right up to the Lucan book of Acts, shows a strong
inclination to tie us down to the fact of Jesus having been seen.
Paul himself expresses this in I Cor. 9.1 and 15.5–8, and John also
emphasizes the fact that the Logos became flesh, and that 'we have
beheld his glory' (John 1.14). In these statements 'seeing' in a
metaphorical sense is certainly mixed with a non-metaphorical
sense, but the two are indeed combined. However, we are concerned here with propositions which are no longer pure proclamation, but are at the same time confessions. Moreover, they
in part belong to doctrine, and in part are the expression of a
mood of joy, which is in accordance with the certainty of faith.

There is no generally unequivocal term for this *certainty* in the
New Testament. But this lack of a concept serves merely to

emphasize its power and significance. Certainty is peculiar to the faith which, like Abraham, does not doubt (Rom. 4.20). The famous passage: I believe, help thou mine unbelief, does not provide a justification for doubt (Mark 9.24). It just means that the person who begins to believe needs Jesus' help, when he is still divided and cannot yet really believe. The antithesis to this is Jesus' word of reply to Thomas, who, in the same way, has not yet really attained to faith: blessed are those who have not seen, and yet believe (John 20.29). True faith shares in God's omnipotence (Mark 9.23). But this does not unite what is God's with what is man's; instead, it keeps the two apart (cf. Mark 10.27). The phrase about mustard-seed faith, which has indeed been 'distorted' (Matt. 17.20; 21.21 par. Mark 11.22f; cf. with Luke 17.6), makes a similar distinction between God's miraculous power and man; but at all events it emphasizes that faith is sure of God's strength, in the same way that the similitude of the mustard-seed itself is (Matt. 13.31f par.). If we want to be on safe ground in the exposition of these sayings which have been attributed to Jesus we must bring them into the context in which the certainty peculiar to faith is made manifest (cf. Matt. 5.48). The certainty of faith depends on the 'object' of faith. But just because it is 'certainty', it can be detected only in faith itself, that is, in man. Nevertheless we are not simply directed to human 'subjectivity', and certainly not to 'correct' doctrinal statements. The certainty of faith is rather the *consequence* of faith in faith, not after faith. Certainty of faith is established in the hearer, when he hears in such a way that he is no longer divided; when instead, as a hearer, he is wholly struck by what he himself is then able to say (Rom. 14.4f, 22). He recognizes this by his ability to describe to others what has struck home to him, in such a way that they can likewise find it striking them (Rom. 14.7–9). The fact of having heard provides the believer with a new *command of language*. Why? Because he is himself able to look beyond himself, when he abides by what he has heard and what can and should be heard by others. For him, his own situation is then transformed into the norm of his language.

There is an analogy which corresponds to this process. In Matt. 5.28 Jesus emphasizes that a man who merely looks at a woman lustfully has already committed adultery in his heart. Will he who loves do this? No. For the lover is entirely filled with love;

he has no desire for another woman. It is the same with faith. The man who is entirely filled with the word which, because of faith, both reached him and means to be passed on, is no longer tied to a variety of things—he is no longer divided and uncertain about what he should listen to. He hears the one word which everyone should want to hear (Luke 10.38–42). He is 'completely filled' with this. It would be interesting to turn at this juncture to a detailed examination of Paul; for he is concerned to show what it is that completely fills man (as 'flesh') when he does not believe (e.g. Rom. 13.14). However, we mean to keep to the question of how Jesus himself can become this word. We can answer the question if we keep in mind that the word (of faith) is a word which can and will be said to *everyone*, since, from the outset, it is a word which in its origin was already heard. This sentence seems to amount to a paradox. But does the New Testament not say of Jesus that he looked beyond himself (e.g. Mark 10.45)? Is Jesus himself, then, on the side of faith? With regard to terminology, we cannot say this, since Jesus never spoke of his faith. In reality he does portray faith, for example in his parables, though for his listeners and not for himself. Jesus *makes* faith into the word, in the form of a parable, for example, and in other ways, too (e.g. Luke 17.33 par.). Jesus reveals faith for a new age (this is the meaning in Gal. 3.23–25). Thus, in regard to Jesus himself, word and faith cannot be separated. They must, however, be distinguished. What faith has heard has, since Jesus, been said; and in this way faith is related to Jesus. Jesus does not invent the word which faith knows. Instead he mints the word for faith. He does not recast it; he says what is to be heard from now on. Therefore he says above all that it is now possible and essential to hear (cf. Mark 4.9 *et al.*). In other words, he says that God speaks through him, indeed that God *has* spoken (Matt. 11.6 par.). Jesus *summons* to faith.

Faith, in the New Testament sense, therefore means that God finally, once and for all, makes himself heard in Jesus. He does this in such a way that man can and must make this word of God his own in faith. If Jesus is to be called God's word, it follows that faith could make Jesus as God's word its own. If Jesus has portrayed or stamped this faith in advance, and if we assume that the New Testament, in its statements *about* Jesus, is firmly determined by this faith, then Jesus' conduct was such that he had to become the image of God's word for faith. In fact, Paul, for example, indicates that God appeared in Jesus in such a way that, in Luther's words, we see into the heart of God (cf. II Cor. 4.4). To 'see the Lord' therefore means the same as to hear God's spoken word (cf. II Cor. 2.17). This is why Paul determines to 'know' only Christ crucified (I Cor. 2.2). By means of this image, he impresses God's word on the communities (Gal. 3.1). Paul regards the crucified Christ as the word of God's love (Rom. 8.32, 39), and in the same way John's Gospel makes God's love the theme of faith in the Logos (John 3.16). God's word is God's 'yes' to man. Man is thereby accepted, recognized, and chosen as God's 'property'. Whoever has dealings with men, has from now on dealings with God—with the God who is revealed in this word and is therefore hidden outside of this word. God himself will be *revealed* as love through faith in this word which is to be proclaimed (I John 4.16). This is what faith has to say. This is why the word both has and retains precedence over everything else, even over the text. Must we add that this word can only be proclaimed as an event, if it is indeed to be believed? A considered 'yes' would remain silent. Jesus *was* God's 'yes' (II Cor. 1.19f).

3. THE TASK OF PROCLAMATION

If the word has precedence over the text, because the word intended in the text is God's word, as it was heard and could be said in Jesus as God's 'yes' to man, faith then has to proclaim this word by repeating Jesus. The task of proclamation is to repeat Jesus.

In this way proclamation participates in God's omnipotence (I John 4.16a). For this very reason the greatest danger threatens at this point. For proclamation must not confuse, but must at this stage strictly distinguish between God and man, between word and text. Only on the basis of this distinction does it become quite clear that proclamation participates in God's omnipotence. The distinction between God and man is not to be equated with a distinction between power and weakness, as if man were innately weak and God, by contrast, the sole power. Religion is usually not just a case of adapting oneself to the inevitable, but also of effecting something—only religions generally prefer to effect the extra-ordinary. Even in the New Testament there are a number of tendencies in this direction. However, they are blocked rather than encouraged, with the result that the New Testament writings stand out from the apocryphal writings by reason of their greater moderation. Along with Jesus and Paul, Christian faith considers instead that what is normal and ordered is extraordinary. For example, it does not reject the 'law' (of Moses); instead it em-phasizes it as God's law. But it indicates that man must make a *new* beginning, if he wants to avoid having God's law against him. Faith thus understands the difference between God and man on the basis of a 'turning' from old to new, which takes place in God as well as in man, but which only comes about in such a way that the new takes place by making everything previous to it old (II Cor. 5.17; Rom. 7.6; II Cor. 3.6).

Even this last assertion remains a pure postulate, as long as it is formulated only in thought. Quite often, and indeed at central points, the New Testament employs a mythical language, so as to avoid surrendering its assertions to the realm of pure thought. It even accepts the inconsistencies of these mythical statements. It is only because of this that a demythologizing of such statements is demanded by the New Testament itself. As is well known, demythologizing does not mean rationalizing, but derationalizing of those mythical statements which, as mythology, have already fallen victim to rationalization. Its intention is to maintain the occurrence-character of the new—an event which is, indeed was, actual—though without allowing the elimination of faith in favour of a purely observable facticity. Only language can accomplish this kind of thing. In accordance with its intention, theology in the New Testament is the conflict between a thinking based on right or order, which threatens from the beginning, and language itself. In accordance with its nature, language in the New Testament speaks on the basis of the event which it passes on. It may thus, in fact, be termed, along with Humboldt, a 'flash' of the spirit.[1] But in this event the language of the New Testament does not repeat reality as our world, in which we consciously find our bearings in language. The intention of the New Testament is to have marked out the root of all language, the

[1] *Ibid.*, p. 249.

word itself (as distinct from the concept or conception), as that event which has its back to everything, even our world—as Helmut Franz rightly stresses in regard to Jesus' sayings.[1] This word hastens on, or goes ahead of all else. The proof of this is precisely the proclamation.

How is the proof of the proclamation achieved? Simply in this way—that everything that man knows becomes so disposable that the word is able to reduce everything else to propositions. Strictly speaking, propositions are self-contained statements, language-constructions in the spirit of objectification. That which allows itself to be put in the proposition has been objectified; I have placed myself at a distance from it. The decisive object of the objectification undertaken in the proclamation of the New Testament, in spite of its mythical ingredient, is not God but man, in the world of his deeds and works which enclose him. Without the word of faith, he can never fully objectify this world, as surely as the word itself belongs primarily to language. Before faith, man lives in the conflict between the deed or work and the word, with the result that, as in the Old Testament, even God meets him only in the sphere of this conflict. By contrast, the New Testament proclamation settles this conflict in favour of the word. It makes the deed subject to the word, through distinguishing first of all between demand and narrative and thus giving the freedom of the word to those who are until then held fast in the compulsion to the deed. This word allows everything to be what it is. For the word satisfies itself simply by speaking. The word certainly still 'strikes home' to me within the old context of the conflict. But it releases me from it, because it fills me completely; that is, it allows me to travel with God along a path which I no longer need to prepare, because it has paved its own way in the word itself. The Old Testament had, of course, already recognized this criterion of the word (Ps. 119.105).

Must the objectification of the New Testament language not, then, lead to the expression of what it is, of which the word is really capable? In fact, the soteriological confessional statements declare what happened 'for us', by including everything, τὰ πάντα, within their radius (e.g. Rom. 8.32). But here the capacity of the word is more clearly demonstrated. When 'everything' becomes

[1] H. Franz, *Kerygma und Kunst*, 1959, p. 91

new, then the propositional truths simultaneously secede from material things (II Cor. 5.17; cf. with I Cor. 3.22f). The earth and its fullness (I Cor. 10.26), Jesus himself, his language of faith—these all merge anew with the word in our existence; they appear as God's property and household. Thus the word is word, inasmuch as it 'identifies' rather than just 'expropriating'. It divides off the old as new from the old as old, and thus makes lasting what can momentarily be said. At this point we move both at a distance from the past and at the same time in intercourse with the present, and thus allow ourselves and what is ours to be measured by this intercourse. In the proclamation of the word, therefore, our intercourse with the present is constantly put to the test. Community is formed. This was the intention.

This means that the text is transposed in the proclamation. There is, of course, no parallel with a commodity which is for sale (II Cor. 2.17; 4.2), but rather with the way the New Testament transposes the Old Testament. This results in the demonstration of what was abolished, although it is still valid for sinners (Gal. 3.25), and of what was confirmed (Gal. 3.6–9). In the same way, the proclamation of faith in God's word transposes the New Testament, with the result that the company of faith understand themselves in community with Jesus, and from this relation everything gains light and colour for them (cf. even Gal. 4.1–7). The proclamation does *not* confront the text with the congregation, but it does make use of the text in such a way that the community with Jesus, the 'word-shaped' nature of faith, its 'capacity', is reflected in it. This is because one person is able to hand on to another the word which all have received in Jesus. The proof of this was Jesus' own word, which can now become the mirror of Jesus. He himself is revealed as God's pledge, as the pearl, the mustard-seed and all his other similar references. His word is revealed as self-witness.

4. THE FULFILMENT OF PROCLAMATION

If proclamation transposes the text through determining its position by faith's community with Jesus, then its particular hermeneutical principle is quite simply the question of whether it can identify the word of Jesus and the 'apostles' with Jesus himself. The 'translation' of the text can therefore never be final, so certain is it that the proclamation will always occur anew. However, the proclamation requires the text, because it only continues what was revealed through Jesus: the event of God's word, which was heard, which was believed because it was heard, and which basically is just one word: God's revelation, the 'yes' by which God accepts, recognizes and chooses all that is his own as his own, as surely as God himself means to be present to man (Gal. 4.9), and gives him presence, so that he may live with God (Rom. 4.17). The above-mentioned analogy of love (Matt. 5.28) is at this point set aside as an analogy, so that love 'fulfils' all in all (Eph. 1.23). He who wants to proclaim correctly must then translate the text of love back into the word of love. To this end he need only ask himself what love is able to do in the congregation as a community. He will then find the word, of which the historical Jesus will remain the image and expression, as long as the New Testament can be read aloud and as long as it is translated, as long, therefore, as a congregation knows that it lives by faith in the word. Word and faith belong together, because love has a text which allows their unity to be brought into language only in the faith of those who are called to love, and which also wants to be brought into language as the word of love. The word finds faith as soon as faith has found the word which precedes the text. Proclamation should therefore keep to the path of the text and be faithful to scripture, in so far as it translates the text into the word which produced the text, because it was the word of loving faith, and the word which constantly demands new faith, because faith always originated only in the hearing of the believer himself. Consequently, only that word of faith can qualify as *text* which will assist the proclamation of the word, which knows, therefore, that it is not the fact of having heard but only the hearing itself which determines the truth of the text. The text, then, subserves the proclamation of faith and thereby the revelation of love, and delivers to faith as the decisive gift of love the word which was vicariously portrayed in the text.

If the word of faith which is alive in the proclamation is understood as the gift through which love gives its pledge to us, we have at last found a hermeneutical principle which binds together translation and proclamation. This principle, which maintains the word as a gift, has achieved its expression in the New Testament in the Lord's Supper. Good exegesis is exegesis in the light of the Lord's Supper. Proclamation accords with the sacrament when the preacher translates and speaks in such a way that the congregation are aware of being included with their dead. Then nothing is prematurely separated, but everything in its place is submitted to God. The task of proclamation, which is laid on faith by the phenomenon of the text, is not what men expect or even demand, but what God expects from the proclamation of his word—the fostering of his gift, of the word. He who, through proclamation, passes on the gift which, right up to the text, God meant to give, gives the word and speaks in love. It is the passing on of the word of love which fulfils love. For the other side of love begins with death. God is not dead—he is not the moral root of metaphysics, although he makes use of metaphysics in the course of the world of nature created by him, in order to provide faith with an image of his faithfulness in nature also—instead, God *is* death. However, death, as it is understood here, is not the death of love, but the essence of love, because love has its own time. Love remains. Love therefore reveals itself as death only at the point where it has already everlastingly given life. Love is not perfected in itself —it has no need of this—it is perfected at the point where, along with its word, it emerges from itself as the all-deciding power. The man who abides in love by following love, because he hands on its word with which it gives its promise, because it *unites* life and death—this man abides in God and God in him. The New Testament means to say that God takes us back to himself through his word. Is this not the meaning of the 'kerygma' in the textual context of the New Testament (Rom. 1.1–7)?

At this point the task of proclamation is once again and finally revealed to us. The task is falsely represented when death is understood as something which always concerns me alone, and is considered 'irreplaceable' as an *'existentiell'* event. The kerygma says instead that Jesus has died 'for us'. That is not a mythological statement. If it is to be understood, the positive meaning of death must be disclosed. Death belongs unavoidably to the rule of the love which alone fully earns the name of love—to the love which makes all things 'new'. Death is God's deed, God's epiphany, because it is said that Jesus has died (and has been raised from the dead) for us. As the turning-point of existence, it has become no longer my death but my life. This life is no longer the far side (*das Jenseits*) of a sinful isolated existence, but the near side (*das Diesseits*) of God, who, in Jesus, has begun anew to accompany us on the path of life. What has to be proclaimed is the gift that God gave to faith. Its proof, which has constantly to be tested, is certainly found in face of the phenomenon of death, but not primarily at the grave: death is conquered, because it has become replaceable (Rom. 8.2; I Cor. 15.55–57).[1] Death's exclusively personal nature (*Jemeinigkeit*) has been replaced by the wide-embracing life before God, the 'earnest' of the Spirit which creates life, because it says: Jesus is Lord. Proclaim this. Then you yourself are translated (Gal. 4.9).

[1] For another view, and one which agrees with Bultmann, see H. Conzelmann, 'Die Überwindung der Weltangst durch den Glauben', in *Mensch und Kosmos* (Eine Ringvorlesung der theologischen Fakultät Zürich), 1960, p. 59.

IX

WHAT IS A 'LANGUAGE-EVENT'?

A Letter
1960

. . . Bultmann accuses me of confusing language and speaking, because I talk of a 'language-event' instead of contenting myself with the expression 'speaking-event' which, according to his view, would be adequately suited to what I mean. I wonder. The question which is directed to being (*Sein*) would surely have advised him otherwise. Certainly if being is abruptly equated with 'actuality', and if one is content to investigate the respective structure of an entity, then naturally the only point of departure is that in language an entity is clarified for what it is. But it is just this that I guard against. I could only consider this conception to be positivism. By the term 'actuality' I understand a being that is always already objectified. Objectified being in fact provides action with its possibilities. If one deals with Christian faith from this point, one will not be content to allow the possibilities for faith to be conditioned by the actuality which is at everyone's disposal. One will instead attempt to claim the actual as a special instance of the possible. Thus Bultmann came to speak of the historicality (*Geschichtlichkeit*) of human existence. But here there is still the threat of theology unilaterally reserving for itself a phenomenon which is demonstrable quite apart from all theology. This is why I took up the quest for being itself, and thus in my own way came upon language, whereas Bultmann contented himself in this quest with a transcendental philosophy and applied Heidegger's *Sein und Zeit* accordingly. In Bultmann the core of 'historicality' is not time, but the will (Kant).

What does language do? It justifies being. How does it do this? It permits being to be 'present' in time; it makes being into an event. If language were to be content just with an entity, if it were without ado to assign being to thought and so render being 'significant' only as an entity, then Bultmann would be right. But language does more. It makes not just the entity but being itself into an event. What is happening here? To put it briefly: an admission. If I use your example and say, 'These sheep are beautiful', then I most certainly point out the beautiful sheep. But by means of this sentence I have already admitted that the beauty of the sheep is the essential thing between them and us, that it is the ruling factor, in so far as I enter upon this essence. In this way is preserved the '*existentiell*' condition of the access to the entity, with which Bultmann also is concerned. There is no weight to the objection that this is particularly the case in aesthetics. Rather: such a thing always happens *as* language. Language assumes the essential characteristic of being—that is, that it gathers together. This requires language, in order to be. Only in language is being by its nature necessarily an event, as a 'path' (Wilhelm von Humboldt).[1] When this is seen, new possibilities are gained, for example for the genitive interpretation. Bultmann is inclined to interpret the Χριστοῦ εἶναι in Gal. 3.29 as a possessive genitive. But if the σῶμα Χριστοῦ conception is based on the genitive, then the possessive is no longer adequate. We now more probably have a partitive genitive for consideration, because the believers belong not only along with Christ but to Christ. We must, then, ask where Christ is accessible in this way. Even the σῶμα conception is no longer adequate. Christ means to be understood as the one to whom we belong as *believers*. This happens in the proclamation. But the proclamation does not just bring a conception into language; it decides where Christ, as the one who gathers us, is present, assuming that we give heed to the proclamation and so believe. This is not just a speaking-event, because the proclamation does not just make real a conception which is in itself available to us, and because faith does not just practise what it believes. The relation between the indicative and the imperative of faith by no means forces a return to the possessive circumstances; even the assertion that there is a paradox here would be inadequate and liable to be overturned. Christ means instead to be proclaimed, and the question is whether *we* are ready for this proclamation. As the proclamation gathers around Christ, there is no faith with-

---

[1] Cf. my *Hermeneutik*, pp. 109f (Herodotus's mouse). Being is what comes to light. This means to enter language.

out the community of Jesus Christ. And this community has its being, its 'togetherness', in the possibility of its being able to speak the kind of language in which the event of its community is fulfilled. This language-*activity* is the mark of the community. *The language of faith brings into language the gathering of faith and thereby Christ.* It admits Christ into that existence which we ourselves enter upon in the *name* of Jesus. We are then repeatedly able to name Jesus as our Lord, to each other and to the world. Now we ourselves are able to say what God does in Phil. 2.9. This is a language-event. For example, the mistaken usage of the name 'brother' both conceals and also quite clearly demonstrates this same matter. The other person is not simply called a brother because he is; he would not be a brother, if I did not so call him. Through my calling him brother I certainly do not make him into one, but I admit him as a brother among us by myself entering this community with him. This event is the very happening with which language is concerned. The concrete word is what first raises being into being, admits gathering as gathering and therefore also allows it. Language is thus concession (*Zulassung*) in admission (*Einlass*). The language-event can, then, be described as 'permission' (*Erlaubnis*).

The concrete 'here and now', with which Bultmann was once concerned, is thus disclosed in language itself. But language is not the handmaiden of the 'here and now'. Being without language is nothing; it is not even nature. Even nature is meant to enter language through our formulation of natural laws. This very example shows that language does not just belong to the poets, but that for its part it is under obligation; not an obligation to the entity, but rather to being, because being and language 'need' each other. The meanings of an entity are not always already there; they are for their own part historical, and therefore bound to the event of language. If Jesus was to be brought into language, because God wanted to enter language in him, this was by no means a concrete possibility, for example for the Old Testament.

Language certainly has man as its object, and being is bound in relation to existence. In this I most certainly agree with Bultmann. But conversely both being and also man have language as their object. And accordingly we are bound in relation to God. Only then is it meaningful to say that God has always spoken and that we are sinners because we would not hear. Now indeed every gift, our nourishment, for instance, speaks to us as a word. Hence I can describe the 'sacramental' happening as the hermeneutical principle of faith. The sacrament is not a speaking-event but a language-event. The word of God admits the living *with* the dead, in order that we may enter upon this eschatological gathering. This is the real meaning of talk about the resurrection of the dead, of the crucified Christ. Whoever really wants to demythologize New Testament eschatology must understand it as a language-event. The New Testament understanding of the sacrament does this. It abides by the word of the Creator which calls to life.

The responsibility for speaking already rests on language and is not outside language. This is my thesis. Whoever takes note of this recognizes that language 'imparts'. Language is not the abbreviation of thought; thought is the abbreviation of language. Language is giving. It assimilates and acquires through its taking place. When someone says 'yes' he bestows that admission in which he himself is imparted. So God says his 'yes' not to strangers but to his own, and in this he imparts himself as the one who belongs to us. This is not an addition or application which God makes of himself or adds to himself. It is the event in which God himself takes place as love and so imparts love.[1] Therefore, because in the case of both God and man the 'yes' really permits understanding, I maintain that the 'yes' is the word of all words and that the Johannine ἐγώ εἰμι is that particular language-event in which God quite simply expressed himself as the word, as the 'yes'. Faith can wish only to correspond to this, by holding fast on its part to what it has heard, and making confession here and now to God's 'yes' in the crucified Christ. Confession means being able to call by name. We have just as little control over this as we have over language. Language is present as language only where it takes place. The fact that we tame language by forcing it into a position inferior to thought simply means that we are sinners, because we supplant the God who speaks by man, who, to be sure, is able to act. But action is in itself devoid of language, just as science is action in the imperative. Language, however, does not accept orders, not even from science; instead it admits everything within its boundaries, and thus reveals the boundaries and possibilities

[1] Cf. my article 'Logos' in *RGG* IV, cols. 439f (exposition of John 1.1ff).

of existence. It is only from the language-event that we gain the
freedom to act and to think within the correct bounds. Only now
is a basis provided for the way that Bultmann correctly related
thought to existence and thereby sought to distinguish thought
and conceptions from each other. I am not suffering under any
misapprehension, but I must charge him with an astonishing lack
of consistency, because he is content with Wilhelm Herrmann's
categories of the historicality of existence. Why can Luther describe the existence of the believer as 'word-formed'? Surely not
for the sake of *mortificatio activa*. The struggle between 'fact' and
'word' must be resolved in favour of the word.[1]

Like Bultmann I also deny that anyone could have 'control'
over faith. But the basis for this lies not in the factuality of sin,
but rather in faith's dependence on the word, on God's word.
Bultmann's talk of the historicality of existence certainly suffices
to illuminate for us this relation between word and faith as one
tied to the text.[2] But it does not make clear that the fact that faith
is not a matter of our disposing is founded not just on the factuality of sin. This is why I went on to demonstrate the historicality
of existence as the language-character of existence, and to claim
the text itself as an aid to this endeavour. For this reason also it
seems to me that, for example, the popular talk of the 'originality'
of the text and the proclamation is inadequate. The hermeneutical
problem has thus been altered. What matters is not just to explore
the conditions under which the text becomes comprehensible, but
equally to enquire what is to be disclosed *through* the phenomenon
of the 'text'. The text is therefore not just the servant that trans-
mits kerygmatic formulations, but rather a master that directs us
into the language-context of our existence, in which we exist
'before God'. I do not say that language is a work of the Holy
Spirit. But the Bible, as the text of proclamation, might, in fact, be
a work of the Holy Spirit. It must be read critically so that it
corrects our criticism of God. Thus the Church on its part is a
hermeneutical condition of biblical interpretation, but not its
guardian, and it must certainly be said that the decisive part in the

---

[1] For Luther's theology cf. Ebeling's detailed article in *RGG* IV, cols. 495–516.
[2] The text binds faith to the *verbum externum*. Jesus' parables reach the same point
by means of the image which appears in the parable. The 'text' therefore represents
Christ's cross, Jesus' historicity, as an *externum*, which compels us to hear, in order
that Jesus might enter language.

illuminating of our existence belongs to the biblical text. The text itself (as a 'language-gain') is a hermeneutic, with the result that exegesis must always be continued, because at any one stage it concludes with the proclamation. Proclamation and the language-character of existence belong together. *Therefore it is really the present that is interpreted with the help of the text.* This is the hermeneutical step which Bultmann's work inevitably demands if exegesis and proclamation are not to be wrongly confused, that is, if exegesis is, in fact, to remain research (criticism), too—as Bultmann has given such an exemplary lead in doing. My opponent is not Bultmann, but those who by their nature are hostile to the word—the historical theology which despairs of the word, which confuses faith and thought, with the result that both suffer damage. . . .

X

THE ESSENCE OF THE 'LANGUAGE-EVENT' AND CHRISTOLOGY[1]
1962

I. THE PROBLEM

IN the last few years our enquiries have again been directed to the historical Jesus. Rudolf Bultmann, who in 1926 himself published a book about Jesus which remains the best up to the present day, has rejected the new quest as theologically irrelevant. At least it is in his opinion not in keeping with the essence of faith in Jesus Christ. His main argument is that the enquiry into the historical Jesus cannot and indeed should not contribute to faith in Jesus Christ. The enquiry should not contribute anything to faith, because faith in Jesus Christ dispenses with every security or support; and it cannot contribute anything, because the certainty peculiar to faith is not to be mixed up with the uncertainty and relativity of historical research. The basis and content of faith are identical. For faith in Jesus Christ is obedient rendering up of the self. Such rendering up of the self is obedient response to the paradoxical truth that the historical event of Jesus Christ is the eschatological event. This means that the believer is aware of being asked whether he will recognize that the crucified Jesus is to be proclaimed as the resurrected Christ; and whether he is therefore willing to recognize that Jesus becomes present for us as the word of God only through this proclamation. If then Jesus is present only in this marvellous manner, he is present for us in no other way, not even through historical research.

I am not quite sure if I have done justice to Bultmann's view in this presentation of it. And I openly admit that it is not clear to me whether in this matter Bultmann has a firm view at all, or whether he wavers about how he should make up his mind. Is he giving up his book on *Jesus*? In my own opinion it must, in fact,

[1] From *Theologia Viatorum* 8, 1961–2, pp. 38–50. Cf. *Theology Today*, 19.3, 1962, pp. 341ff.

be stated that faith responds to the proclamation of the word of God in this way, that he who is questioned and grasped by the proclamation confesses for his part—Jesus is God's word. Without a confession of this kind the hearer of the proclamation would not become a 'partner' of the proclamation. The proclamation, however, is intended to have or win its hearer as a 'partner'. All of us, and not just the apostles of long ago, can become partners of the Christian proclamation.

In the word which is to be proclaimed there is therefore contained a question which is addressed to the hearer. The hearer is, however, not simply asked if he will accept and hand on a list of doctrinal points which is presented to him. Otherwise the Church of the word of God would simply be a union of theologians imposing their will on the world. What the hearer is asked is if he will, through his own decision, give precision to the proclamation. The proclamation then consists not simply in the recital of doctrinal points, nor even in the repetition of facts which have at some time taken place. Instead, the proclamation poses the question which the hearer has to answer by his faith. This means that only the faith of the hearer makes evident as the word of God the word that is proclaimed to him. For this reason the proclamation is consummated in the confession of faith, and it is a contradiction of the free nature of the word which is to be proclaimed when in worship we come forward with the confession of faith before the proclamation takes place. The dynamic circle which links proclamation and confession of faith must include the active attitude of the hearer. The hearer should not be constrained to limp into place behind a previously established unity of preaching and confession. For the word of God sets free. But it only sets free the man who, having heard, is able himself to acknowledge the proclamation as the liberating word of God. The word of God is certainly not made into the word of God by the hearer. But the word of God does not reveal itself as such, it does not appear as the word of God, unless it is believed as the word of God. This only happens when the hearer realizes that he is placed in the position of answering the proclamation with his own confession. The confession of faith should not then be forestalled by the preaching. However, the question now arises, why the believer continually needs preaching, although the issue was always the further confession of faith.

What, then, is proclaimed when the resurrection of Jesus is proclaimed? There meets us in the proclamation of the resurrection of Jesus the stumbling-block of his cross. This stumbling-block has always to be overcome anew, and therefore it keeps reappearing. In actual fact our reason refuses to believe things that cannot be conceived. Does reason know what sin is? How are we to conceive of a man without sin? As an angel perhaps? But what is an angel? In mythological language is there not also a fallen angel? Obviously reason and its criteria by-pass what we actually have in mind when we speak of sin. Nor is sin simply immorality, though it may lead to immorality. Probably we only really recognize sin when we are freed from it. Sin is then a mark of the 'whole' man. What the 'whole' man is—one who can be not only sinful but also free from sin—first appears in the moment of self-confrontation. Something like this happens too in a secular judgment. But it also happens in the Christian proclamation, as soon as it is recognized that the stumbling-block of the proclamation of the resurrection of Christ is, in fact, the proclamation of the stumbling-block of his crucifixion. We reject the crucified Jesus as the word of God, if we maintain that his being proclaimed as the resurrected Christ is senseless. But the crucified Jesus *must* be proclaimed as the resurrected Christ, because he is not to be swallowed up in death, but is to remain present as the word of God. In terms of this apostolic insight, are we to attribute only one meaning or significance to Jesus (in the way that all historical phenomena can become meaningful)? What, for example, is the difference between Leonidas, who fell fighting for his fatherland, and the crucified Jesus? Leonidas gains his significance from the fact that he did what perhaps anyone else should have done, as soon as the battle had been joined. From the start we are in agreement with Leonidas, for we see in him one of us, and the result is that Leonidas has necessarily to become a prototype. In the case of Jesus it is quite different. His death on the cross is not an example, but a stumbling-block. The proclamation therefore asks us if we are prepared to let the stumbling-block of Jesus' crucifixion become a judgment on our own existence. The question shows that, as soon as our life is at stake, we reckon not with the defeat but with the victory. When we sacrifice ourselves for others we hope that they will be victorious as the result of our sacrifice. We want to be victorious, because we understand ourselves as being worthy of life. But Jesus' crucifixion shatters our worthiness.

If we submit to that, then the proclamation tells us that this judgment emanates from God. In this judgment God intends to demonstrate his graciousness towards us. We must let it come to this, then—the message thrusts us right into the 'nothingness' of our existence, in order to declare God as the sole saving power. As this power is in Jesus, so it extends to us. That is to say, it is 'for us' for Jesus' sake. God bestows life through bringing death (I Cor. 15.36). Consequently God has revealed himself in Jesus as the paradox of our correctly understood existence, an existence received through obedience which is the rendering up of ourselves. If someone enquires after God, then the Christian believer must say to him: God is the paradox of our existence. The paradox is in the first instance the expression of an '*existentiell*' antithesis between spirit and flesh, between surrender and self-assertion. But within this contrast God is the power of any one life, a power which is beyond the realm of our disposal, and which only encounters the man who, in response to its bidding, repeatedly accepts and recognizes that his personal being (*Dasein*) is, in fact, under the power of death; a man therefore who wills to exist in faith in this word or bidding of God. That is, authentic existence, which can already be comprehended by the philosopher, can be realized only in faith. I am asked how I understand myself, if I want to have a future. My relation to the future decides whether or not I exist authentically.

Bultmann's reference to a philosophy which clarifies the structure of existence has often caused concern. However, theology, if it is to be *doctrina* (i.e. if it is to preserve truths), also requires concepts. For the expositor of the New Testament there arose the hermeneutical problem of how he, as an historian, could do justice to the documents handed down to him. As these documents proffered and at the same time removed their subject, so they posed for the historian the question of his own existence. Bultmann understands this question of one's own existence as one which also motivates historical study precisely because it is a demanding question. The consciousness, say, of the Apostle Paul as the author of his letters, may well have been one which was continually different, and which was immediately accessible at most for those to whom he then wrote and for those who signed the letters with him. However, the self-understanding which directed his ministry (διακονία) is accessible also to the reader of today, because Paul considered it important that he should without exception (even in the case of a congregation he did not know) be understood as a believer, and that his letters should be read by people who were committed to faith. The question of what self-understanding this faith implies is therefore prompted, and at least in part demanded, by the documents themselves. Basically therefore (i.e. with regard to method), the situation of the expositor of the New Testament could be explicated as the endeavour to work out an existential interpretation of the documents. Such an 'existential interpretation' was understood simply as knowledge of the distinction between authentic and inauthentic existence, so that the question could be asked: When did the documents have authentic existence in mind? What features in the New Testament would be characteristic of authentic existence? 'Fear and trembling' perhaps? Or a state of tranquillity in one's consciousness, achieved through peace of conscience? Or both together? In addition the expositor had to keep in mind that such questions confronted him also outside the New Testament. Exposition became the contribution of the theologian to the present-day philosophical interpretation of existence, in so far as the expositor had indeed to concern himself with the task of disclosing the structure of our existence, that is of our personal being (*Dasein*), as historical (*geschichtlich*): historical in the sense that it always converges on the moment of our decision concerning ourselves. Therefore, if it was stated that man is always concerned with his own self, then in this thesis, with its relation to conscience, the essence of human personal being was described as that which is always completely at stake. In this hermeneutic, authentic existence is to be understood as my existence which I have to decide in the moment of existing. 'What am I living for?' man must ask, if he wants to exist authentically. Is it that for which I die? Each individual has received his personal being only in an historical context. It follows then, with regard to the existence of the individual in that moment which is for him decisive, that the context itself in which he conducts his life must be the subject of discussion.

This analysis of human personal being disclosed the present as the meaning of history. One had to say to a person: you live for the present, in the sense that historically (as one existing between past and future) you are responsible for the present. If you want indeed to be a real person, this responsibility must direct your self-understanding. Bultmann added to this that Paul and the author of the Fourth Gospel proclaimed this kind of responsibility for the present as an eschatological event. That is to say, the present, as the object of the responsibility of the individual, and thereby as the content of his personal being, is at the same time the gift of man's being before God (*Sein vor Gott*). If, in the existential analysis of personal being, the future addresses to the individual the question, whether he is willing to understand himself in contemplation of that which is past, by allowing the responsibility for the present as the meaning of history—a responsibility which falls to him in a concrete way—to be disclosed to him, then the message of the New Testament says to the individual that the responsibility for the present sets him free for a future in which man is relieved of the burden of the past. The message of the New Testament therefore radicalizes human existence, with its demand that I accept the present as true, by accepting my responsibility for proclaiming that the end of history always occurs in my own present. The result is that the past then sinks away, because it is the will of God himself, *extra nos*, to be our future. God is the paradox of our existence, when we become conscious of the present not only as the meaning of history, but as at the same time the end of history. This is what it would mean to have faith in God. The self-understanding of faith then most certainly includes a consciousness. However, in so far as faith, in this understanding of the present as the end of history, understands God as the one who bestows on us 'presence' as a gift, then God becomes that which corresponds to authentic human existence. The believer is responsible before God, while he is at all times accountable for his understanding of the present; and that is responsibility for choosing whether or not he lives out the present as the wonderful gift and work of God. If the believer lives out the present as the gift and work of God, then he also gives up the past of his own works in favour of the future, without allowing himself to be led astray by death. Faith therefore continually requires renewal, in order to go into the future with the present, that is, in order to remain present faith. Faith, therefore, continually requires the word which calls to faith. That is the meaning of Christian baptism, for example. (For baptism delivers us from the coercive course of history, that is, from the law of sin and death.)

So the *problem* arises: How is the proclamation, required by faith, to be provided? In my opinion this problem can be resolved by an understanding of the connexion between the essence of the 'language-event' and Christology. We can now pose the question: Why does the preaching of faith have a text?

2. THE HERMENEUTICAL SIGNIFICANCE OF THE 'SITUATION'

The question why the preaching of faith should have a text can indeed be answered simply thus: because the preaching of faith is the preaching of the gospel. And the preaching of the gospel, as in the case of Paul, is relatively easily paraphrased as the proclamation of grace, in terms of the contrast between faith and the works of the law. Indeed, this procedure leads also to the concept to which I shall be referring in what follows: the concept of the 'situation'. This procedure has, however, the disadvantage that it is dogmatically weighted, because we assume we know that the situation of man before God is the being of man under the law. As a result of this assumption one becomes involved in the discussion of the usage or *usus*, of the law, which is also variously applied exegetically; in the light of faith in the gospel the law appears other than it does apart from faith.

Is there, however, for the question which investigates the text of preaching, any other procedure than that of the distinction between law and gospel? From the exegetical point of view, some other is to be expected. For the Pauline antithesis between faith and the works of the law is not dominant, for example, in the Synoptic Gospels (although it is taken into consideration in the Fourth Gospel; compare John 1.17 with 6.28). The Synoptic Gospels still preserve for us some insight into Jesus' own proclamation. Jesus' proclamation shows us that he understood himself as the one who 'brought into language' the call of God in the final hour. 'Leave the dead to bury their dead' (Luke 9.60). 'Whoever would save his life will lose it' (Mark 8.35). 'Whoever gives heed to Jesus will find in God a father' (Luke 15.11ff). 'Blessed is he who takes no offence at me' (Luke 7.23 par. Matt. 11.6). One could take offence at Jesus. For in his attitude to those publicans and sinners who were prepared to hear him he portrayed God's rule, and thereby excluded from God's saving word the representatives of the law of Moses, who rejected him (so the Sermon on the Mount). We must try to see this conduct of Jesus in harmony with the keen accent of his language.

I understand Jesus' proclamation as a 'language-event'. That is not to say that Jesus created new concepts. It is his parables which are typical of Jesus. These parables certainly contain the same proclamation as the 'logia' quoted above. But they go further than the 'logia' in this respect at least, that in the parables Jesus' understanding of his situation 'enters language' in a special way. The special characteristic of the parables becomes clear as soon as we try to 'objectify' them. Matthew has already done this by relating the parables directly to the rule of God. He probably provides in this way the correct exposition, so long as we hold simply to his key-word, and not to his occasional commentaries and additions (as, for example, his explanations of the parables of the wheat and the tares, and of the net, Matt. 13.36–43, 49f). Without doubt Jesus' parables summon to decision, just as his 'logia' do. Like the man who found treasure, or the pearl merchant who found the one pearl of great price, the hearer must stake all on one thing— that he win the future which Jesus proclaims to him. But this 'all' is not restricted to external possessions. What is meant is that one must allow oneself to be laid hold of. This can happen in no other way than that the man who is addressed understands himself anew, in that he receives himself from God as a new creature, who is able to love even his enemy (Luke 6.27bf; Matt. 5.44f). It is clear that this kind of conduct simply corresponds to Jesus' conduct to obvious sinners. Thereby it is also made clear that the rule of God already begins to be effective in the presence of Jesus, so that one can speak of 'blessed eyewitnesses' (Matt. 13.16f par. Luke 10.23f).

Jesus does not put his own words into other people's mouths. They themselves have to be able to say what they have understood. This is why he speaks to them in parables, which simply portray the new situation. Between the present which they share with Jesus, and the future in which God is to accomplish his rule, they find themselves, as between a tiny beginning and a magnificent end: that is the intention of the similitude of the mustard-seed and the leaven (Matt. 13.31f par.; 13.33 par.). But all of them, together with Jesus, move *within* this occurrence, when they understand and have faith; even though, in relation to the rule of God, their faith itself appears like a grain of mustard-seed (Matt. 17.20 par.).

This is the decisive achievement of the parables of Jesus: whoever understands and goes this way moves already in a new context, in being before God. He can then relate God to himself in a relationship like that of the prodigal son to his loving father, and like that of the labourer who actually came too late to the generous lord of the vineyard. Thus Jesus intends to 'bring God into language'. Whoever goes this way—the Gospels call this 'following', or the way of discipleship—will then himself be in the position to appeal to God as Jesus did. From this there arises his all-embracing prayer (Matt. 6.9–13; Luke 11.2–4, cf. 5–8; also 18.9–14, cf. 1–8). Jesus' proclamation bestows on these people 'freedom for the word'.

The 'language-event' of this proclamation is thereby already described. We notice that every 'speaking' has a content. What is the presupposition for being able to speak in terms of content? The statement that all speaking is related to our conceptions of the subjects spoken of would hardly be sufficient. For our conceptions come not only from our own observations, but also from the stock of conceptions which has accumulated both unnoticed and openly in our consciousness. In relation to our current observations we bring also a pre-understanding, upon which our language capacity has extensively played. However, it cannot be denied that current observations continually bring a fresh impetus to our language. Hence a new observation can throw all our previous conceptions into confusion, or rearrange them completely; as, for example, our observing the slaughter of an animal, and the way this is done. What has been observed in other ways and preserved in conceptions comes into conflict with that which is newly observed, and so demands a comparison. This comparison requires from us a decision. Only when the decision is made can I speak further. My language is therefore never solely the expression of single conceptions, but is always at the same time the expression of a decision. In this decision there takes place the adjustment which supersedes the differences in my conceptions. This power of language which creates unity is what I call the 'language-event'. For in language I do not remain self-contained as I do in thinking. In language I expose those conceptions which I have unified to the agreement or contradiction of others. That is by no means to say that we live dialectically. Our language moves rather in a being which, as that decision concerning the unity of our conceptions, is indeed always my being; but in that it is always my being it reveals the situation, in which the being of others strives after an adjustment with my being. This means that we have a common understanding, whether friendly or hostile, of how we conceive ourselves, *because* we speak with each other. The real content of language, that which is an event not only in language but also precisely as language among men, is therefore being itself. But because being itself discloses in language something like our situation, as that which is ever and again understood between us, I term being itself *situation*. Situation is the essence of the 'language-event'.

3. THE CHRISTOLOGICAL REFERENCE OF THE 'LANGUAGE-EVENT'

The concept of the situation, which is understood as the essence of the 'language-event', is able to reveal that Jesus' person belongs to the content of his proclamation. This makes it possible to answer the question of how Jesus' person belongs to his proclamation and to the proclamation of faith in Jesus. Then it will also be clear why the preaching of faith has a text.

Whoever speaks of God as Jesus does alters and fixes the situation of man, and thereby of being, as the content of language. Unless his hearers were firmly determined to listen to him, Jesus' proclamation, just like Paul's, had necessarily to throw their traditional conceptions into confusion. This can be seen from the antitheses of the Sermon on the Mount in Matt. 5. Had, then, the word of the law of Moses, delivered to those of old, been invalid? No, it had become invalid. Under what condition? At the point when the situation of man before God had changed. This is just what Jesus said: 'But I say to you . . .' We can therefore speak of a claim of Jesus, which met and meets everyone's situation.

This claim of Jesus leads to catastrophe, as is seen in the peri-copes relating the assertion of authority in Jerusalem (Mark 11.27–33 par.; 12.13–17, 18–27, 28–34, 35–37 par.). Here indeed is more than Jonah or Solomon (Luke 11.29–33 par.), and even more than the Baptist (Mark 11.33 par.; Matt. 11.11 par.). It is certainly possible, and from an outward point of view even pro-bable, that Jesus was, so to speak, accidentally arrested, as a result of a riot in the forecourt of the temple in Jerusalem, which may even have been caused by his followers; and that Jesus was for this reason crucified by the Romans. It is also quite possible that the cause of the riot was a temper of immediate eschatological expectation on the part of Galileans who knew Jesus. However, it is hardly permissible simply to gainsay the presentation of the evangelists, even that of the Fourth Gospel, when their presenta-tion of Jesus' passion lends to the events the interpretation which is, in fact, in principle appropriate. Jesus' claim to being heard was from the beginning openly made, in the same way that the Baptist openly appeared in the Jordan region outside Jerusalem. It would have contradicted the whole proclamation of Jesus if in Jerusalem he had asserted his claim only in seclusion. Jesus' claim was radical, for he conceived the situation of man before God as 'presence'. Only he who gave heed to Jesus could, according to Jesus' claim, be certain that he found himself *within* a saving relationship to God. This proclamation was a direct challenge to the Jewish cult and to the ruling operation of the law, because Jesus claimed to bring God himself decisively 'into language', while offering to each of his hearers a new self-understanding before God, because it was a 'being to God'.

Whoever made the decision for this new self-understanding had given heed to God, in that he believed in Jesus' proclamation (cf. Mark 1.15). However, Jesus had not in any way made special claims for his own person. Obviously he fully accepted the offence of his person (Matt. 11.6 par.). It will then be correct for us to set out from some point other than Jesus' authority. This concept is better suited to the critique of opponents, and to the proclamation of the early Church. The Church awaited the crucified Jesus as the messianic Son of Man coming to judgment; just as Paul, too, could proclaim him as the Lord and the Son of God at God's judgment seat (II Cor. 5.10; cf. Rom. 1.4). In the case of the historical Jesus himself one has solely to hold fast to the fact that he was conscious of the scandal of his claim, and wanted therefore to justify himself purely on the grounds of his proclamation. But the legitimation of Jesus' proclamation lay completely in the future; and that remained so, however near this future may have approached (cf. Luke 11.20 par. Matt. 12.28). This is why Jesus demanded decision in regard to his own person—this much at least can be gathered from those sayings of disputed authenticity which tell of the judgment of the coming Son of Man (Luke 12.8f; Mark 8.38). For Jesus' conduct towards those publicans and sinners who were prepared to hear him (Matt. 11.19 par. Luke 7.34; cf. also Mark 2.14f par.) cannot be separated from his parables which summon to decision, any more than it can from the 'logia' which summon to decision, and from his calls of woe.

As his conduct shows, Jesus clearly did not want to be understood apart from his proclamation, but rather in it. His whole proclamation is one single self-testimony, not as witness for his possible messianic consciousness (for in my opinion Jesus spoke definitely of the future Son of Man), but because this proclamation presupposes a new being of man, in which God speaks with the individual; and as a result, the individual also is able to speak freely of God, as the parables of the labourers in the vineyard and the prodigal son do. (The early Christian formula *Maranatha*—I Cor. 16.22—could quite conceivably also have been used by Jesus, when it is understood as an appeal to God.) Jesus did not claim for himself a special position before God. He understood himself as the *witness of a new situation*, as the authentic witness for the exposition of the future of the rule of God; an exposition which is valid now in his own presence (Luke 11.20 par. Matt. 12.28). He therefore summoned men, his contemporaries, to the rule of God (Matt. 5.3–12; cf. Luke 6.20–23). These were men who had everything to expect from God and nothing more from the world—and therefore men like Jesus himself. God would recompense them all in wonderful measure (Mark 10.29f par.; cf., however, also the parable of the sower, Mark 4.1–9 par.; further Matt. 6.1–18).

The criterion for Jesus' understanding of his being and for his self-understanding, in short, for his understanding of the situation, is not a psychological one. Nor may it be sought in individual eschatological conceptions. Form-critical dissection has indicated the twofold nature of the tradition, of Jesus as a teacher of wisdom and Jesus as an eschatological prophet. And when Bultmann enquires after the essential unity of this dual tradition, he has, with the formulation of this question, already taken the decisive step towards understanding Jesus' proclamation. If we separate the genetic question of the development of the individual parts of the tradition and their forms from the question of the essential reference to the entire proclamation of Jesus, then it at once becomes clear that Jesus understands everything he says as bound up with the situation. He refers back to himself in so far as he carries the responsibility for his summons to the decision, with which the situation before God must be answered. Only *within* the situation can the situation before God be proclaimed and answered. This means, each person can in truth only answer by understanding himself in relation to the proclamation, within the situation before God, and therefore from the situation before God. Otherwise he rejects Jesus. Jesus therefore demands decision, particularly in the 'logia'; but he brings the situation itself only indirectly 'into language' in the parables, with the result that each individual has the responsibility of understanding where he is prepared to be encountered. Therefore the criterion for Jesus' understanding of his being and for his self-understanding is solely *the 'language-power' of his proclamation*. Especially in the parable form, this 'language-power' expresses the obedience of Jesus in relation to God. For in his proclamation Jesus preserves God's liberating freedom. Only then can we correctly assess Jesus' conduct in terms of Jesus' own intention, when on the strength of this we are able to bring God himself 'into language'. That happened, for example, with the conception of the Son of Man, which was transferred to Jesus himself.

Without doubt the early Christian proclamation also intended to bring God 'into language'. The attempts to do this have become the *text* for the entire subsequent Christian preaching of faith. It was thereby decisive that Jesus' own person moved definitely into the centre of the proclamation. That was, on the one hand, the consequence of Jesus' crucifixion, which raised the question of his authority. But what was conclusive was that the early Christian proclamation for its part expressed in God's name its conviction about Jesus, by believing in the crucified Jesus as him who had been exalted to the position of the Son of Man; as the resurrected Christ; as the Lord over sin and death, who had been made into the word of God decisive for all men (Acts 2.36). God had spoken in Jesus; or as Paul says, God had in Christ reconciled the world to himself and established the preaching of reconciliation (II Cor. 5.19). The being between God and man, the situation before God, would in the future be determined by the Spirit of God as the Spirit of Christ. Whoever understood himself out of this situation would bring Jesus Christ 'into language'. Jesus would in the future speak to his community as its Lord. From the *witness* of faith in God there had arisen the *basis* of this faith. Why? Because in the future also Jesus would place himself before God, though now as he who intercedes for us before God (Rom. 8.34; Heb. 7.25); as he whom we understand in our faith in God, as the Fourth Gospel shows. The historical Jesus had become the Jesus whom we understand.

Thereby it was, in fact, stated that no one can talk of God, if he intends somehow to do this and still by-pass Jesus. Jesus therefore became the text of the proclamation. But the written word does not replace the proclamation. It simply preserves the situation in which we have to speak of God. We have to speak of God in that Jesus himself is proclaimed as the word of God; in such a way that faith in God sets free the 'language-power' which is presented to it, and with this power faith is able to speak of Jesus, because it has understood him. Through this freedom in its character as an event, it becomes ever and again clear that faith in God speaks out of that self-understanding to which Jesus once summoned his hearers. The text of preaching has therefore a hermeneutical task, namely to lead us to that point in the proclamation where it is ever anew decided whether we are at one with Jesus; whether we therefore, like Jesus, speak the language of faith. This is the language which for its part presupposes the being of man before God, just as Jesus did, and thereby is the cause of Jesus' relationship to God becoming an event for us also. The time of the parable has now been superseded by the time of confession to Jesus, just as in worship the text makes way for preaching. This is because Jesus' obedience preceded faith in Jesus. The

Church of faith then moves towards a future which ever anew confirms the Church's unity with Jesus, when the Church through its own obedience is able to invoke God as the Father of Jesus Christ and through Jesus Christ as our Father. Therefore the Church prays for the Holy Spirit as the power of her word, too. The being which Jesus revealed is fulfilled as being before God, by means of the word which, in the name of Jesus, is spoken as our word in faith.

What situation has now become central? The situation in which the historical Jesus himself appears delivered over to God's mortal judgment on all our lives? Or the one in which Jesus opposes this judgment, because something entirely new, the rule of God, will come? Jesus' proclamation says that he considers the time of God's rule to have come. His words and actions are said and done for the sake of his hearers—those who listen to him because they understand him. Therefore, we have to speak of Jesus' love. But this love means not just to continue, but to be believed in as the power which is stronger than God's judgment. It is brought into language so that it might be believed in, so that we might believe that its hour has come. This faith will then always be its first part. If God holds fast to this love, he will then have held fast to Jesus. If God has held fast to Jesus, then he wants to have our faith in the time for love—our faith, not only the faith of the Apostles. God's word will then for Jesus' sake be that 'yes' to Jesus which for us means faith in the time for love. This is the situation in which the language of faith becomes confession, even though this confession may love in silence. The situation certainly does not become an ideal scene; it remains the situation of Jesus, the situation of proclamation by which Jesus himself appealed to God, the temporal announcement of God's rule, of the rule of love. Through the time of Jesus time itself becomes the content of faith and therefore of proclamation. In the world the final hour will always have struck.

The quest of the historical Jesus then reveals to us our own time as a time conditioned by the situation of the preaching of faith. Who has asked us the question about the historical Jesus? And what is it about time, if our own time is itself to become the content of faith? Where will theology derive her understanding of time? In terms of a history? But how can this be, if faith is directly opposed to history, since, in regard to history's inexorability, faith submits to no further deception? Has our future begun to speak in the historical Jesus? Jesus' resurrection could then become a word to us only through our future entering language in this word. And this would mean—our death.

INDEX

INDEX OF NAMES

INDEX OF NEW TESTAMENT REFERENCES

233